Crochet
your way

Crochet

your way

A Learn-to-Crochet Afghan

Over 40 Projects for Home and Family

Easy-to-Understand Text and Symbols

Special Instructions for Left-Handers

EZ Reference Crochet Shorthand Chart

GLORIA TRACY *and* SUSAN LEVIN

The Taunton Press

Front cover photo by: Jack Deutsch
Back cover photos by: Jack Deutsch
Author photo by: Pacific Light Studios
Publisher: Jim Childs
Acquisitions Editor: Jolynn Gower
Assistant Editor: Sarah Coe
Copy Editor: Peter Chapman
Cover Designer: Carol Singer
Interior Designer: Kay Green
Layout Artist: Kay Green, Rosalie Vaccaro
Photographers: Jack Deutsch, Scott Phillips
Illustrator: Mario Ferro
Indexer: Lynda Stannard

Taunton
BOOKS & VIDEOS
for fellow enthusiasts

Printed in the United States of America
10 9 8 7 6 5 4 3 2 1

The Taunton Press, Inc.
63 South Main Street, PO Box 5506
Newtown, CT 06470-5506
e-mail: tp@taunton.com

Distributed by Publishers Group West

Library of Congress Cataloging-in-Publication Data
  Tracy, Gloria.
    Crochet your way : a learn-to-crochet afghan, over 40 projects for home
and family, easy-to-understand text and symbols, special instructions for left-
handers / Gloria Tracy and Susan Levin.
      p.   cm.
    ISBN 1-56158-310-3
      1. Crocheting. 2. Crocheting—Patterns. I. Levin, Susan. II. Title.
    TT820.T694   2000
    746.43'4043—dc21   99–058398

To all of you
Who crochet by symbols or by text,
Use your right hand or your left,
Who yearn to learn new stitches and tips,
Design, techniques and patterns and hints.
Beginners, advanced, or even brand-new,
Whatever *your* way, this book is for you.

Acknowledgments

When we think about gratitude in conjunction with our book, our thoughts go first to Jolynn Gower and Sarah Coe, our editors at The Taunton Press, for their incredible patience and understanding. Both the project and our business grew in scope as deadlines came…and went. We're happy to report both have benefited from the passing time.

Next we think of Ruthie Marks. Ruthie attended a crochet class Gloria taught in 1996, became our second employee, and has been our right hand since. We should say, "our left hand." Ruthie and Susan, both left-handers, have raised Gloria's handed-consciousness to the point that directions for left-handers have become a significant feature of the book. Ruthie's other contributions include designing, editing, crocheting, and serving as an always insightful sounding board.

Not to be forgotten is Deb Dietz, our accountant, who is a prolific knitter, but, alas, not yet a crocheter. Her good nature and willingness to pitch in as needed (as well as her ability to keep the office humming while we were otherwise engaged) also contributed greatly to the success of the book.

We bow down to Karen Manthey's unique talent for creating international symbols. Her contribution enables the readers of *Crochet Your Way* to learn a skill that simplifies pattern reading and brings the whole world of crochet to their fingertips.

Hélène Rush and Anne Reed are both crochet editors par excellence. Their I-dotting and T-crossing attention to detail give us confidence that the patterns will be as error-free as a book of patterns can be.

The crocheters who pitched in to make models quickly, often from unedited patterns, were indispensable to creating this book. We thank Barbara Thurber, Ellen Dreschler, Karen Frazer, Carol May, and Barbara Kervin for their help.

We also want to thank the many talented crocheters, old and new, professionals and hobbyists, who took the time to send us tips. We learned a few things from them, and we are sure you will too.

We also couldn't have completed this book without our families, who patiently put up with us crocheting through every occasion as we rushed to meet our deadlines, who smiled as we spent our weekends editing instead of visiting with them, and who praised us in spite of it all. Thanks so much for understanding.

Finally, we acknowledge each other. Our various skills are, most of the time, complementary. Even though there were a few jugular discussions, as often happens on projects, this book has reconfirmed our gratitude in having each other as a partner.

GLORIA TRACY AND SUSAN LEVIN

Contents

PART ONE: Beginnings and Basics 8

PART TWO: Learn-to-Crochet Afghan 64

PART THREE: # Creative Projects 122

Introduction

When people asked what our book was about, we reflected over words and descriptions that would summarize *Crochet Your Way*. It isn't a stitch dictionary, although it does contains dozens of different stitches, techniques, and stitch patterns. It isn't just a pattern book, although it does contain over 40 different projects that both novice and expert crocheters will enjoy. *Crochet Your Way* is an experiential book. It is a book that will be a resource for years to come in addition to providing you with hours of pleasure as you complete the projects and develop your crochet skills.

Whether you are a novice or an experienced crocheter, the 20 crocheted blocks that make up the Learn-to-Crochet Afghan featured in Part Two will provide you with hours of enjoyable crocheting as you are guided through increasingly more intriguing stitches and techniques.

For additional applications of what you learn in the Learn-to-Crochet Afghan blocks, the stitches and techniques are used in inspiring wearables and home decorating projects. Each block is cross-referenced to the project using those stitches or techniques, and the projects are cross-referenced back to the block that teaches the stitch or technique. If you've particularly enjoyed working one of the blocks, go to the referenced project to see how else the technique may be applied. You may even want to consider taking a project detour to make it!

We went about writing *Crochet Your Way* as if we were teaching a class—a one-on-one class with you as the student. Since Gloria is right-handed and Susan is left-handed, there was constant interaction as we made sure that each of us understood the other and that all the directions were clear, no matter which hand you use. Susan, especially concerned that beginners understand every step as they go, developed the "In Other Words..." guidelines. Since often times crochet directions make the assumption that the reader has experience, these guidelines explain the standard text directions in greater detail.

The "In Other Words..." guidelines will be especially helpful for newer crocheters, but even experienced crocheters may want to refer to them when trying a new technique or a different approach to a familiar one. We placed the guidelines to the side of

the text directions rather than in the midst of the text so that those crocheters already knowledgeable in the technique being discussed won't be distracted by additional text.

Gloria, an advocate of reading patterns from international symbols, campaigned to have them included. If working from international symbols is new to you, following the easy instructions on how to read them will open up the entire world of patterns to you.

When you browse through the book you will also find numerous tips from other crocheters, alternative crochet stitches, and clever techniques such as how to work the chain and first row at the same time. The projects and fibers chosen are varied too. They include home decor, accessories, and wearables that range from a homey bath mat and lid cover made of easy-care acrylic to a chenille scarf and hat, a fabulous merino wool reversible jacket, and an elegant evening tunic. In two of the projects, we've shown you a model in a designer yarn and also one in a more economical version.

If you decide to start with one of the projects and it calls for a stitch or technique that is new to you, go to the block referenced to see how it is worked. If you decide to make the block even though you don't plan to make the whole afghan, you can turn individual blocks into pillow tops.

If you are new to crochet, you'll probably want to complete the blocks in the order they are presented. Anyone who completes all 20 blocks will not only be fluent in the "Language of Crochet" but will also be able to display and enjoy their efforts when they assemble the blocks into an afghan.

Crochet Your Way is truly a crochet book for anyone of any experience level. If you are already a crocheter, we hope you will be inspired to try approaches, stitches, techniques, and projects that are new to you. If you are a novice or an aspiring crocheter, get ready for fun! Go ahead—right-handed or left-handed, novice or expert—grab your hook, and get started crocheting *your* way!

The Language of Crochet

Some people learn more easily with text instructions, others by symbols, still others through pictures and illustrations. Throughout the book, we've provided instructions in text, symbols, and beginner guidelines with accompanying photos and information for both right- and left-handers!

Abbreviations

alt	alternate
approx	approximately
beg	begin(ning)
blo	back loop only
BP	back post
BPdc	back post double crochet
BPtr	back post treble crochet
c	crossed stitch
CC	contrast color
ch(s)	chain(s)
ch sp	chain space
cl	cluster
cm	centimeters
cont	continue
dc	double crochet
dc2tog	double crochet two together
dsc	double single crochet
dsc2tog	double single crochet two together
dE	double Elmore
dec(ing)	decrease(ing)
dtr	double treble crochet
E	Elmore
E d tr	Elmore double treble
E tr	Elmore treble
ea	each
eor	every other row
est	established
flo	front loop only
FP	front post
FPdc	front post double crochet
FPtr	front post treble crochet
frt	front
hdc	half double crochet
hE	half Elmore
hk	hook
inc	increase
Ldc	linked double crochet
lp(s)	loop(s)
MC	main color
pat st	pattern stitch
Psc	picot single crochet
rf	relief stitch (see post stitches)
rem	remain(ing)
rep	repeat
rnd(s)	round(s)
RS	right side
Rsc	reverse single crochet
s	spike
sc	single crochet
sc2tog	single crochet two together
sk	skip
sl	slip
sl st	slip stitch
sp(s)	space(s)
st(s)	stitch(es)
tch	turning chain
tog	together
tr	treble crochet
tr2tog	treble crochet two together
tr tr	triple treble
TT	Tall Texan
WS	wrong side
yo	yarn over
yrh	yarn round hook (yarn over)

Symbols and Punctuation

* † ★ Asterisks, daggers, and stars may all be used to indicate that you should repeat the instructions that immediately follow the symbol the number of times indicated *in addition to the first time*.

In Other Words...

"*dc in the next 3 sts, ch 3, rep from * 3 times" means to work three double crochets, and then three chains a total of four times.

( ) [ ] Parentheses and brackets may be used several different ways.

1. They are sometimes used instead of an asterisk to indicate the number of repeats.

In Other Words...

"(dc in the next 3 sts, ch 3) 4 times" means that you will work three double crochets, then three chains a total of four times. The same number of stitches is worked as in the asterisked example above, but it is stated differently.

2. They are used to list a number of different sizes and the corresponding number of stitches or inches that should be worked for each size.

In Other Words...

"Sizes 4(6, 8, 10)" indicates the number of different sizes in which the pattern is written. In the pattern it may say "work even on 25(30, 35, 40) sts." You should have the corresponding number of stitches for the size garment you have chosen. (It sometimes helps to review a pattern before beginning and highlight the corresponding numbers throughout the pattern for easy reading.)

3. In some complicated patterns, parentheses and brackets may be used together to signify a repeat within a repeat.

In Other Words...

"[(sc, ch 1 in the same st)3 times, ch 3, skip 3 st] 4 times" means that the instructions within the parentheses are repeated three times, then chain three and skip three stitches, and repeat that entire sequence four times.

4. Parentheses or brackets may also mean that you are to work several stitches as a unit.

In Other Words...

"(dc, ch 1, dc) in the ch sp" means that you work all the stitches within the parentheses in the next chain space.

5. Parentheses or brackets may also contain explanations.

Terms

Back loop	The loop that is away from you at the top of the stitch.
Free loops	The ridge of unused loops that remain in a previous row after working that row in the front or back loops only. Often these are used later to form decorative patterns.
Front loop	The loop that is closest to you at the top of the stitch.
Leg(s)	The vertical portion of the stitch (also see *post*). This term is used most frequently when a stitch will have multiple legs, such as a cluster stitch or textured patterns that often have multiple legs worked into one stitch.
Multiple	The number of stitches required to complete one repeat of a pattern.
Multiple +	The number of stitches required to complete one repeat of a pattern plus the number of extra stitches required to center the pattern on the row.

In Other Words...

A multiple of 4+3 means that each repeat is 4 stitches and that a total of 3 extra stitches must be included either at the beginning or end of the row in order to center the pattern. If you want your fabric to be approximately 36 stitches wide and the multiple is 4+3, you must have either 35 stitches or 39 to center the pattern.

Parts of the stitch as viewed from begininng of row

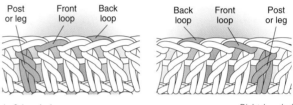

Left-handed   Right-handed

Working in front, back, and both loops

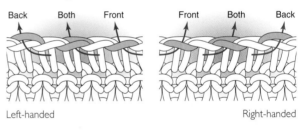

Left-handed   Right-handed

Working in free loops

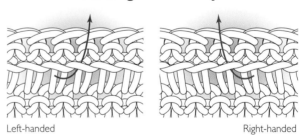

Left-handed   Right-handed

Working in the post from the front and back

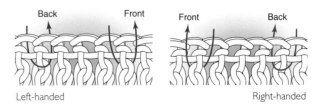

Left-handed   Right-handed

Post The vertical part of the stitch. Decorative stitches may be worked into or around this part of the stitch from either the front or the back.

Right/Left Refers to the side of the garment as if you were wearing it.

Right side The right side of the garment is the side that you want to show when the piece is finished. Most patterns indicate which side will be the right side (RS) and which is intended to be the wrong side (WS). However, patterns often have interesting textures on both sides. Feel free to use the "wrong" side as the "public" side if you like it better. Just remember to make all your garment pieces the same!

Work even Continue to work the pattern as established in the row or round just completed without decreasing or increasing.

Wrong side (WS) The side of the work that will not show when the project is complete.

Understanding International Symbols

Many new crocheters feel that international symbols are particularly helpful. There are not many and they are quite easy to learn. Knowing these few, simple symbols will make all of your crocheting life easier and more fun. Not only is it faster to read from the symbols, but it opens the whole world of crochet design to you. By the time you finish this book you will be able to read Japanese patterns (some of the best designs in the world) as if you were...well, Japanese.

International symbols assume you are a right-handed crocheter. Row 1 begins on the right-hand side of the pattern and assumes that Row 1 will be the right side or "public" side of your project. When you encounter a pattern that shows Row 1 beginning on the left side, it indicates that the first row of the pattern will be on the wrong side.

Look at the symbols on the facing page. As you might expect, a chain (ch) is an open oval. A slip stitch (sl st), which is often used to fasten a stitch, is a solid oval. A double crochet (dc) is a vertical line with two horizontal marks, one across the top and a slanted one in the middle. That a double has two lines is logical. A half double (hdc) has half the lines of the double, or only one horizontal line across the top. A treble (tr) has three lines. Again, it's logical. An "x" or "+" sign is used for a single crochet. Although instructions are provided in both symbol and text form, try working from the symbols before reading the text. It won't take you long to become a convert!

Take, for example, the crumpled griddle stitch. Before you look at the text directions, try reasoning it out by the symbols.

You can see that 12 chains were used to start and that a double crochet (dc) was worked into the fourth chain from the hook followed by 8 more dc to form Row 1. You can see that a ch 3 is worked at the beginning of Row 2, then a single crochet (sc) is worked into the second stitch and a dc into the third. These two stitches form the repeat that is worked across the row ending with the last sc worked into the top of the 3 chains that were skipped at the beginning. Row 3 is a repeat of Row 2.

The traditional text directions are written below the symbols chart, but we think you'll soon agree that following the International Symbols is faster and easier.

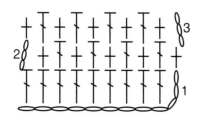

International Symbols

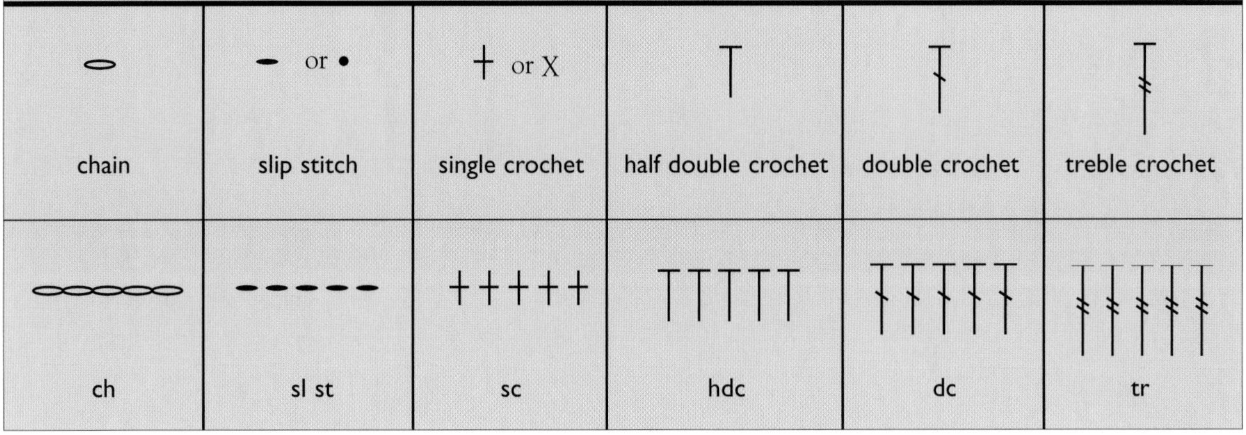

chain	slip stitch	single crochet	half double crochet	double crochet	treble crochet
⬭	— or •	✝ or X	T	⸸	⸸
⬭⬭⬭⬭⬭	– – – – –	✝✝✝✝✝	TTTTT	⸸⸸⸸⸸⸸	⸸⸸⸸⸸⸸
ch	sl st	sc	hdc	dc	tr

Weights and Measures

1 gram (g) = 0.03527 ounce (oz)

1 kilogram (k) = 2.2016 pounds (lb)

50 grams = 1.7635 ounces

1 ounce = 28.35 grams

1 pound = 0.4536 kilogram

1 centimeter (cm) = 0.3937 inch (")

10 centimeters = 3.937 inches

1 meter (m) = 39.37 inches

1 inch = 2.54 centimeters

1 foot (') = 3.048 decimeters

1 yard (yd) = 0.9144 meter

Approximate Equivalents

10 centimeters = 4 inches

1 meter = 1.1 yards

1 kilogram = 2.2 pounds

25 grams = 0.9 ounce

50 grams = 1.75 ounces

100 grams = 3.5 ounces

100 meters = 109 yards

PART ONE
Beginnings and Basics

The first part of this book is the foundation for all the wonderful techniques and projects to come. If you are new to crochet, take the time to read this carefully so you learn correct techniques and habits from the start. If you are an experienced crocheter, we suggest that you also take the time to review the information offered here. You may find one little tip or technique that will be an "aha!" that makes all your future crochet projects even more fun.

Getting Started

It's important to be familiar with all the basic crochet techniques and information on the following pages before you attempt to make a project. If you practice each of the techniques illustrated, when you do begin your first project it will go much more quickly and smoothly.

Crochet requires so little in the way of tools—only a crochet hook and your favorite yarn in your favorite color. With these two simple ingredients you are ready for hours of pleasure.

The Crochet Hook

Crochet hooks are most commonly made of steel, bone, plastic, aluminum, or wood. Each has its place and purpose. Whatever brand or shape you prefer, the basic parts are essentially the same. After crocheting for a while, if you are like most of us, you'll probably end up with quite an assortment of hooks as you try out different types and sizes to find your favorites.

The anatomy of the hook

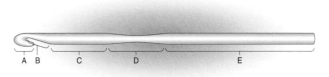

A = Head
This end is used to catch the yarn or thread and pull it through the stitch.

B = Throat
This shaped section guides the yarn or thread up into the working area. Different brands of hooks may have different-sized and different-shaped throats. It is personal preference which style you prefer.

C = Shank
This is the section that determines hook size. Each loop on the hook is pulled into this area as it is worked. It is the circumference of this area, measured in millimeters, that determines how large the finished stitch is.

D = Grip
The section indented for gripping the hook with thumb and index or middle finger.

E = Handle
The end that rests in the crook of the thumb and index finger or in the palm of the hand.

Hooks for every project. (All notions courtesy Bryson Distributing.)

LEFT-HANDERS UNITE!

Left-handers can be just as successful at crochet as right-handers, and there's no reason for any left-hander to be forced to attempt to crochet right-handed if it is frustrating or awkward. Gloria, a right-hander, and Susan, a left-hander, wrote this book together and even worked on several projects together. Here are some tips to help you crochet successfully if you are left-handed.

◆ If you are new to crochet, or want to learn a new technique from a right-hander, sit opposite the right-handed crocheter and mirror their actions.

◆ If you are trying to follow a printed picture of an action, keep in mind that you will be doing everything from the opposite direction that the picture shows. If you prefer, you may take the directions to a copy shop and ask them to print a mirror image that will show everything from the left-handed view. We have tried to include left-handed pictures for every action in *Crochet Your Way*.

◆ If you are reading instructions that indicate a specific direction, such as "insert hook from right to left" or "with right side facing, begin at lower right-hand corner," *you will be working in the opposite direction*, so you will need to re-interpret the instructions for yourself. A left-hander will "insert the hook from left to right" and a left-hander will "with right side facing, begin at the lower left-hand corner."

◆ All left-handed crocheters' stitches slant or twist in the opposite direction to right-handers'. On most stitches the difference isn't even noticeable. If you are working stitches such as a diagonal spike stitch or a crossed stitch, the difference may be more obvious, but it doesn't matter as long as you are consistent.

◆ International symbols are always written from the right-handed perspective, even though you may occasionally see directions that appear to begin on the left. In the drawing below, you can see that the number 1 is in the lower right-hand corner of the diagram. If you see an international symbol that shows Row 1 on the left side, it doesn't mean that the directions were written for left-handers. It means that the first row of the pattern will be on the wrong side. (See "Understanding International Symbols" on p. 6 for more details.)

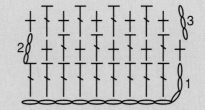

◆ A left-hander has two choices when working with international symbols: Begin at the number in the lower right corner and follow the chart from right to left as if you were right-handed or begin at the lower left corner and follow the chart to the opposite end of the row. The only difference between the two methods is that if you begin at the lower right corner and follow the chart as written for a right-hander, your finished piece will be a mirror image (i.e., your stitches will slant in the opposite direction).

◆ If you are following directions for a shaped piece, your piece will angle in the opposite direction. For example, if the directions were for the right front of a sweater, you would actually be making a left front.

◆ As long as your work is consistent, it makes no difference if you are left-handed!

Steel hooks usually have the smallest shanks and are used primarily for working with threads or fine yarns. Larger size hooks are made out of a variety of materials but are most commonly aluminum or hollow plastic to reduce the weight. Most hook sizes are designated with both a letter or number and a millimeter size. There is no standard universal numbering system for hooks, so it is imperative to make a gauge swatch and check the hook shank with a needle or hook gauge. If you change hooks during a project, you can't assume that hooks marked the same size actually are the same size. Confirm the size with your gauge measure.

Gauge measure.

Unfortunately, there is little standardization among hooks made by different companies. The comparison of hook sizes shown in the chart at right is the one most commonly used, but it is always best to experiment before beginning each project to be sure you are matching hook and yarn to desired gauge.

> TIP: When choosing a hook size, there is occasionally a discrepancy between the imprinted letter or number on a crochet hook and the actual size of the hook. Even if your hook is imprinted with the millimeter number, take the time to slide the shaft of the hook down the hole of a gauge measure to double check the circumference. Be especially careful if changing hooks in the same project.
>
> *Contributed by Ingrid Reed*

Approximate Hook Sizes*

Steel Crochet Hooks

U.S. (American)	Continental (metric)	U.K. (English)
00	3.50	-
0	3.25	0
1	2.75	1
2	2.25	1.5
3	2.10	2
4	2.00	2.5
5	1.90	3
6	1.80	3.5
7	1.65	4
8	1.50	4.5
9	1.40	5
10	1.30	5.5
11	1.10	6
12	1.00	6.5
13	0.85	7
14	0.75	-

Plastic and Aluminum Crochet Hooks

U.S. (American)	Continental (metric)	U.K. (English)
B/1	2.5	12
C/2	3	11
D/3	3.25	10
E/4	3.5	9
F/5	4	8
G/6	4.25	7
7	4.5	7
H/8	5	6
I/9	5.5	5
J/10	6	4
K/10.5	7	3
L/11	8	-
M/13	9	-
N/15	10	-
P/16	15	-
Q	16	-
S	19	-

* May vary by company.

Holding the Hook

There are two basic ways to hold the hook—in the pencil position, with the end of the hook in the well between your thumb and index finger; or in the knife position, with the hook held as though grasping a knife. Whichever option you choose, your thumb and either your index finger or third finger grasp the hook in the flattened finger rest. Either position will provide good support and allow you to develop a comfortable rhythm. Try both positions to determine which one you like the best. Your free hand will control the yarn supply.

The pencil position

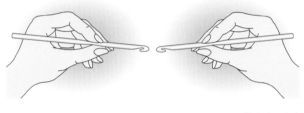

Left-handed   Right-handed

The knife position

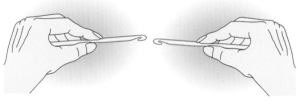

Left-handed   Right-handed

Making a Slip Knot

Every crochet project begins with a simple slip knot. Most of us learned this basic technique years ago—you probably make them without even thinking about what they are called. If you didn't learn the technique before, you are sure to find many uses for the technique in addition to starting your crochet projects.

Leaving about a 6" length of yarn, make a loop and allow the end of the yarn to hang down behind. Reach through the loop with your crochet hook and catch the yarn, pulling it forward through the loop and tightening the knot.

Making a slip knot

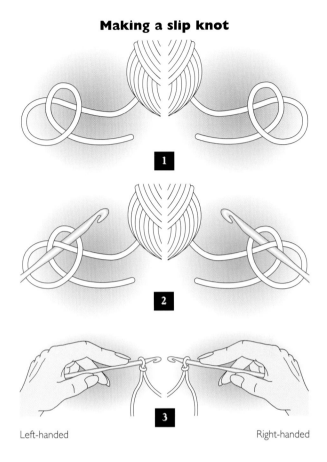

Left-handed   Right-handed

Holding the Yarn

There are almost as many ways to hold the yarn as there are crocheters. Below is one tried-and-true method that will give you even tension and good control. If you find that holding the yarn in a different way is easier, then do it—as long as you are able to maintain control.

Loop the working yarn over the index finger of your free hand and hold it loosely with your last two fingers, or loosely wrap it around your little finger. Grasp the slip knot with your thumb and middle finger. As you crochet, the yarn will feed through your fingers to form new stitches.

Holding the yarn

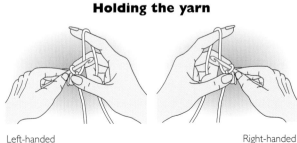

Left-handed   Right-handed

Yarn-Overs and Making the Chain

Catching the yarn with the hook and drawing it through to form a stitch is part of every crochet stitch. It is important to always catch the yarn in the same way so your stitches look consistent.

Bring the yarn over the top of the hook from back to front, catching the yarn in the throat of the

Correct yarn-over

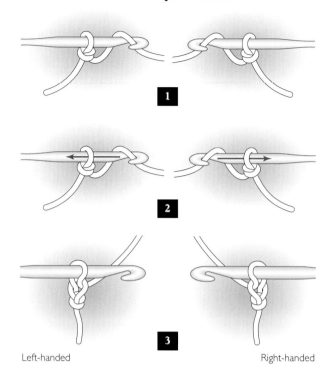

Left-handed   Right-handed

Incorrect yarn-over

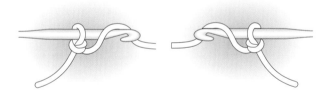

hook (yarn over made). Turn the hook slightly toward you to help prevent the yarn from slipping off the hook.

Pull the yarn through the hook and onto the shank. One chain is made, and one loop remains on the hook. Continue making chains in this manner, moving up the thumb and middle finger that are grasping the chain every few stitches to keep the tension even. This is the foundation chain. If the hook slips off the loop, be sure to re-insert it through the front of the stitch without twisting.

The chains formed should be loose enough for the hook to go back through easily, and should be even in appearance. It is important that they are the same size as the shank of the hook. If they tighten up to the size of the throat, they will be too tight.

Working with the Chain

The loop on the hook and the slip knot are NEVER counted. The front of the chain looks like a series of little V's or hearts. The back of the chain has a bump behind each chain, forming a spine.

When the foundation chain has the desired number of stitches, you are ready to work the first row. This row will be worked into the foundation chain. You can work into the bumps along the back spine, under the top strand of the front Vs, or you can insert the hook under the top strand and the back spine bumps. Unless a pattern calls for a certain method, it makes no difference which method you choose as long as you are consistent.

Counting stitches on the front of the chain

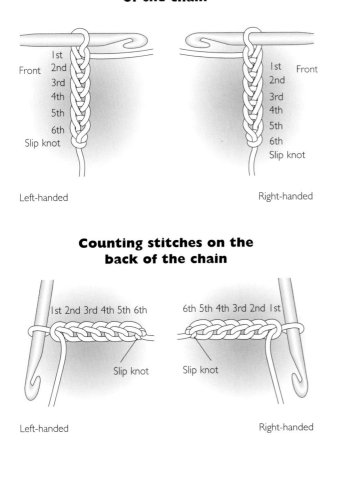

Left-handed   Right-handed

Counting stitches on the back of the chain

Left-handed   Right-handed

As the Chain Turns

Crochet stitches are formed by making various loops that give each stitch a different height. At the start of each row or round, and at the end of the starting chain, chains are worked to raise the hook to the height of the first stitch of the next row or round. Each basic stitch has a recommended number of chains to equal the height of the stitches to be worked on the coming row or round. See the EZ Reference chart on p. 213 for the recommended number of chains to equal the height of each stitch.

Chains at the beginning of a row or round When moving from row to row, the chains are called turning chains (abbreviated as tch), because you are actually turning the piece in order to have the opposite side facing you to work the next row. Some directions tell you to work the turning chain before turning the work; some tell you to work it after turning the work. Either will do the job; just be consistent. Our personal preference is to work the turning chain at the beginning of each row because the chain isn't twisted when you turn your work.

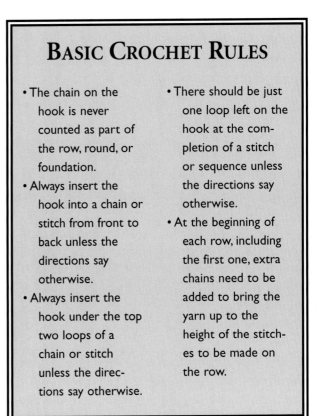

BASIC CROCHET RULES

- The chain on the hook is never counted as part of the row, round, or foundation.
- Always insert the hook into a chain or stitch from front to back unless the directions say otherwise.
- Always insert the hook under the top two loops of a chain or stitch unless the directions say otherwise.
- There should be just one loop left on the hook at the completion of a stitch or sequence unless the directions say otherwise.
- At the beginning of each row, including the first one, extra chains need to be added to bring the yarn up to the height of the stitches to be made on the row.

When working in the round, even though you don't actually turn the work, you still need to raise the hook to the height of the first stitch unless you choose to work in a continuous spiral. The spiral works well in a solid color, but will create jogs when working with color changes. The most common transition from round to round is to end with a slip stitch into the top of the beginning chain or into the top of the first stitch of the round. Start the next round with a chain equal to the height of the first stitch to be worked.

On both rows and rounds, when the first stitch is a half double crochet or taller, the turning chain is usually counted as the first stitch. In such cases, the instructions will indicate this and will direct you to start in the second stitch. Single crochet and double single crochet are usually considered neater when started in the first stitch. When counting the beginning chain as a stitch, however, to maintain the correct stitch count you need to make the last stitch into the top of the beginning chain of the row or round below to compensate for the skipped first stitch (see "The Crochet Master Rule" on p. 18).

Chains added to the end of the starting chain The number of chains needed to start your piece will be equal to the stitches needed to work the pattern of the first row or round, plus enough chains to equal the height of the first stitch to be worked. Some directions add the two numbers together and others do not. Understanding what you want to end up with may help cut through the confusion.

The number of chains suggested to equal the height of each stitch (as given in the tch column of the EZ Reference Crochet Shorthand chart on p. 213) is the number of chains to be added to the beginning chain. This is also the number of chains to skip before starting the first stitch in the first or foundation row or round. Directions will commonly read: "Starting in the X chain from the hook…" This number will be the chain height of the first stitch plus one stitch. If the chain is to be counted as the first stitch, the number of chains remaining will be one less than what is needed for the stitch count of the first row or round.

For certain stitch patterns that start with chains or an open area, an additional number of chains will be added to the beginning chain count. The directions will usually indicate when this is the case.

Turning chains Since a slip stitch adds little or no height to a row, it does not need a turning chain. Slip stitches are usually used only to attach new yarn, join pieces, or move the yarn across a group of stitches without adding height.

Turning Chains and Stitch Height

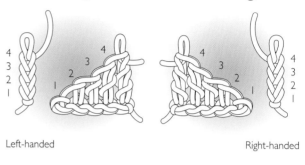

Left-handed   Right-handed

0 – Slip stitch
1 – Single crochet
2 – Half double crochet
3 – Double crochet
4 – Treble crochet

A single crochet stitch is the height of one chain stitch, so one chain is made when moving to the next row; it does not count as the first single crochet so the first stitch is usually made into the first stitch of the previous row.

Taller stitches are the same height as two, three, or more chains. For these taller stitches, the turning chain usually counts as the first stitch of that row or round.

> **TIP:** Think of the turning chain (tch) as a ladder to climb to the next row. If you chain tightly, you may notice that the edges of your rows "cup in." If so, you may need to add a chain to the usual count. A person who chains loosely may need to omit a chain. Use the number of chains that works for you.
>
> *Contributed by Mary Jensma*

Working in the Round

When you want to make a flat, round project like a doily or a shaped project like a hat, or perhaps even a pullover sweater, you will need to work in the round.

When working in the round, your project will not have a visible beginning or end. This makes it more attractive, and, if you are making booties or hats, it also eliminates the bulge that a seam would produce.

Make a foundation chain of the desired length, usually four or more, and close it into a ring by making a slip stitch into the first chain.

Begin each round by making a starting chain that matches the height of the first stitch to be made in that round. Always insert the hook into the center of the foundation circle when working the first round of stitches.

Beginning with the second round, insert the hook under the top two loops of the stitches in the previous round unless the pattern instructs otherwise.

After completing each round, insert the hook into the starting chain or first stitch as desired and make a slip stitch to join.

Do not turn your work after each round. Keep the same side toward you and mark it as the right side.

> **TIP:** If you have ever crocheted a very long starting chain, only to find you're one or two chains short after you completed the first row and have to start all over, just chain a few more than the pattern calls for. It's easy to undo the extras once you see they're not needed.
> *Contributed by Ruthie Marks*

Joining a New Yarn

You may need to begin using a new strand of yarn for a variety of reasons: your skein ran out, your pattern asks you to cut the yarn and rejoin in a different place, or you are changing colors.

If your old skein runs out and you are continuing to work with the same color, it is always best to try to change yarn at the end of a row. Leave a 4-in. to 6-in. tail so you have enough yarn to weave in the ends later, or place the ends along the stitches of the previous row and work over them.

When joining a new yarn, work the previous stitch until there are two loops left on the hook. Complete the stitch by drawing the new yarn through the last two loops.

Joining new yarn

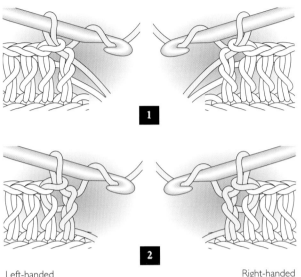

Left-handed   Right-handed

Decreasing Stitches

Working two stitches together is the most common way to decrease stitches. Other methods include decreasing stitches by ending a row before all the stitches are used, working slip stitches to the end of the row or skipping stitches intentionally. Patterns that require unusual decreases will explain the specific technique to be used.

To make a decrease by working two double crochet stitches together, work a double crochet stitch into the next stitch until two loops remain on hook.

THE CROCHET MASTER RULE

If you count the turning chain as a stitch and start work in the second stitch as many patterns instruct, you must work the last stitch of the row into the top of the turning chain of the previous row.

If you do not count the turning chain as a stitch and start work in the base or first stitch, do not make a stitch in the top of the turning chain at the end of the row.

Patterns that break this rule will indicate that the stitch count will be different.

Crochet isn't fun when you've added or decreased stitches not called for by the pattern. This happens to everyone when you start. Once you understand the crochet master rule and understand which is the first stitch, you'll know how to prevent this common crochet complaint.

The first stitch is the stitch at the base of the turning chain (tch). The two drawings at right are of two four-stitch-wide strips. In the drawing at near right, six chains were worked for the foundation chain. The first double crochet was worked into the fourth chain below the hook, *counting the first three chains as the first stitch.* Two more double crochet were worked for a total of four stitches (the turning chain plus three double crochets).

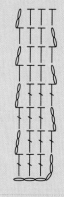

In the second row, three chains were worked for the turning chain. The three chain stitches are counted as the first stitch, and the first actual double crochet is made into the top of the second stitch, then another double crochet is made into the third stitch. To continue to have four stitches, the final double crochet must be made *into the top of the turning chain of the previous row.*

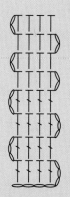

The drawing at the right shows another equally valid method of working. It is also a four-stitch-wide strip, but the turning chain is ignored. Seven chains are worked for the foundation chain, with the first double crochet worked into the fourth chain from the hook, and then three more double crochets are made. The chain counts only as a ladder to bring the hook to the height of the new row. As you can see on row two, the first double crochet is placed into the first stitch at the base of the turning chain.

If you start in the second stitch, as many patterns instruct, but omit the stitch into the turning chain at the end, you will lose one stitch. Also, if you start in the first stitch *and* place a stitch in the turning chain, you will increase a stitch. Locating the turning chain at the end of the row can be confusing. Even experienced crocheters count their stitches frequently to maintain the correct stitch count. The turning chain will be the loops at the very end of the row. Work the final stitch through the top chain rather than into the space.

Why use one method over the other? Some designs are counted more easily when started in the first stitch. Some designers like the look of the actual stitch rather than the thinner chain and may use that method when the turning chain can become a design feature on the edge or be hidden in the seam. There is often an unattractive hole at the beginning of the row when the first stitch is skipped. Neither method is right or wrong. It is what suits your needs. Understanding the concept, however, will make losing and gaining stitches less likely. You will have an opportunity to use both methods when making the squares and the projects in the chapters that follow.

Decrease in double crochet

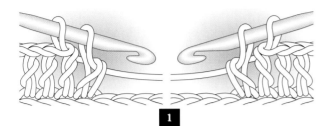

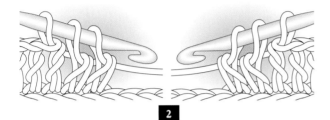

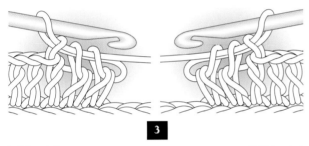

Left-handed   Right-handed

TIP: Which is it? Right side or wrong side? Often both sides of crochet can look quite similar. Decide which is to be the right side (RS) or wrong side (WS) of your work. Mark the right side with a safety pin or piece of yarn. Note if it is an odd- or even-numbered row. Knowing this can help you keep track of your place. Always try to complete a row, round, or repeat before stopping and make a written note of the date and row, round, or repeat where you ended.

Contributed by Liza O'Reilly

TIP: Use a split ring marker in the top of the turning chain so you don't miss that all-important final stitch of the row. Even if you don't have a problem finding this stitch, it makes it easier to crochet and watch TV.

Contributed by Jean Blaine

Keeping these two loops on the hook, work a double crochet into the following stitch until a total of three stitches remain on the hook. Yarn over and draw through all three loops on the hook. This method of decreasing may be used with any type of stitch. The same technique may be used to decrease three or more stitches.

Increasing Stitches

To increase the width of a piece, it is necessary to increase stitches. Increasing is easily achieved by working two stitches in the same stitch or space or by adding chains to the end of a row.

Always make the increase stitch in the same type of stitch as your others and pay close attention to how the increased stitch(es) may affect your pattern repeats.

Basic Crochet Stitches

There are seven basic crochet stitches and six interesting half-step variations on the basics. If you take the time to familiarize yourself with these stitches, you will soon be manipulating them to form all the variations and combinations of interesting and fun crochet stitch patterns found throughout this book and others. See EZ Reference Crochet Shorthand Chart on p. 213 for shorthand explanations.

Slip Stitch

Symbol − − − − − −
Text: sl st
Shorthand: (-1)

The slip stitch is the shortest of all the crochet stitches and is not used to produce fabric. It is used for joining, shaping, and carrying the yarn from one place to another.

To form a slip stitch, insert the hook into the second chain from the hook or insert the hook into the first stitch as shown in example below.

Yarn over the hook and draw through both the work and the loop on the hook. One loop remains on hook and one slip stitch complete.

Single Crochet

Symbol + + + + + +
Text: sc
Shorthand: (-2)

To form a row of single crochet stitches onto a chain, insert the head of the hook from front to back into the *second* chain from the hook. Bring the yarn over the hook from back to front and pull the yarn through, forming two loops on the hook.

Bring the yarn over the hook again from back to front and draw it through both loops. One single crochet complete. Repeat in each chain across row.

Single crochet

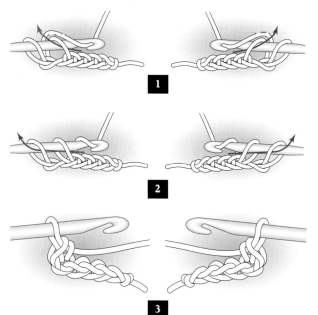

Slip stitch

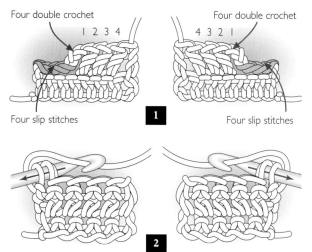

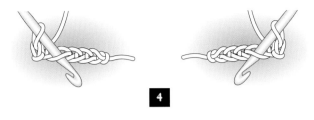

4

To make another row of single crochets, turn work, chain *one* for turn chain. (This turning chain is used only to bring the yarn to the height of the next row of single crochet; it does not count as a stitch.)

Insert hook under both top loops of the first single crochet stitch to begin row. Work a single crochet in each single crochet across row, making sure you work in the last stitch in the row below, but not in the turning chain. Continue making additional rows in the same manner.

Making the single crochet turning chain

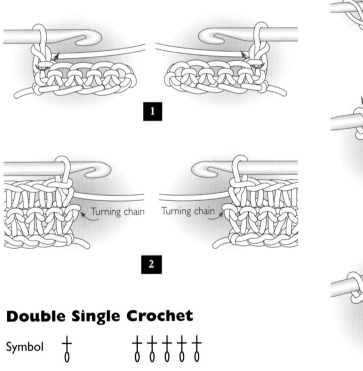

1

Turning chain   Turning chain

2

Double Single Crochet

Symbol   †   † † † † †

Text: dsc
Shorthand: (-1-2)

To form a row of double single crochet stitches onto a chain, insert the head of the hook from front to back into the *second* chain from the hook. Bring the

yarn over the hook from back to front and pull the yarn forward to form two loops on the hook. Bring the yarn over the hook from back to front again and draw it through *one* loop. Two loops on hook. Yarn over the hook and pull through both loops on hook. One loop remains on the hook and one double single crochet complete. Repeat in each chain across row.

To make another row of double single crochets, turn work, chain *two* for turning chain. Insert hook under both top loops of the *first* double single crochet stitch to begin row. (The turning chain does not count as a stitch in double single crochet stitches.) Work a double single crochet in each remaining stitch across row.

Double single crochet

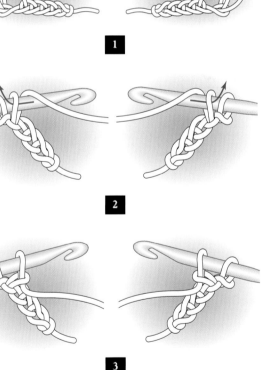

1

2

3

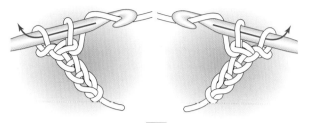

4

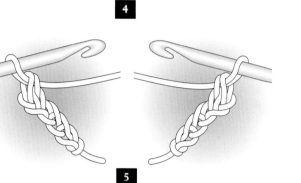

5

Half double crochet

Symbol T $\quad$ $\mathsf{T T T T T}$

Text: hdc
Shorthand: yo(-3)

To form a row of half double crochet stitches onto a chain, yarn over, then insert the head of the hook from front to back into the *third* chain from the hook. Yarn over and pull the loop through the chain, but not through the two loops on the hook. Three loops on hook. Yarn over and draw through all three loops on the hook at once. One loop remains on hook and one half double crochet complete. Repeat in each chain across row.

To make another row of half double crochet, turn work around, chain *two* for turning chain. The turning chain for half double crochet usually counts as the first half double crochet of the row.

Bring the yarn over the hook, then insert the hook under both top loops of the *second* half double crochet stitch in the row. Bring the yarn over and through all three loops on the hook.

Half double crochet

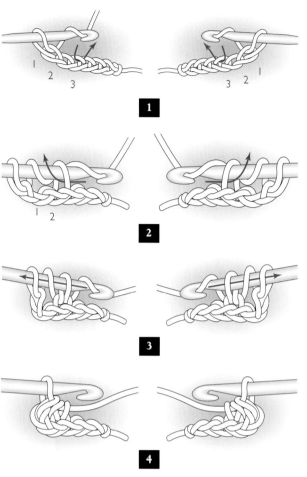

1

2

3

4

Work a half double crochet in each remaining half double stitch across row, working the last half double crochet in the top of the turning chain. Continue skipping first stitch and working in turning chain on following rows.

Making the half double turning chain

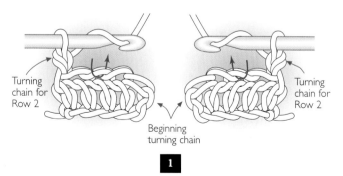

Turning chain for Row 2

Turning chain for Row 2

Beginning turning chain

1

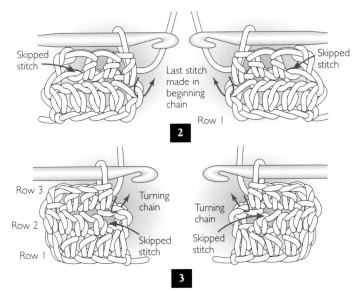

2

Row 1

3

Row 3
Row 2
Row 1

Turning chain
Skipped stitch

Turning chain
Skipped stitch

Last stitch made in beginning chain

Skipped stitch

Skipped stitch

TIP: *As an option, when working in half double crochet, try making your first stitch in the first stitch of the row and do not use the turning chain, which is easy to overlook in half double crochet.*

Contributed by Ruthie Marks

Double crochet

Symbol †   †††††

Text: dc
Shorthand: yo(-2-2)

To form a row of double crochet stitches onto a chain, yarn over, then insert the head of the hook from front to back into the *fourth* chain from the hook.

Yarn over and pull the loop through the chain, but not through the loops on the hook. Three loops on the hook.

Yarn over and draw through *two* loops on the hook at once. Two loops remain on the hook. Yarn over and draw through *two* loops on the hook at once. One loop remains on the hook and one double crochet complete. Repeat in each chain across row.

Double crochet

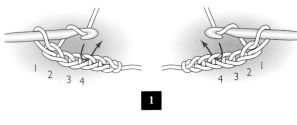

1   2   3   4   4   3   2   1

1

2

3

4

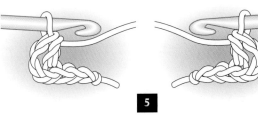

5

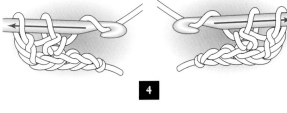

To make another row of double crochet, turn your work around, chain *three* for turning chain. The turning chain for double crochet usually counts as the first double crochet of the row.

Bring the yarn over the hook, then insert the hook under both top loops of the *second* double crochet stitch in the row. Bring the yarn over and through two loops on the hook, then yarn over and bring through remaining two loops. One double crochet complete. Work a double crochet in each remaining double crochet stitch across row, working the last double crochet in the top of the turning chain.

Making the double crochet turning chain

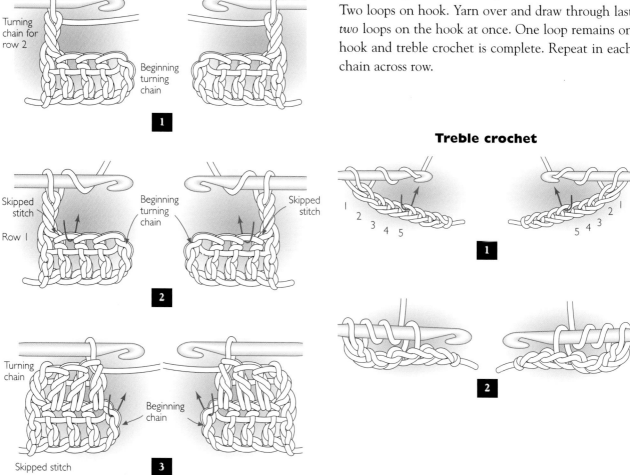

Treble Crochet

Text: tr

Shorthand: yo2(-2-2-2)

To form a row of treble crochet stitches onto a chain, yarn over *twice*, then insert the head of the hook from front to back into the top two loops of the *fifth* chain from the hook.

Yarn over and pull the loop through the chain, but not through the loops on the hook. Four loops on hook.

Yarn over and draw through two loops on the hook at once. Three loops on hook. Yarn over and draw through next two loops on the hook at once. Two loops on hook. Yarn over and draw through last *two* loops on the hook at once. One loop remains on hook and treble crochet is complete. Repeat in each chain across row.

Treble crochet

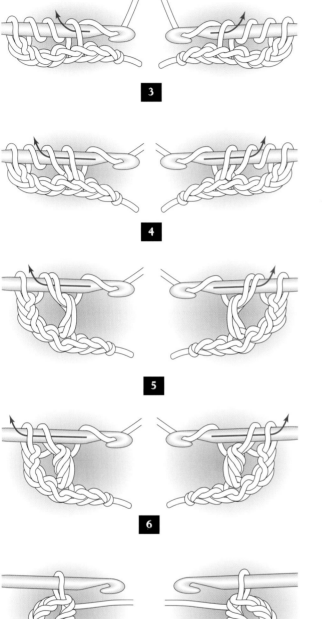

3

4

5

6

7

To make another row of treble crochet, turn your work around, chain *four* for turning chain. The turning chain for treble crochet usually counts as the first treble crochet of the row.

Bring the yarn over the hook twice, then insert hook under both top loops of the *second* treble crochet stitch in the row. Bring the yarn over and through two loops on the hook, then yarn over and bring through next two loops.

Yarn over and bring through last two loops on the hook. One loop on hook, and one treble crochet complete.

Work a treble crochet in each remaining treble crochet stitch across row, working the last treble crochet in the top of the turning chain.

Making the treble crochet turning chain

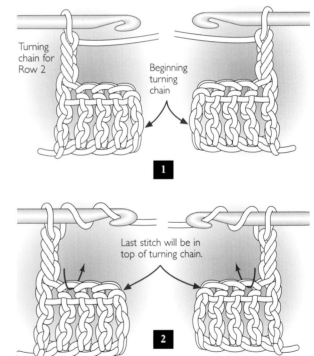

Turning chain for Row 2

Beginning turning chain

1

Last stitch will be in top of turning chain.

2

Double treble crochet

Symbol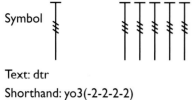

Text: dtr

Shorthand: yo3(-2-2-2-2)

Yarn over *three times* before inserting hook into the top two loops of the *sixth* chain from the hook. Continue working as for treble crochet, working two loops off the hook four times.

Double treble crochet

TIP: For neater long stitches, keep the loops close together and hold them with your finger around the hook until you have worked them off. Also, hold your work at the base of the stitch with the middle finger and thumb of your tension hand so that it will not stretch the fabric. Move your fingers up after each or every other stitch.

Contributed by Bonnie Blackburn

TIP: To make UK patterns come out right, you need to know that the British call their crochet stitches by names a "step up" from American definitions. For instance, the stitch called single crochet in the US is called a double crochet in British publications. See the EZ Reference Crochet Shorthand Chart on p. 213 for the UK names. Some UK patterns have been especially printed with American terms for US distribution. Some may contain a sheet stating which terms have been used and how to translate the patterns. Just knowing you need to watch for this discrepancy can save you countless hours of frustration.

Contributed by Chelsea Stevenson

Half-Step Stitches

Crochet innovator Bill Elmore categorized a series of stitches that fall between the traditional single, half double, double, and treble stitches. They allow for more graduated height changes and are very useful when a subtle height change is needed. They are rarely listed in crochet books, but form a useful addition to any crocheter's library of stitches.

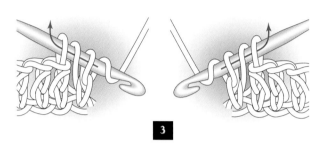

3

Half Elmore

Symbol

Text: hE
Shorthand: yo(-1-3)

To form a row of half Elmore stitches onto a chain, yarn over, insert the hook from front to back into the chain and draw through.

Yarn over and pull through one loop. Three loops on the hook. Yarn over and draw through all three loops. One half Elmore complete. Repeat in each chain across the row.

Elmore

Symbol

Text: E
Shorthand: yo(-1-2-2)

To form a row of Elmore stitches onto a chain, yarn over, insert the hook from front to back into the chain and draw through. Yarn over and pull through one loop. Three loops on hook. Yarn over and draw through two loops. Two loops remain. Yarn over and draw through two loops. One Elmore complete. Repeat in each chain across row.

Half Elmore

1

2

Elmore

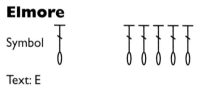
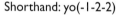

1

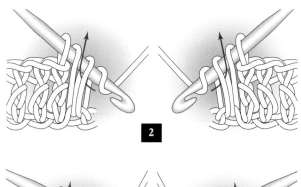

2

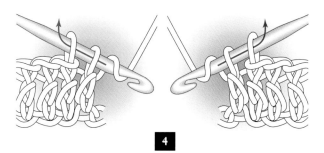

3

4

Double Elmore

Symbol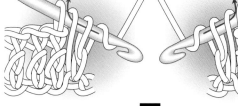

Text: dE
Shorthand: yo(-1-1-2-2)

To form a row of double Elmore stitches onto a chain, yarn over, insert the hook from front to back into the chain and draw through. Three loops on the hook. Yarn over and draw through one loop two times. Yarn over and draw through two loops two times. One double Elmore complete. Repeat in each chain across row.

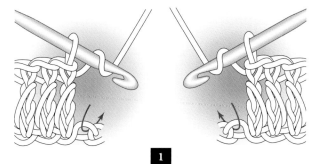

1

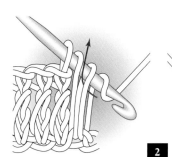

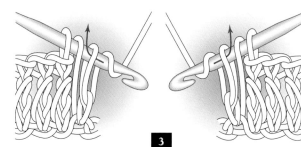

2

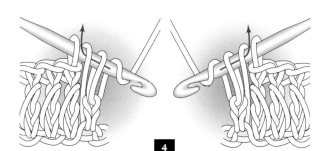

3

4

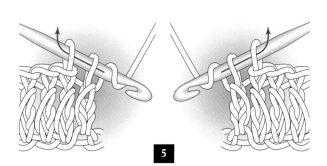

5

Elmore Treble

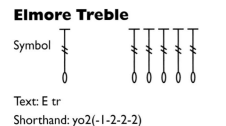

Text: E tr
Shorthand: yo2(-1-2-2-2)

To form a row of Elmore treble stitches onto a chain, yarn over twice, and insert the hook from front to back into the chain and draw through. Yarn over and pull through one loop. Four loops on the hook. Yarn over and draw through two loops three times. One Elmore treble complete. Repeat in each chain across row.

Elmore treble

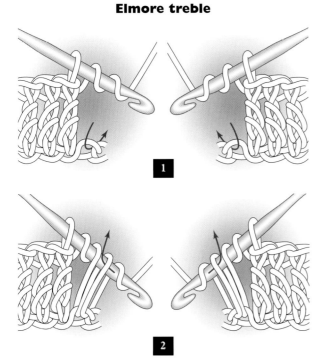

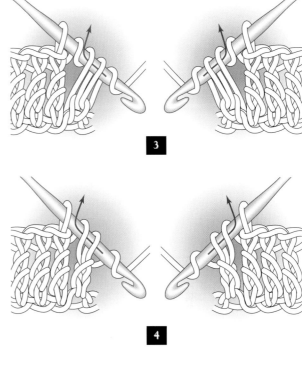

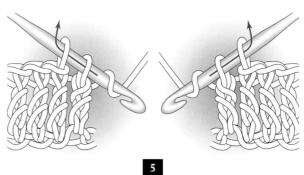

Elmore Double Treble

Symbol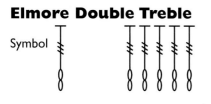

Text: E d tr

Shorthand: yo2(-1-1-2-2-2)

To form a row of Elmore double treble stitches onto a chain, yarn over twice, insert the hook from front to back into the chain and draw through. Yarn over and pull through one loop two times. Four loops remain on hook. Yarn over and draw through two loops three times. One Elmore double treble complete. Repeat in each chain across row.

Elmore double treble

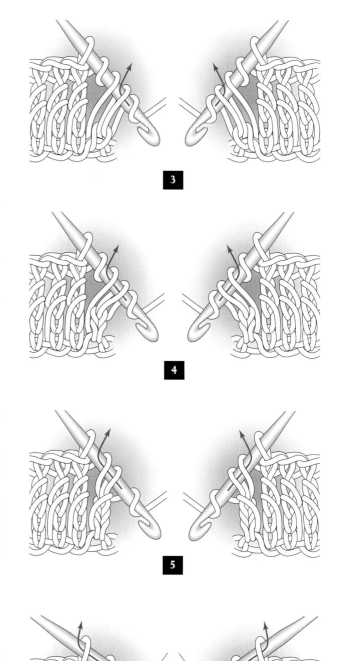

Tall Texan

Symbol

Text: TT

Shorthand: yo2(-1-2-1-2-1-2)

To form a row of Tall Texan stitches onto a chain, yarn over twice, insert the hook from front to back into the chain and draw through. (Yarn over and pull through one loop, yarn over and pull through two loops) repeat between ( ) two times.

Tall Texan

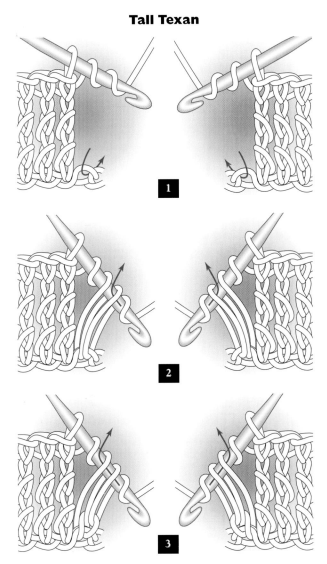

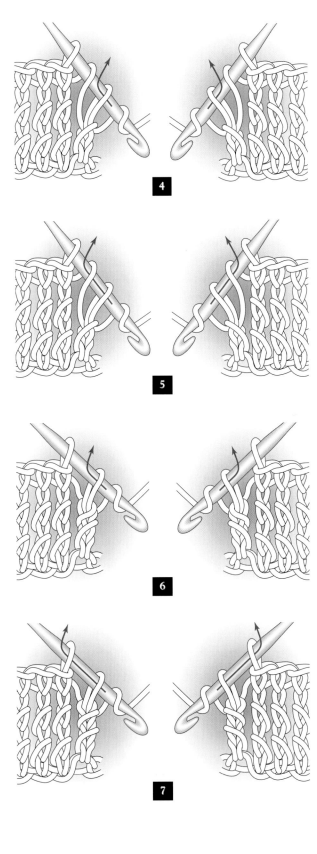

Simple Stitch Alternatives

Adding simple stitch alternatives to your basic crochet stitch skills will enable you to make even more interesting crochet fabric. These simple stitch variations may be used alone to form crochet fabric, or they may be combined with the basic crochet stitches to form the foundation of even more interesting and creative patterns. If you take the time to learn these stitch alternatives, you'll be confident when combining all the elements to create unique crochet patterns and projects.

Working into the Front or Back of the Stitch

Working into only the front or the back of the stitch forms horizontal bands that provide a decorative ledge. Working into only the back loop results in a horizontal band across a row; if worked vertically as an edging, it has the appearance of ribbing. Working into the front and back loops alternately creates a basketweave effect. The loop *not* worked in is called the "free" loop and may be worked on another row to create additional interesting patterns. See p. 5 for an illustration of the parts of the stitch. The illustrations show this pattern worked in single crochet, but you can use this technique with any stitch.

Front Porch Pattern (or working into the back loops only)

Text: blo or blpo

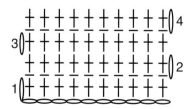

Any number of stitches plus 1 for turn.

Row 1 (WS): Single crochet in second and every chain across, turn.

Row 2 (RS): Chain one, single crochet in each stitch working into back loops only, turn.

Row 3: Chain one, single crochet in each stitch across, turn.

Repeat Rows 2 and 3 for pattern.

**Front porch pattern
(working in the back loop only)**

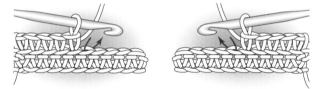

Alternating Front and Back Porch Pattern (or working alternately into back and front loops)

Text: alt flo and blo or alt flpo and blpo

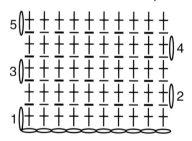

Multiple of 2+1 plus 1 for turn

Row 1 (WS): Single crochet in second and every chain across, turn.

Row 2: Chain one, single crochet in back loop of first stitch, *single crochet in front loop of next stitch, single crochet in back loop of next stitch, repeat from * to end, turn.

Row 3: Chain one, single crochet in front loop of first stitch, *single crochet in back loop of next stitch, single crochet in front loop of next stitch, repeat from * to end, turn.

Repeat Rows 2 and 3 for pattern.

Alternating front and back porch pattern

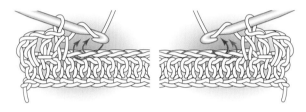

Linked Stitches

All the basic stitches (except single crochet) may be linked to make a fabric that is firmer and more stable. Linking stitches offers the possibility of eliminating the openness of longer stitches without creating a fabric as dense as single crochet. The stitches are linked by inserting the hook into the horizontal bars of the previous stitch instead of using yarn overs.

Linked Double Crochet

Symbol

Text: Ldc

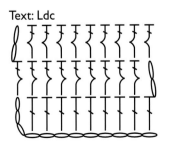

After working a foundation row in any stitch of your choice:

Chain three, insert hook through *second* chain from hook and draw through loop. Insert hook through second stitch and draw through loop. Three loops on hook. Yarn over and draw through two loops twice. First linked double crochet completed. *Insert hook through horizontal crossbar of stitch just worked, yarn over and draw through loop. Insert hook through next stitch and draw through loop. Two loops on hook. Yarn over and draw through two loops twice. Repeat from * for as many stitches as instructed ending last stitch in top of turning chain.

Longer stitches may be linked in the same way by inserting the hook through the horizontal bars of the previous stitch and pulling a loop through for each step.

Linked double crochet

1

2

Reverse Single Crochet

Symbol

Text: Rsc

This stitch is also referred to as crab stitch, shrimp stitch, or corded stitch. It is most commonly used to make an attractive finished edge that resembles cording, but it can also be worked anywhere that an attractive twist is desired. It is always worked with the right side facing and in the opposite direction, i.e., left to right for right-handers, right to left for left-handers.

With right side facing and one loop on hook, *beginning on the opposite end from where you usually start*, insert hook into the first stitch. With head of hook pointing downward, catch yarn and draw through loop, twisting hook so head faces up. Two loops on hook. With head of hook facing down, yarn over and pull through two loops. One reverse single crochet complete. Repeat in each stitch across.

Reverse single crochet

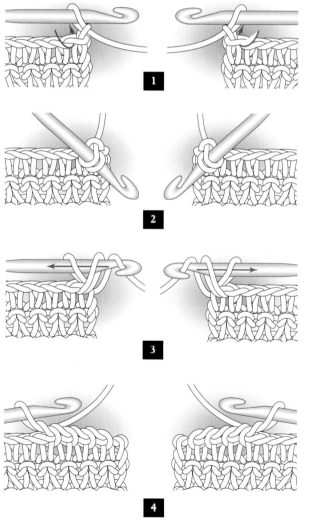

Working in the Stitch Space

Text: st sp

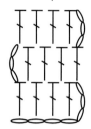

Note that the symbol shows the stitches worked between the stitches on the previous row.

Some patterns may call for working in the space between the posts of adjacent stitches. This will form a more open, compressed fabric with a wider stitch gauge and a shorter row gauge. Be sure to make your foundation chain loose enough to accommodate this extra width.

Working in the stitch space

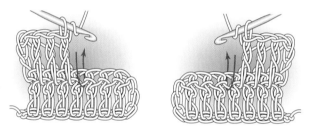

Post Stitches

Interesting color effects, patterns, and special textures such as ribbing or aran looks are created by working a stitch around the post (the body of the stitch between the top two loops and the base) instead of under the top two loops of the stitch. A pattern may specify that the hook be inserted from either the front or the back. Post stitches are also known as relief stitches.

Front Post Double Crochet Stitch

Symbol:

Text: FPdc

To make a double crochet post stitch from the front, yarn over, insert the hook from the front around the post of the next stitch in the row below.

Yarn over, draw through a loop. Yarn over and draw through two loops twice. One Front Post double crochet complete.

Back post double crochet

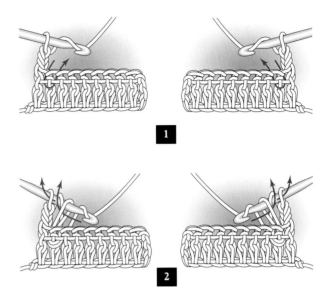

1

Front post double crochet

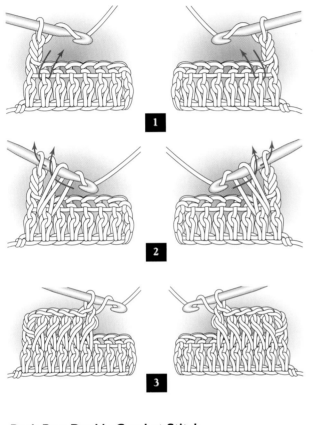

1

2

3

2

Spikes

Spike stitches are made by inserting the hook into one of the rows below as instructed. They may be made vertically by inserting the hook into a stitch directly below, or they can be made on an angle by inserting the hook to the left or right. Often spikes are combined with the use of a different color yarn to provide texture and color interest. Spikes may also be worked singly or in clusters. It is very important to work spike loops loosely so that the finished stitch is at the proper height and doesn't compress the fabric. Work at least one row before beginning spike stitches.

Back Post Double Crochet Stitch

Symbol:

Text: BPdc

Work as for front post except insert the hook from back to front.

Treble crochet stitches are formed in the same way except that the yarn is wrapped around the hook twice before inserting the hook around the post.

Spikes in the row below

Symbol:

Text: S

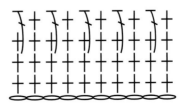

Work three rows of single crochet, changing color in the last stitch. Turn.

Chain one, *single crochet, insert hook into the front of the next single crochet two rows below. Yarn over and draw up loop even with loop on hook. (Yarn will be wrapped around fabric.) Yarn over and draw through both loops on hook. One spike complete. Repeat from * for as many spikes as desired.

Spikes in the row below

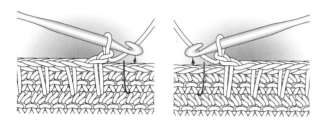

Crossed Stitches

Symbol:

Text: C

Crossed stitches offer a simple way of adding texture to almost any surface. The simplest variation is made by inserting the hook into a skipped stitch or space. The crossed stitches can be intertwined by inserting the hook through the previously made stitch, or the stitches can remain separate by inserting the hook behind the previously made stitch.

Skip one stitch. Work one double crochet into next stitch. Work one double crochet into stitch that was previously skipped.

Crossed stitches

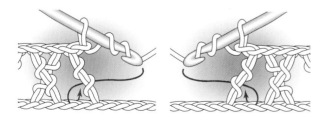

Things That Go Bump

All these stitches are real standouts! Try variations using more or less stitches than indicated for taller, shorter, or "bumpier" stitches than those shown. You can also combine different stitches in the same space, and you can work them from the right side or wrong side. Some patterns add an extra chain stitch at the end of larger "bump" stitches to close them securely.

Bobbles

Symbol:

Text: Bobble or dc5tog

A bobble is a cluster of stitches worked into the same stitch and joined together at the top.

Work five double crochet into the same stitch, leaving the last loop of each stitch on the hook. Yarn over and draw through all six loops on the hook. Ch1 to complete stitch.

Bobbles

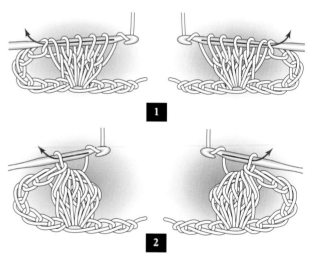

1

2

Clusters

Symbol: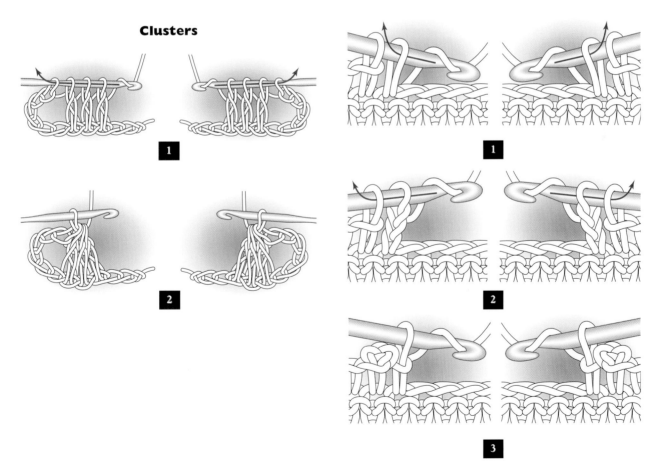

Text: CL

Clusters are two or more stitches worked into separate stitches and then joined together at the top. This technique may be used for decorative purposes or as a method of decreasing stitches. Any combination of stitches can be joined into a cluster simply by leaving the last loop of the previous stitch on the hook until they are all worked off together at the end. You may even skip stitches in between the legs of the cluster. Experiment with different numbers and sizes of stitches and techniques to find ones you like that are uniquely your own.

Work a double crochet into the next three stitches until one loop of each stitch remains on the hook. Yarn over and draw through all four loops on hook.

Picots

Symbol:

Text: Psc

Picots are a series of chains that are closed into a loop by a slip stitch or single crochet stitch. Traditionally, they are made up of three chains, but they can be any length. They may be worked on either side of the fabric since the picot is easily pulled through to the other side if desired. You can vary the number of chains in a picot to make larger or shorter "bumps."

Insert hook into next stitch. Yarn over and draw loop through. Chain three through first loop on hook only. Yarn over and draw through both loops on hook. Single crochet in next stitch to anchor. If necessary, pull picot to right side of fabric.

Clusters

Picots

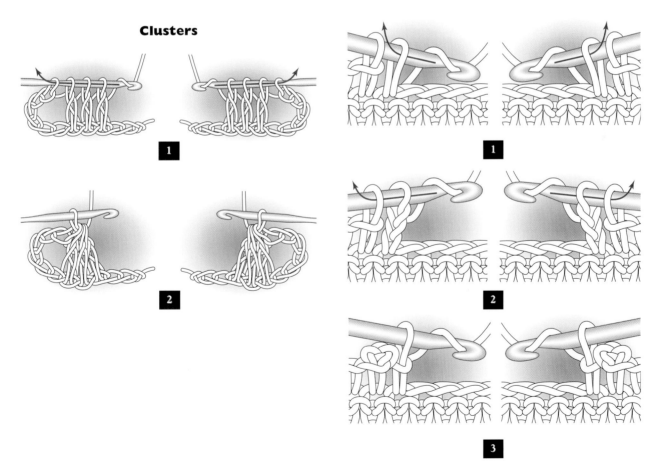

Popcorns

Symbol: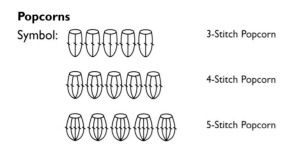

3-Stitch Popcorn

4-Stitch Popcorn

5-Stitch Popcorn

Text: Popcorn

Popcorns are groups of complete stitches worked into the same stitch and then gathered together.

Work three to five double crochet stitches into the same stitch, completing each stitch (the illustration shows a 4-stitch popcorn). Remove the hook from the working loop and insert it from front to back through the first stitch of the group. Pick up the working loop again, yarn over and draw through to complete stitch.

Puffs

Symbol:

Text: Puff

Puffs are similar to bobbles but are made using half double crochet stitches. Since it isn't possible to work a half double crochet until only one loop remains on the hook, the stitch has a different appearance.

Yarn over and insert hook into next stitch. Yarn over and draw through. Yarn over and draw through same stitch two more times. Seven loops on hook. Yarn over and draw through all loops on hook. Yarn over and draw through loop on hook to anchor stitch.

Popcorns

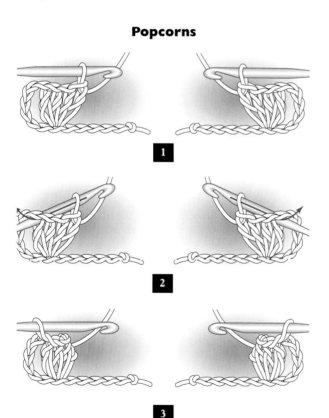

Puffs

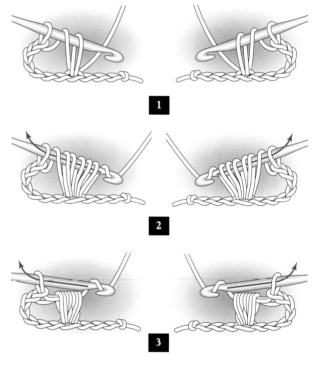

Pattern Stitches

Pattern stitches combine the basic crochet stitches and the simple variations into unique sequences. The pattern stitches on the following pages (listed in alphabetical order) were used to create the projects in this book. In addition to the ones presented here, there are many books with thousands of other pattern stitches that have been created over the years. If you are new to crochet, you'll soon find that a reference library of these patterns will provide you with unlimited opportunities to create your own unique projects.

Crochet patterns are usually written using text abbreviations and/or international symbols to conserve space. Starting now, we will write the patterns using these standard abbreviations and symbols. In some cases, we also list special abbreviations used in a pattern. If you don't remember a text abbreviation or symbol, refer to "The Language of Crochet" on p. 4.

Alternating Front and Back Porch Stitches

See "Simple Stitch Alternatives" (p. 32).

Bobbles

Multiple of 4+3 plus 3 for turn[1]

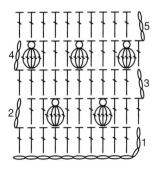

Special abbreviation

DcBobble (double crochet bobble): (bobble may be worked using from 3 to 5 sts) Work indicated number of dc inserting the hk into the same st and leaving the last lp of ea st on hk, yo and draw through all lps on hk.

Row 1 (RS): Dc in 4th ch from hk and then every ch across.

Row 2: Ch 3, skip 1 st, 2 dc, DcBobble 3dc, rep from * to end, working last st in top of tch, turn.

Rows 3 and 5: Ch 3, dc in ea st across, turn.

Row 4: Ch 3, skip 1 st, *DcBobble, 3 dc, rep from * to last 2 sts, DcBobble, dc last st in tch, turn.

Rep Rows 2–5 for pattern.

In other words...

[1] It takes four stitches to form one complete repeat of this pattern plus another three stitches. It takes three chains to reach the required height to match the other stitches in the row.

Chained Cross

Multiple of 3 plus 2 for turn

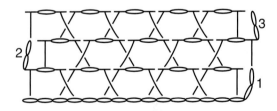

Special abbreviation

Chdc (crossed half double crochet): sk 1 st, hdc into next st, hdc into sk st working back over hdc just made.

Row 1: Hdc into third ch from hk, *ch 1, sk 1 ch, work Chdc over next 2 chs[1], rep from* to last 2 ch, ch 1, sk 1 ch, hdc into last ch, turn.

Row 2: Ch 2, hdc into 1st ch sp, *ch 1, Chdc working 1st st into ch sp of prev row and 2nd st into st before ch sp, rep from * ending ch 1, hdc into top of tch, turn.

Rep Row 2 for pattern.

In other words...

[1] You skip a total of two stitches. When the pattern is complete, there will be one skipped stitch left between each pattern repeat.

Chevrons

We used this pattern in the Learn-to-Crochet Afghan (beginning on p. 64) and the Chevrons Cap-Sleeved Tee Top or Long-Sleeved Tunic (p. 156). Since we wanted our afghan square to have a flat bottom edge and we wanted the Chevrons Tunic to have a wavy, or ripple, lower edge, we wrote the pattern in two different ways.

Chevrons, version #1 for straight bottom edge
Multiple of 6+1 plus 1 for turn

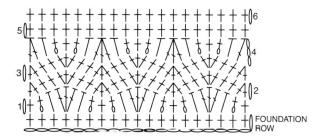

Pattern is written for four colors. Change color every 2 rows beg after Row 1.

Foundation Row: Sc in 2nd ch from hk, sc into next and ea ch to end, turn.

Row 1: Ch 1, sc in 1st st, *dsc into next st, hdc into next st, 3 dc into next st, hdc into next st, dsc into next st, sc into next st; rep from * to end changing color on last st, turn.

Row 2 (RS): Ch 1, sc 2tog, sc into ea of next 2 sts, *3 sc into next st, sc into ea of next 2 sts, over next 3 sts work sc3tog, sc into ea of next 2 sts;

rep from * to last 5 sts, 3 sc into next st, sc into ea of next 2 sts, over last 2 sts work sc2tog, sk tch, turn.

Row 3: Rep Row 2 changing color on last st.

Row 4: Ch 3, sk 1st st, dc into next st (counts as dc2tog), *hdc into next st, dsc into next st, sc into next st, dsc into next st, hdc into next st **, over next 3 sts work dc3tog; rep from * ending last rep at ** with 2 sts rem. Work dc2tog, sk tch, turn.

Row 5: Ch 1, sc in ea st across changing color on last st, turn.

Row 6: Rep Row 5 without changing color on last st, turn.

Rep Rows 1–6 for pattern ending final rep after Row 5.

Chevrons, version #2 for wavy bottom edge
Multiples of 8+1 plus 1 for turn

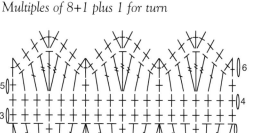

Foundation Row: Sc2tog in 2nd and 3rd ch from hk, sc into ea of next 2 ch, * 3 sc into next ch, sc into ea of next 2 ch, over next 3 sts work sc3tog, sc into ea of next 2 ch; rep from * to last 5 ch, 3 sc into next ch, sc into ea of next 2 ch, over last 2 ch work sc2tog, turn.

Row 1: Ch 1, over 1st 2 sts sc2tog, sc into ea of next 2 sc, * 3 sc into next sc, sc into ea of next 2 sc, over next 3 sc work sc3tog, sc into ea of next 2 sc; rep from * to last 5 sc, 3 sc into next sc, sc into ea of next 2 sc, over last 2 sts work sc2tog, changing color on last st, turn.

Row 2: Ch 4, sk 1st st, tr into next st (counts as tr2tog), dc into next st, hdc into next st, * sc into next st, hdc into next st, dc into next st, over next 3 sts work tr3tog, dc into next st, hdc into next st, sc into next st. Rep from * to last 4 sts, hdc into next st, dc into next st, over last 2 sts work tr2tog, sk tch, turn.

Row 3: Ch 1, sc into ea st across, changing color on last st, turn.

Row 4: Rep Row 3 without changing color on last st, turn.

Row 5: Ch 1, sc into 1st st, * hdc into next st, dc into next st, 3 tr into next st, dc into next st, hdc into next st, sc into next st; rep from * to end of row, changing color on last st, turn.

Row 6: Ch 1, rep Row 1, turn.

Rep Rows 1–6 for pattern, ending final repeat after Row 1.

Cluster Pattern Single Crochet

Multiple of 2+1[1] plus 1 for turn

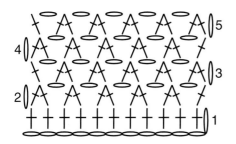

Special abbreviation

Sc2tog (single crochet two together)[2]: insert hk into 1st st, yo and pull lp through (2 lps on hk), insert hk into next st, yo and pull lp through (3 lps on hk), yo and draw through all 3 lps completing sc2tog.

Row 1 (WS): Sc in 2nd and every ch across, turn.

Row 2: Ch1, *sc2tog, ch 1, rep from * ending sc into last st, turn.

Row 3: Ch 1, *sc2tog inserting hk into 1st sc and then into next ch sp, ch 1, rep from * ending sc into last st, sk tch, turn.

Rep Rows 2 and 3 for pattern.

In other words…

[1] Another way you may see (multiple of 2+1) written is "any odd number."

[2] This stitch is sometimes also referred to as a **sc decrease**.

Comma Pattern (Spike Double Single Crochet)

Multiple of 4+3 plus 2 for turn

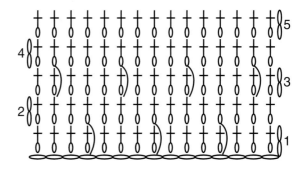

Special abbreviation

Sdsc (spike double single crochet): insert hk below corresponding st 1 row below, yo, draw lp through and up to same height as current row, yo, draw through 1 lp, yo, draw through 2 lps.

Row 1: Dsc into 3rd ch from hk, dsc into ea ch to end, turn.

Row 2: Ch 2, dsc into 1st and next 2 sts, *Sdsc below next st, 3 dsc, rep from * to end of row, turn.

Row 3: Ch 2, dsc into 1st and ea st across, turn.

Row 4: Ch 2, dsc into 1st st, *Sdsc below next st, 3 dsc, rep from * to last 2 sts, sdsc below next st, dsc, turn.

Row 5: Rep row 3.

Rep Rows 2–5 for pattern.

> **TIP:** When making a spike stitch, make sure the loop is drawn up loosely so that your work doesn't pucker.
>
> *Contributed by Stephanie Hicks*

Crosses and Bars in Two Colors

Multiple of 10 plus 1 for turn

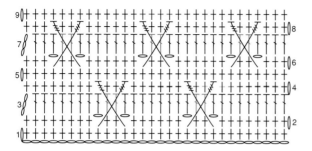

Note: On Rows 3 and 7 work dc into ch, *not* ch space.

Row 1: With A, sc into 2nd ch from hk and ea ch to end, changing to B in last st, turn.

Row 2 (RS): Ch 1, sc into 1st 8 sc, *ch 1, sk sc, sc into ea of next 2 sc, ch 1, sk sc, sc into ea of next 6 sc; rep from * to last 2 sc, sc into ea st, turn.

Row 3: Ch 3 (count as dc), sk 1st st, work dc into ea sc and ch to end, changing to A on last st, turn.

Row 4: Ch 1, sc into ea of 1st 8 dc, *dtr into 2nd sk sc 3 rows below, sk dc, sc into ea of next 2 dc, dtr into 1st sk sc 3 rows below (thus crossing 2 dtr), sk dc, sc into ea of next 6 dc; rep from * to last 2 sts, sc into last st and tch, turn.

Row 5: Ch 1, sc into ea st to end, changing to B on last st, turn.

Row 6: Ch 1, sc into ea of 1st 3 sts, *ch 1, sk sc, sc into ea of next 2 sc, ch 1, sk sc, sc into ea of next 6 sc; rep from * ending with 3 sc, turn.

Row 7: Ch 3, sk 1 st, dc into ea st and ch to end, changing to MC on last st, turn.

Row 8: Ch 1, 3 sc, *dtr into 2nd sk sc 3 rows below, sk dc, sc into ea of next 2 dc, dtr into 1st sk sc 3 rows below (thus crossing 2 dtr), sk dc, sc into ea of next 6 dc; rep from * ending with 3 sc in last rep, turn.

Row 9: Ch 1, sc into ea st to end, turn.

Rep Rows 2–9 for pattern.

Crumpled Griddle Stitch

Multiple of 2+1 plus 3 for turn

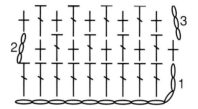

Row 1: Dc in 4th ch from hk and into each ch to end, turn.

Row 2: Ch 3 (counts as dc), sk 1 st, *sc into next st, dc into next st; rep from * ending with sc into top of tch, turn.

Rep Row 2 for pattern working sc in dc and dc in sc of previous row.

Crunch Stitch

Even number plus 2 for turn

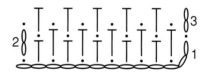

Row 1: Sk 2 ch (counts as hdc), *sl st into next ch, hdc into next ch; rep from * ending sl st into last ch, turn.

Row 2: Ch 2 (counts as hdc), sk 1 st, sl st into next hdc, hdc into next sl st; rep from * ending sl st into top of tch, turn.

Rep Row 2 for pattern.

Diagonal Spike

Multiple of 4+2 plus 2 for turn

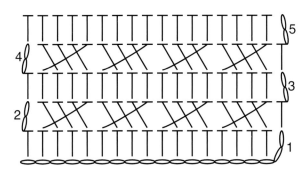

Special abbreviation

DS (diagonal spike): yo, insert hk from front to back into sk st before hdc block, yo, draw lp through and up to same height as current row [yo, draw through 2 lps] twice.[1]

Row 1: Hdc in 3rd ch from hk and into ea ch across, turn.

Row 2: Ch 2 (counts as 1 hdc), sk 1 st, *hdc into ea of next 3 sts, sk next st working DS in sk st[2]; rep from * ending 1 hdc into top of tch, turn.

Row 3: Ch 2 (counts as hdc), sk 1 st, hdc in ea st across, turn.

Repeat Rows 2–3 for pattern.

In other words...

[1] Viewed from the right side, if you are left-handed, your spike will slant up from left to right; if you are right-handed, your spike will slant up from right to left.

[2] There will be one skipped stitch between each three-stitch block of hdc that is used to work the diagonal spike stitch.

Diamond Lace

This pattern was inspired by a Bernat Baby Yarns crochet crib cover pattern and was adapted with permission.

Multiple of 20+17 plus 1 for turn

Row 1 (RS): Sc in 2nd ch from hk, [ch 5, sk 3 ch, sc in next ch] twice, *sk 1 ch, 5 dc in next ch, sk 1 ch, sc in next ch, ** [ch 5, sk 3 ch, sc in next ch] 3 times, rep from * ending last rep at ** when 8 ch remain, [ch 5, sk 3 ch, sc in next ch] twice, turn.

Row 2: *[Ch 5, 1 sc in next ch-5 arch] twice, 5 dc in next sc, sc in 3rd of next 5 dc, 5 dc in next sc, 1 sc in next arch, rep from * ending ch 5, 1 sc in next arch, ch 2, dc in last sc, sk tch, turn.

Row 3: Ch 1, sc in 1st st, sk ch-2 sp, *ch 5, sc in next ch-5 arch, 5 dc in next sc, 1 sc in 3rd of next 5 dc, ch 5, 1 sc in 3rd of next 5 dc, 5 dc in next sc, 1 sc in next arch, rep from * ending ch 5, 1 sc in 3rd ch of tch arch, turn.

Row 4: Ch 3 (counts as dc), 2 dc in 1st st, *1 sc in next ch-5 arch, 5 dc in next sc, 1 sc in 3rd of next 5 dc, ch 5, 1 sc in next arch, ch 5, 1 sc in 3rd of next 5 dc, 5 dc in next sc, rep from * ending 1 sc in next arch, 3 dc in last sc, sk tch, turn.

Row 5: Ch 1, sc in 1st st, *5 dc in next sc, 1 sc in 3rd of next 5 dc, [ch 5, 1 sc in next arch] twice, ch 5, 1 sc in 3rd of next 5 dc, rep from * ending 5 dc in next sc, sc in top of tch, turn.

Row 6: Ch 3, (counts as dc), 2 dc in 1st st, *1 sc in 3rd of next 5 dc, 5 dc in next sc, 1 sc in next arch, [ch 5, 1 sc in next arch] twice, 5 dc in next sc, rep from * ending 1 sc in 3rd of next 5 dc, 3 dc in last sc, sk tch, turn.

Row 7: Ch 1, sc in 1st st, * ch 5, 1 sc in 3rd of next 5 dc, 5 dc in next sc, 1 sc in next arch, ch 5, 1 sc in next arch, 5 dc in next sc, 1 sc in 3rd of next 5 dc, rep from * ending ch 5, sc in top of tch, turn.

Row 8: *Ch 5, 1 sc in next ch-5 arch, ch 5, 1 sc in 3rd of next 5 dc, 5 dc in next sc, 1 sc in next arch, 5 dc in next sc, 1 sc in 3rd of next 5 dc, rep from * ending ch 5, 1 sc in next arch, ch 2, dc in last sc, sk tch, turn.

Row 9: Ch 1, sc in 1st st, sk ch-2 space, ch 5, 1 sc in next ch-5 arch, ch 5, 1 sc in 3rd of next 5 dc, * 5 dc in next sc, 1 sc in 3rd of next 5 dc, [ch 5, 1 sc in next arch] twice**, ch 5, 1 sc in 3rd of next 5 dc, rep from * ending last rep at ** in tch arch, turn.

Rep Rows 2–9 for pattern.

Dots and Diamonds

Multiple of 4+3 plus 1 for turn

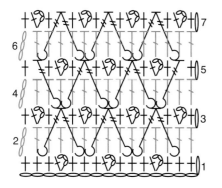

Special abbreviations

Psc (picot single crochet): insert hk, yo, draw lp through [yo, draw through 1 lp] 3 times, yo, draw though both lps on hk. Pull picot ch lps to front (RS) of work.

FPtr (Front Post treble crochet): yo hk 2 times, insert hk from front to back around the post of the st 2 rows below, yo and draw through lp, then complete as a regular tr.

FPtr2tog (Front Post treble crochet working 2 together): work 1 FPtr as indicated until 2 lps remain on hk, work 2nd leg of FPtr including 2 lps from 1st FPtr until only 1 lp rem on hk.

Row 1 (RS): Sc into 2nd ch from hk, sc into ea of next 2 ch, *Psc into next ch, sc into ea of next 3 ch; rep from * to end, turn.

Row 2: Ch 3 (counts as dc), sk 1st st, dc into ea st to end, sk tch, turn.

Row 3: Ch 1, sc into 1st st, *Psc into next st, sc,** FPtr2tog over next st inserting hk around 2nd sc 2 rows below for 1st leg and around 5th sc for 2nd leg (sk 3 sts in between), sc into next st; rep from * ending last rep at ** in top of tch, turn.

Row 4: Rep Row 2.

Row 5: Ch 1, sc into 1st st, FPtr over next st inserting hk around top of 1st raised cluster 2 rows below, *sc, Psc, sc **, FPtr2tog over next st inserting hk around same cluster as last raised st for 1st leg and around top of next raised cluster for 2nd leg; rep from * ending last rep at ** when 2 sts rem, FPtr over next st inserting hk around top of same cluster as last raised st, sc into top of tch, turn.

Row 6: Rep Row 2.

Row 7: Work same as Row 3, except when making new raised clusters insert hk around previous raised clusters instead of scs.

Rep Rows 4–7 for pattern.

FanCee Vees

Multiple of 6+4 plus 3 for turn

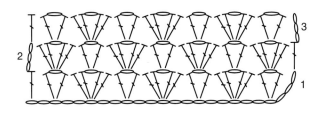

Row 1: Dc into 4th ch from hk, ch 1, dc into same ch as previous st, sk 2 ch, *2 dc into next ch, ch 1, 2 dc into same ch, sk 2 ch, dc into next ch, ch 1, dc into same ch, sk 2 ch, rep from * to last 2 chs, sk 1 ch, dc into last ch, turn.

Row 2: Ch 3, *2 dc in ch-1 sp, ch 1, 2 dc into same ch sp, dc into next ch-1 sp, ch 1, dc into the same ch-1 sp, rep from * to last ch-1 sp, 2 dc in ch sp, ch 1, 2 dc into same ch-1 sp, dc into top of tch, turn.

Row 3: Ch 3, *dc into ch-1 sp, ch 1, dc into the same ch-1 sp, 2 dc into the next ch-1 sp, ch 1, 2 dc into same ch-1 sp, rep from * to last ch-1 sp, dc into ch-1 sp, ch 1, dc into the same ch-1 sp, dc into top of tch, turn.

Rep Rows 2 and 3 for pattern.

Floret Stitch in Three Colors

Multiple of 2+1 plus 3 for turn

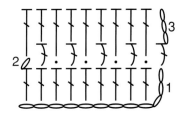

Work 1 row ea in 3 colors.
Row 1: Sk 3 ch (counts as dc), dc into next and ea ch to end, turn.

Row 2: Ch 1, sk 1 st, * dc into next st, sl st into next st; rep from *ending dc into top of tch, turn.

Row 3: Ch 3 (counts as dc), sk 1 st, *dc into ea st across ending last st in tch, turn.

Rep Rows 2 and 3 for pattern.

Front Porch Pattern

See "Simple Stitch Alternatives" (p. 32).

Granite Pattern

Multiple of 2+1 plus 1 for turning chain

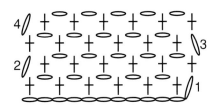

Row 1: Sc in 2nd ch from hk, ch 1, sk 1 ch, *sc, ch 1, sk 1 ch, rep from * to last ch, sc in last ch, turn.

Row 2: Ch 1, sc in 1st ch-1 sp, ch 1, sk sc, *sc in next ch sp, sk sc, ch 1, rep from * to end, work sc in top of tch, turn.

Rep Row 2 for pattern.

Grit Double Single Crochet

Multiple of 2+1 plus 2 for turn

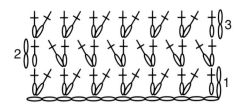

Row 1: Sk 2 ch (counts as dsc), dsc into next ch, *sk 1 ch, 2 dsc into next ch; rep from * to last 2 ch, sk 1 ch, 2 dsc into last ch, turn.

Row 2: Ch 2, dsc into 1st st, *sk 1 st, 2 dsc into next st, rep from * to last 2 sts, sk 1 st, 2 dsc in last st, turn.

Rep Row 2 for pattern.

Jack-o-Lantern Teeth

Multiple of 3+1 plus 1 for turn

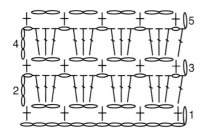

Note: Count sts only after Row 3[1].

Row 1: Sc into 2nd ch from hk, * ch 2, sk 2 sts, sc in next ch, rep from * to end, turn.

Row 2: Ch 4 (counts as dc and one ch), * 3 dc in ch-2 sp of previous row, ch 1, rep from * to last st, dc, turn.

Row 3: Ch 1, sc into 1st ch-1 sp, * ch 2, sc into next ch-1 sp, rep from * to end, turn.

Rep Rows 2 and 3 for pattern.

In other words…

[1] To create this pattern, some rows have extra stitches that are then decreased away before the pattern is complete. You can get an accurate count only after completing Row 3, not including ch-1 spaces. This is also true of other patterns, such as Chevrons.

Open Shells

Multiple of 5+1 plus 1 for turn

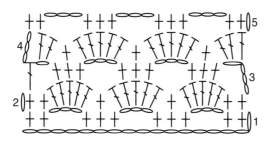

Row 1: Sc into 2nd and 3rd chains from hk, *ch 3, sk 2 chs, 3 sc, rep from * ending 2 sc, turn.

Row 2: Ch 1, 2 sc, *5 dc into ch-3 sp, sk 1 st, sc, sk 1 st, rep from * to last 2 sts, 2 sc, turn.

Row 3: Ch 4 (counts as dc and 1 ch), sk 3 sts, 3 sc, *ch 3, sk 3 sts, 3 sc, rep from * to last 3 sts, sk 2 sts, ch 1, dc into top of tch, turn.

Row 4: Ch 3 (counts as dc), 2 dc in ch sp, *sk 1 st, sc, sk 1 st, 5 dc into ch-3 sp, rep from * ending sk 1 st, sc, sk 1 st, 3 dc into ch-4 sp, turn.

Row 5: Ch 1, 2 sc, ch 3, sk 3 sts; *3 sc, ch 3, sk 3 sts; rep from * to last dc, 2 sc working last sc into top of tch, turn.

Rep Rows 2–5 for pattern.

Picket Fences

Multiple of 2+1 plus 3 for turn
Special abbreviation
FPtr (front post treble crochet): yo hk 2 times, insert hk from front to back around the post of the st 2 rows below, yo and draw through lp, then complete as a regular tr.

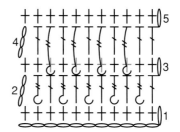

Note: Instructions are given using two colors. This pattern may also be done using one color.

Row 1: With A, sc in 2nd ch from hk and every ch across, turn.

Row 2: Ch 3 (counts as dc), sk 1 st, * FPtr in next st, dc in next st; rep from * to end, skip tch, turn.

Row 3: Ch 1, sc across making last st into tch and changing color to B, turn.

Row 4: Ch 3 (counts as st dc), sk 1 st, * dc into next st, 1 FPtr around the dc in the next st in the row below, rep from * to last 2 sts, dc into ea of last 2 sts, turn.

Row 5: Rep Row 3.

Rep Rows 2–5 for pattern.

Picot Single Crochet Pattern

Multiple of 4+3 plus 1 for turn

Special abbreviation

Psc (picot single crochet): insert hk, yo, draw lp through [yo, draw through 1 lp] 3 times, yo, draw though both lps on hk. Pull picot ch lps to front (RS) of work.

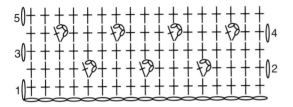

Row 1 (RS): Sc in 2nd ch from hk and every ch across, turn.

Row 2: Ch 1, *4 sc, Psc, 3 sc rep from * to last 4 sts, 4 sc, turn.

Rows 3 and 5[1]: Ch 1, sc in ea st across, turn.

Row 4: Ch 1, 2 sc, *Psc, 3 sc, rep from * to last 3 sts, Psc, 2sc, turn.

Rep Rows 2–5 for pattern.

In other words...

   [1] This a common way of saying work Row 3, then work Row 4, then work Row 5 exactly as Row 3.

Popcorn Pattern

Multiple of 4+3 plus 3 for turn

Special abbreviation

DcPopcorn (double crochet popcorn) (popcorn may be worked using from 3 to 5 sts): Work indicated number of dc inserting the hk into the same st and completing ea st. Remove hk from working lp, insert it from front to back through the 1st st of the

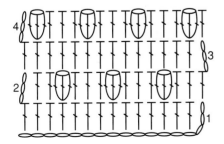

group, pick up the working lp again, draw through to complete st.

Row 1 (RS): Dc in 4th ch from hk and then every ch across, turn.

Row 2: Ch 3 (counts as dc), sk 1 st, 2 dc *DcPopcorn, 3 dc, rep from * to end, turn.

Rows 3 and 5: Ch 3 (counts as dc), sk 1 st, dc in ea st across ending last st in tch, turn.

Row 4: Ch 3 (counts as dc), sk 1 st, *DcPopcorn, 3 dc, rep from * to last 2 sts, DcPopcorn, dc in tch, turn.

Rep Rows 2–5 for pattern.

Puffs Pattern

Multiple of 4+3 plus 2 for turn

Special abbreviation

HdcPuff (half double crochet puff: puff may be worked using from 3 to 5 sts): *yo, insert hk, yo, draw through. Rep from * as many times as desired. Yo, draw through all lps on hk.

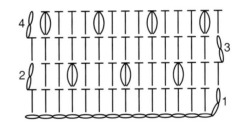

Row 1 (RS): Hdc in 3rd ch from hk and every ch across, turn.

Row 2: Ch 2 (counts as hdc), sk 1 st, 2hdc, *HdcPuff, 3 hdc, rep from * to end, turn.

Rows 3 and 5[1]: Ch 2 (counts as hdc), sk 1 st, hdc in ea st across ending last st in tch, turn.

Row 4: Ch 2 (counts as hdc), sk 1 st, *HdcPuff, 3 hdc, rep from * to last 2 sts, HdcPuff, hdc, turn.

Rep Rows 2–5 for pattern.

In other words...

   [1] This a common way of saying work Row 3, then work Row 4, then work Row 5 exactly as Row 3.

Solid Shells

Multiple of 6+1 plus 1 for turn

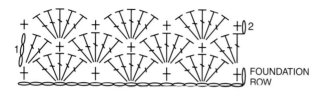

FOUNDATION ROW

Foundation Row: Sc into 2nd ch from hk, *sk 2 ch, 5 dc into next ch, sk 2 ch, sc into next ch; rep from * to end, turn.

Row 1: Ch 3 (counts as dc), 2 dc into 1st st, *sk 2 sts, sc into next st, sk 2 sts, 5 dc into next st; rep from * ending last rep with 3 dc into last st, sk tch, turn.

Row 2: Ch 1, sc into 1st st, *sk 2 sts, 5 dc into next st, sk 2 sts, sc, rep from * ending last rep with sc into top of tch, turn.

Rep Rows 1 and 2 for pattern.

Squares

Even number plus 2 for turn

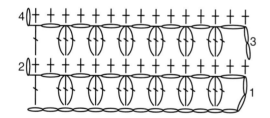

Work 1 row sc as foundation before beginning pattern.

Row 1(WS): Ch 3, starting in 2nd st *[(yo, insert hk, yo and pull through lp, yo, pull through 2 lps) rep between ( ) 2 more times in same st, yo, pull through 4 lps on hk] for square, ch 1, sk 1 st, rep from * to last st, dc in last st, turn.

Row 2: Ch 1, *sc in dc, *sc in ch-1 sp, sc in top of square, rep from * across, sc in top of tch, turn.

Rep Rows 1 and 2 for pattern.

Three-Color Interlocking Blocks

Multiple of 6+3 plus 3 for turn

Special abbreviation

Sdc (spike double crochet): work dc over ch sp by inserting hk into top of next st in row below being careful to keep chs to WS of work on all rows.

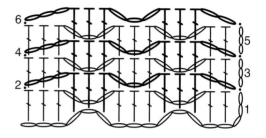

Work 1 row each of color A, B, and C throughout.

Row 1: Sk 3 ch (counts as dc), dc into ea of next 2 ch, *ch 3, sk 3 ch, dc into ea of next 3 ch; rep from * to end, turn.

Row 2: * Ch 3, sk 3 sts, Sdc over ea of next 3 sts; rep from * to last 3 sts, ch 2, sk 2 sts, sl st into top of tch, turn.

Row 3: Ch 3 (count as Sdc), sk 1 st, 1 Sdc over ea of next 2 sts, * ch 3, sk 3 sts, 1 Sdc over ea of next 3 sts; rep from * to end, turn.

Rep Rows 2 and 3 for pattern.

Three-Color Post Stitch

Multiple of 3+2 plus 1 for turn
This pattern uses three colors: A, B, and C.

Special abbreviations

BPtr (back post treble crochet): placing hk in back of work, yo 2 times, insert hk from back to front around the post of the st as directed, yo and draw through lp, then complete as a regular tr.

FPtr (front post treble crochet): keeping hk in front of work, yo 2 times, insert hk from front to back around the post of the st as directed, yo and draw through lp, then complete as a regular tr.

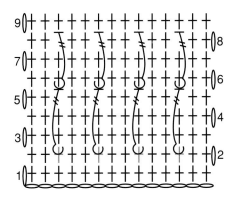

Row 1 (WS): Starting in 2nd ch from hk, with A, sc in ea ch across, turn.

Row 2: Ch 1, sc into ea st to end, turn.

Row 3: Rep Row 2 changing to B on last st.

Row 4: Rep Row 2 changing to C on last st.

Row 5: Ch 1, sc into 1st 2 sts, *BPtr on next st, working around the post of the st 3 rows below, sc into ea of next 2 sc, rep from * to end, turn.

Row 6: Rep Row 2 changing to B on last st.

Row 7: Rep row 2 changing to A on last st.

Row 8: Ch 1, sc into 1st 2 sts, *FPtr on next st working around the post st 3 rows below, sc into ea of next 2 sts, rep from * to end, turn.

Row 9: Rep Row 2 changing to B on last st.

Rep Rows 4–9 for pattern.

Trinity Pattern

Multiple of 2+1 plus 1 for turn

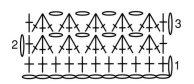

Row 1: Sc into 2nd ch from hk and then every ch across, turn.

Row 2: Ch 1, sc, sc3tog inserting hk first into previous sc, then into ea of next 2 sc, *ch 1, sc3tog inserting hk first into same sc as 3rd leg of previ-

ous cluster, then into ea of next 2 sc; rep from * ending sc into same st as 3rd leg of previous cluster, sk tch, turn.

Row 3: Ch 1, sc into 1st st, sc3tog inserting hk first into same place as previous sc, then into top of next cluster, then into next ch sp, *ch 1, sc3tog inserting hk first into same ch sp as 3rd leg of previous cluster, then into top of next cluster, then into next ch sp; rep from * ending sc into same st as 3rd leg of previous cluster, turn.

Rep Row 3 for pattern.

Triple Tucks

Any number of sts plus 1 for turn

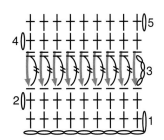

Row 1: Starting in 2nd ch from hk, sc to end, turn.

Row 2 (RS): Ch 1, starting in the 1st st, sc across, turn.

Row 3: Ch 4 (counts as one tr), tr in back lp of 2nd sc and in back lp of ea sc to end, turn.

Row 4: Ch 1, *sc in back lp of ea tr st and in rem lp of corresponding sc in the row below; rep from * ending last st in top of tch, turn.

Row 5: Ch 1, sc in ea sc to end, turn.

Repeat Rows 2–5 for pattern.

Two-Color Basketweave Blocks

Multiple of 16+9 plus 1 for turn

Special abbreviation

FPdc (front post double crochet): Yo hk, insert hk from front to back around the post of the st in the row below[1], yo and draw through lp, draw through 2 lps, yo, draw through two lps. One FPdc complete. Work 2 rows of ea color throughout.

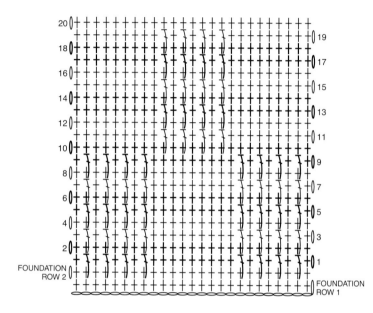

Two Foundation Rows[2]: With 1st color, starting in 2nd ch from hk, sc to end, turn.

Ch 1, starting in the 1st st, sc across, changing to 2nd color on last st, turn.

Row 1: Ch 1 * (sc in 1st st, FPdc in next st) rep three times, ** sc in next 9 sts, rep from * ending last rep at **, sc in last st, turn.

Row 2: Ch 1, sc in ea st across, turn.

Rows 3–10: Rep Rows 1 and 2 four times.

Row 11: Ch 1, *sc in 9 sts**, (sc in next st, FPdc in next st) four times, rep from *, end last rep at **, sc in last st, turn.

Row 12: Rep Row 2.

Rows 13–20: Rep–Rows 11 and 12 four times.

Rep Rows 1–20 for pattern.

In other words...

[1] Right-handed crocheters insert hook from right to left; left-handed crocheters insert hook from left to right.

[2] Since the FPdc stitch is worked into the row below, the first foundation row provides a smooth edge and the second foundation row is used to crochet into the row below.

Twisted Loops

Any number of sts plus 3 for turn

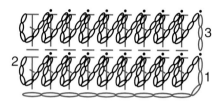

Row 1: Sk 3 ch (counts as dc), dc into ea ch to end, turn.

Row 2: *Ch 7, starting in the 2nd st, sl st into bk lp only inserting hk from back to front, repeat from* ending ch 7, sl st into top of tch, turn.

Row 3: Ch 3, starting in the 2nd st, inserting hk from front to back, dc in rem blo, turn.

Rep Rows 2 and 3 for pattern.

Woven Plaid Pattern

Multiple of 2+1 plus 4 for turn

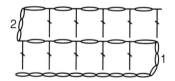

Row 1: Work dc in 5th ch from hk, *ch 1, sk next ch, dc in next ch; rep from * across, turn.

Row 2: Ch 4 (counts as dc and ch 1), *sk 1 st, dc, ch 1; rep from * across, ending dc in top of tch, turn.

Rep Row 2 for pattern.

Unique Techniques

Clever details, special techniques, and nifty tricks all contribute to your own unique crochet style. In this section, we've included techniques such as filet crochet and multicolor crochet, alternative beginnings, and a few nifty tricks to make your crochet more fun.

Fabulous Foundations/ Alternative Beginning Chains

Starting a project with a wiggly, skinny foundation chain may be difficult to count and sometimes ends up being a different gauge than the rest of your project. To increase your crochet enjoyment, try these alternative beginnings. Although a tight chain may be alleviated by chaining with a hook one or two sizes larger, there are several ways of working the chain and first row at the same time that produce a better looking edge and make it much easier to count.

Bill Elmore, who grouped and named a category of stitches that falls in height between the traditional stitches (see "Half-Step Stitches" on p. 27), also detailed several alternative methods of working the beginning chain. Crocheters have used these sts and techniques intentionally and unintentionally throughout the years, but until Mr. Elmore's work, they were referred to only as variations of other techniques.

Double Chain Foundation

The double chain foundation is not used much in the United States but is referred to in books published outside the U.S. The double chain creates a two-row foundation consisting of a chain and a single crochet.

Ch 2, pass hk through 1st st, yo, pull through 1 lp (2 lps on hk), yo, draw through both lps.

To make the next st, *pass hk through lp farthest from hook of st just completed, yo and pull through lp, yo, pull through two lps. Repeat from *.

Double chain

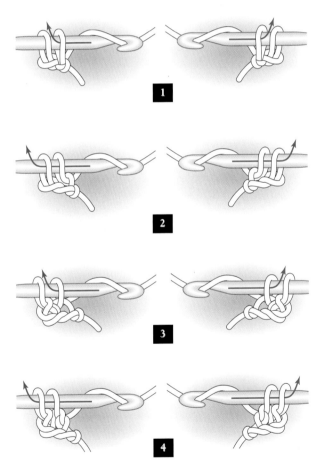

1

2

3

4

Elmore Single Face Variation

This technique creates a two-row foundation consisting of a chain and a taller stitch that could be any stitch of your choice that uses a yarn over to complete the stitch—hdc, dc, E or dE. The illustrations show how to work the stitch using a double crochet.

Ch 3, yo, insert hk into 1st ch, yo and pull through lp (3 lps on hk). Complete by working any st that starts with one yo such as hdc, dc, E or dE.

To make the next stitch, *yo, insert hk into first lp of st just made, yo and pull through lp. Complete st as before. Rep from * for length desired.

Elmore single face

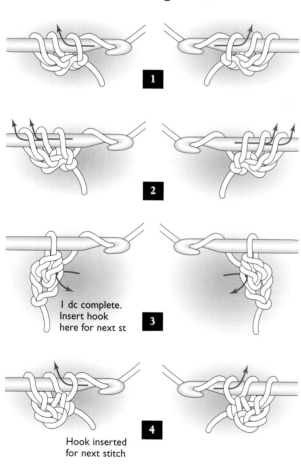

1

2

I dc complete.
Insert hook
here for next st   **3**

Hook inserted
for next stitch   **4**

Filet Crochet

Filet crochet is an easy technique that is usually worked only in double crochet and chain stitches. Basically it is an open-work mesh. Some of the open spaces are filled in with double crochet stitches to form patterns that can range from geometrics to flowers or lettering. Filet crochet is usually worked from charts instead of written instructions, with filled-in black squares representing solid blocks of crochet. Once you understand this concept, it is very easy to make a filet crochet item.

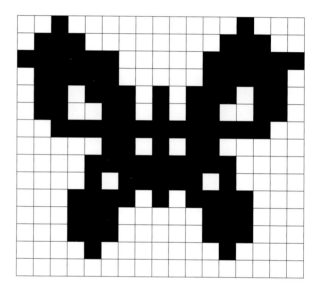

Each square on the graph represents 3 stitches in width. Because filet crochet usually uses double crochet stitches, a square's height would equal three chains or one double crochet.

The butterfly graph above is read with the odd-numbered rows representing the RS of the work and

> **TIP:** Use Post-It notes to keep your place while following pattern directions. When putting your work aside for a time, move the Post-It to where you will resume working the next time you pick it up. The note is also a good place to write down the hook size you are using and any other pertinent information.
>
> *Contributed by Jamie Webster*

the even numbers representing the WS of the work. Even though the finished piece is virtually reversible, we suggest you mark the RS of your work to help keep count of the rows.

There is one edge stitch used on both sides, thus each side edge square represents four stitches. The starting edge stitch will always be the three-chain turning chain.

The two double crochets or chains that make up the center of each square are edged by a double crochet on each side, like side posts.

Since each three-stitch square has either two double crochets or two chains plus the side post double crochet it shares with its neighbor, two adjacent filled squares would be made up of seven double crochets as follows: the first side post double crochet, its own two chains or stitches, the next side post double crochet, then the next square's 2 stitches plus the end side post double crochet. Three adjacent squares would be 10 stitches wide. The number of stitches needed to make up adjacent filled squares will always be 3 stitches for each square plus an ending corner post.

If a square is filled, place two double crochets between the side post double crochet stitches. If it is left blank, chain two between the two side post double crochet stitches.

Since each square represents 3 stitches, most filet crochet is done using fine yarn or thread. The actual size of the piece can be deceptive when compared to the chart.

Increasing and decreasing in filet crochet to maintain the mesh shaping is usually done by working additional chains at the beginning or the end of the row.

TIP: *When crocheting a long chain, such as the base for an afghan, use split-ring markers on every 10th or 20th chain. It's easier to keep track of your count and if you think you have miscounted, you won't have to go back to the beginning each time.*

Contributed by Patricia Lawrence

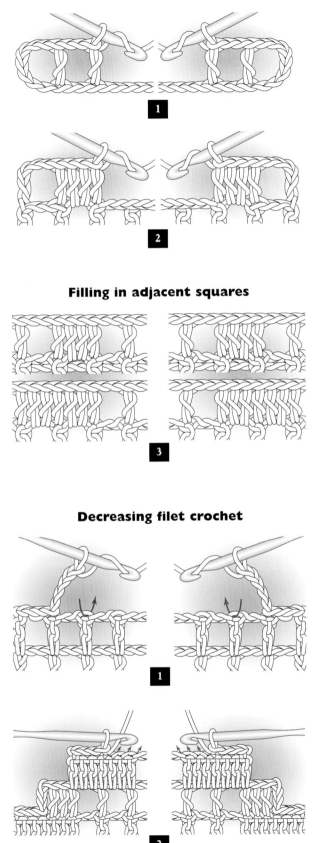

Filet crochet

1

2

Filling in adjacent squares

3

Decreasing filet crochet

1

2

Increasing filet crochet

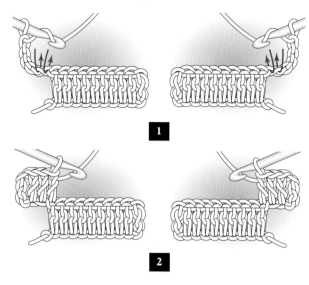

1

2

Making a Center-Pull Skein

There's no reason you can't make a convenient pull skein with any yarn, no matter how it was originally packaged.

Hold one end of the yarn in the palm of your hand and wind the yarn around your thumb and index finger in a figure-eight until your fingers are fairly full of yarn.

Carefully remove the figure-eight and fold it in half. Continue winding the yarn around this core, keeping the center-end yarn free and changing direction frequently to form a ball.

Multicolor Crochet Techniques

The simplest kind of multicolor work is done by changing color at the beginning of a row. This will produce the horizontal stripes that may be very interesting when combined with different stitches or different-width color bands.

However, taking a little time to learn how to work with multicolors in the same row brings a big payoff. And, it's probably much easier than you imagined! Multicolors bring variety and interest to your work, open up a whole new world of patterns, allow you to use up *lots* of leftovers, and are incredibly satisfying.

Bobbins for every project.

There are two main techniques for working with multicolors in the same row: stranding and intarsia.

Stranding

When only two colors are used and the colored areas are alternated across the width of the piece, stranding is usually chosen as the most effective technique. Stranding means both colors are in your hands all across the row, one being used and one being stranded, floated, or carried along at the back of the work. A generally accepted rule of thumb is that you don't carry yarn unworked more than three stitches without securing it or catching it in at the back. The unused yarn is secured by laying it between the back of your work and the hook and enclosing it as you draw the working yarn through the next stitch.

Intarsia

Intarsia is Italian for "inlay." This technique is used when many colors are used in one row or when two colors are separated by more stitches than it would be practical to strand across. To use this method, the necessary amount of several yards of each color to be inlaid are cut from the skein or ball of yarn and allowed to hang at the back of the work. The last two loops are left on the hook at the stitch before each inlaid color. The new color is drawn through and used for as many stitches as called for in the patern or

Back side of Learn-to-Crochet Afghan Block #16 showing intarsia and stranding techniques.

chart. The next color is drawn through the last two loops of the last stitch at each color change. If the amount of inlaid color needed is less than a yard or so, it is usually just left hanging free. If larger amounts are needed, there are a variety of bobbins available to hold various quantities of yarn.

> **TIP:** Ends can be quickly and neatly woven into the back of a finished item with a latch hook. Simply push the end of the hook under or through a few stitches on the back of the finished item (which will open the latch), catch the tail of the yarn, and pull back through in the opposite direction (which will close the latch). Give the end a gentle tug so that the buried yarn doesn't pucker the crocheted stitches. Repeat the procedure in the other direction so that the yarn end is woven in a "U" shape and is well secured before clipping it off. A tiny dab of fabric glue applied with the point of a pin will help to secure the ends of even the most slippery yarns.
>
> *Contributed by B. J. Licko-Keel*

Back side of Learn-to-Crochet Afghan Block #19 showing intarsia technique.

Fringes, Pom-Poms, and Tassels

Fringes, pom-poms, and tassels are among the most popular edgings for afghans, scarves, and hats. They add a nice decorative touch and are a great way to use up leftovers or add a spark of contrasting color to a project.

Fringe

Cut yarn into lengths twice the required length plus about 2". Using four or more strands together, fold in half. Draw the folded end of the loops from the right side through to the wrong side of the edge with a crochet hook. Hook the ends through the loop and draw in gently to tighten the knot.

Repeat, placing fringes close together for a rich, full look. After all the fringe has been placed on the project, lay it flat and trim the ends evenly.

Pom-poms

Many inexpensive pom-pom makers are available in craft stores. If you prefer to make your own, cut out two cardboard circles, making the diameter about ½" larger than you'd like your finished pom-pom.

Cut a circle in the center of each. The larger the inner circle, the more dense your finished pom-pom will be. Using a tapestry needle if desired, wind yarn around and through the center of the two circles until the hole is filled.

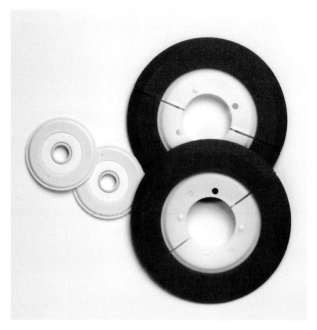

Pompom makers.

Cut through the outer loops between the two disks and separate slightly. Tie a piece of yarn firmly around the loops between the disks. Gently separate the two disks and fluff your pom-pom.

Making a pom-pom

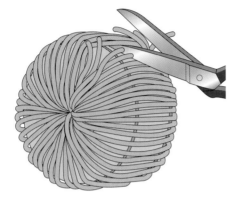

1

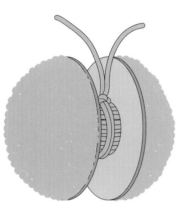

2

Tassels

Measure a piece of cardboard the desired length of your tassel. Wind yarn around the cardboard to desired thickness. Tie loop around yarn at top with yarn at least three times the length of the tassel, remove cardboard, and cut bottom loops. Wind the yarn around all the loops about ½" below the knot and fasten off.

Making a tassel

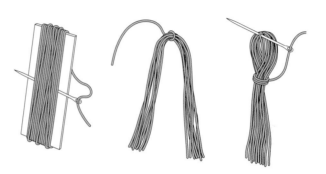

Twisted Cord

The easiest, most fun way to make twisted cording is by using an electric mixer. Kids love to help with this.

Use 8 to 14 strands of yarn in the color(s) of your choice, approximately three times your desired finished length, depending on how tightly you wind the cord.

Hold strands together and knot each end. Fasten a large paper clip through one knot and then into the end of the electric mixer beater. Have someone hold the other end of the yarn or fasten it to a stationary object.

"Mix" until the strands are twisted tightly, gradually moving the ends closer as tension increases. When cord begins to crimp when the tension is slightly relaxed, fold in half and allow to wind on itself. Knot each of the doubled ends, leaving 4" to 6" for tassel.

Get Confident with Color

Deciding which colors to use is the one thing every crochet project has in common. It is also the area in which many of us have the least amount of confidence. Fortunately, help is available. A simple, inexpensive, and effective tool for choosing color combinations is a color wheel. In this section, you'll find an overview of how a color wheel works and how it will help you choose balanced color combinations. You can check "A Glossary of Color Terms" on the facing page for explanations of any terms with which you are not familiar.

The sequence of colors on a color wheel isn't happenstance; it is based on the order in which color appears in the spectrum of light from the shortest wavelength to the longest. Red, orange, yellow, green, blue, and violet is the sequence you see when looking at a rainbow. When those colors are arranged in a circle, they make a color wheel. Use your color wheel to create harmonious combinations by laying various symmetrical shapes in its center. For harmonious combinations, combine the colors indicated by the points of each shape.

> **TIP:** Laying symmetrical shapes in the center of a color wheel and combining the colors at their points will always result in harmonious combinations.

In addition to a straight line that points to pairs of complementary colors (those colors that lie opposite each other on the color wheel), the symmetrical shapes most commonly used are an equilateral triangle, an isosceles triangle, a square, and a rectangle. As the shapes rotate on the wheel, the combinations change, but the spacing of the colors in each combination does not. For instance, an equilateral triangle invariably points to every fourth color on the wheel even though the colors in the combination change. It is the symmetrical spacing that consistently ensures a harmonious combination.

The Rainbow Pick, Point & Match Color Selector shown above is an inexpensive, simple-to-use tool that will help you choose winning color combinations every time. What makes it different from other color wheels is that each of the 12 color families also includes seven numbered values, from pastels to deep jewels, encircling a cutout window. When starting your combination with an existing fabric, fiber, paint chip, or other material, place it under the windows until you find the closest color and value

A Glossary of Color Terms

Analogous Colors next to each other on the color wheel.

Color A broad term referring to any color sensation when light falls on the retina of the eye. This includes black, white, gray, and grayed colors.

Complementary Colors that lie opposite each other on the color wheel.

Cool colors Colors in the green, blue, and violet range. They denote coolness and look calm, clean, and inviting. They recede and are restful. Red to violet and yellow to green contain elements of both warm and cool colors. These colors become warmer or cooler as they travel toward red or blue on the color spectrum.

Counterpoint The adjacent color to the right or left of a color's complement.

Intermediate colors See Tertiary colors.

Intensity The brightness or dullness of a color. Intensity refers to how much of the pure pigment is in the color. The less a color has been tinted or shaded, the greater its intensity. Sometimes used interchangeably with saturation or chroma.

Monochromatic Multiple values of one color.

Primary colors Red, yellow, and blue. These three colors cannot be made by combining other colors. Also, mixtures of the primaries, together with black and white, theoretically can make all other colors.

Quartic colors A mixture of two tertiary colors. The quartic mixtures produce 6 colors in addition to the traditional 12 colors of the color wheel: russet, cinnamon, citron, olive, forest, and eggplant.

They are the most sophisticated and fashion-oriented of the colors.

Secondary colors A mixture of two primary colors resulting in orange, violet, or green.

Shade A color darkened by adding black.

Split complement A three-color combination consisting of a starting color plus the adjacent two colors on either side of its complement.

Tertiary (Intermediate) colors A mixture of one primary and one secondary color, resulting in yellow-green, blue-green, blue-violet, red-violet, red-orange, and yellow-orange.

Tetrad A four-cornered shape. Squares and rectangles are tetrads commonly used to form four-color combinations on a color wheel.

Tint A color lightened by adding white.

Tone A color darkened by adding a gray that is of the same value as the color to which it is added.

Triad A three-cornered shape. Equilateral and isosceles triangles are triads commonly used to form three-color combinations on a color wheel.

Warm colors Colors in the yellow, orange, and red range. They denote warmth and make a color scheme look cheerful and exuberant. Warm colors come forward with vibrancy.

Value The lightness or darkness of the color as measured against a gray scale that runs from white to black. Black, white, and gray are values that contain no color.

match. Then turn the inner dial to see a series of color combinations, all perfectly balanced and harmonious. Based on your project and the number of colors you wish to use, you can choose from the following color combinations:

Complementary (6 two-color combinations based on a straight line): Choose a starting color on the color wheel. The color directly opposite is called its complement and is used to accent your main color.

Triad (4 three-color combinations based on an equilateral triangle): Combine every fourth color on the color wheel to form four beautifully balanced three-color combinations—a bright and youthful primary triad, a more subtle triad made up of the secondary colors, and two triads using all tertiary colors.

Split Complement (12 three-color combinations based on an isosceles triangle): Choose a starting color on the color wheel. The other colors of the combination are the two colors on either side of its complement. This forms a quite striking three-color version of the two-color complementary combination.

Rectangular Tetrad (6 four-color combinations based on a rectangle): Choose a starting color on the color wheel. A rectangle placed on the color wheel will point to two positions separated by three colors and two positions separated by one color. Move the rectangle around the wheel to form six different combinations.

Square Tetrad (4 four-color combinations based on a square): Combining every third color on the color wheel forms these combinations. Each Tetrad's double pair of complementary colors make a bold statement.

Four additional color combinations are:

Monochromatic (any number of tints and shades of the same color): The Fans and Vees Tunic and Juliet Hat, shown on p. 163, is a monochromatic combination.

Analogous (three- and five-color combinations): Choose a starting color on the color wheel. The starting color, plus the one or two colors on either side, are analogous. The Chevrons Cap-Sleeved Tee Top, shown on p. 160, is an analogous combination.

Multicolor (up to 12 colors): Use matching values from each color around the wheel. You can also create a six-color combination by using matching values of every other color. The Chevrons Long-Sleeved Tunic, shown on p. 156, is a multicolor combination using mid-value colors. You could make the same project using all light or all dark colors.

> **TIP:** Use matching values in multicolor combinations that include more than two primary colors, or range beyond four colors in either direction on the wheel. Mixing values results in a spotty look and is distracting.

Dividing the Space and Colors

As you look at the combinations suggested by a color wheel, don't forget that the division of space and the colors that fill them are usually more pleasing when they are not used in equal proportion. Notice that when our book projects use blocks of color, the color is used disproportionately. The Loopy Bath Mat and Lid Cover and the Popcorns, Picots, and Puffs Pullover and Hat are examples of this guideline.

> **TIP:** Think of the colors you are assigning to your spaces as a gallon of your main color, a quart of your supporting color, and an ounce of accent.

> **TIP:** Space is more pleasing when sections are divided disproportionately, such as two-thirds/one-third, than when they are divided in half.

Make It So It Fits!

Every designer, every magazine, and every pattern company has its own set of standards. That's why a medium from one company may fit, but another company's medium may be too long, too short, too wide in the shoulders, too narrow at the waist…well, you get the point. Although standard measurements based on extensive testing are available, every manufacturer and designer is free to interpret them however they wish.

What Shape Are You?

Large or small, everyone tends to fall into one of three different body types. We call them the "glass shapes." Three people may weigh the same, but their height and proportions may make them look very different:

The Hourglass This figure type is what many consider a "typical" woman's shape. It really just means that this body type has hips and bust that are about the same size and the waist is defined. Even with extra pounds, this body type carries weight evenly distributed all over.

The Wineglass This body type carries more weight through the shoulders, chest, and midriff. Often this body type has narrow hips, a flat derriere, and thin legs.

The Decanter Larger hips, derriere, and heavy legs characterize this body type. Just the opposite of The Wineglass, this body type usually has narrow shoulders and a relatively small bust.

These are just general body types. You may be basically one of these body types with tendencies toward another. If you are a Decanter shape, you may find that a pattern with the proper bust size will be too tight in the hips. Wineglass shapes may find the right bust size, but the hips are too wide. If you are taller or shorter than average, you may need to make your sweater longer or shorter.

> **TIP:** When making a sweater out of thick yarn, the outside finished measurement may be up to 2" larger than the inside measurement because of the thickness of the fabric. Try this: Lay a heavy cardigan sweater down on a flat surface. Measure its width while closed. Now open the sweater and measure the back width. How much difference did you find? If you want 3". of ease in your sweater, you may need to make the finished width 4" or 5" more than your body measurement.
>
> *Contributed by Doris Schwartz*

Measure Twice, Crochet Once!

Most patterns have a schematic that shows the finished measurements of the garment. For best results, choose a garment in a similar style and fiber that you already have made or bought and measure that garment. Compare the measurements of your garment to the one you plan to make. Uh-oh! Do you see places where your measurements are quite different from the sweater you plan to make? Some adjustments may be in order, but don't just make a larger size because you want a looser fit across the chest or hips. In most patterns, as chest size increases or decreases, so do shoulder width, armhole openings, and length.

> **TIP:** Make a paper pattern for each piece from either an existing garment whose fit you like or a simplified sewing pattern that you have made and know will fit. Then it's a simple matter to crochet away in the stitch of your choice while frequently comparing each piece to the paper pattern to get the proper shaping and dimensions. In most cases, this eliminates the need for written instructions—a nice bonus on a car trip or when a mindless project is warranted.
>
> Contributed by Joan McGowan

EASY TRICKS FOR BETTER FIT

If you are a Decanter Shape and want the hip portion of your sweater to be larger, try using a hook two sizes larger for the hips, switch to one size larger for the chest, and then use the called-for size for the shoulders.

If you are a Wineglass Shape, reverse the above suggestion so that you use the largest size hook on the top portion of the garment.

Most garments look best if they end at your high hip or don't drop below your widest hip measurement. Garments that end at the widest part of the hip or below, especially if they have ribbing, will "cup" under your derriere.

To change the length of a pattern, lengthen or shorten the body of the sweater between the lower edge and the armhole by one or two pattern repeats.

If your pattern repeat isn't complicated and you want to increase the hip width of your pattern, try starting your garment using the directions for the next larger size and gradually decrease stitches until you have the correct number for the next smaller size at the armhole. Then begin following the directions for the next smaller size from the armhole up.

If the sleeves need to be more than 1" shorter or longer than the directions call for, change your rate of increases.

If your pattern is multicolored, use the darkest shades at the bottom with lighter shades around your face. This will pull the viewer's eye toward your face and make the lower portion of your body recede.

If your garment goes over your hips and you plan to sit or drive in it, make sure you leave plenty of ease, at least 4" to 5", so that you can move comfortably.

"En-gauging" Ideas

Probably more than any other one thing, gauge is the reason that handmade garments don't fit properly. Always take the time to check the gauge before beginning your sweater. Your pattern will have a gauge given, but every crocheter is different. If you don't believe us, try this. Using the same yarn and hook size, have several of your friends chain 20 stitches and then work 10 rows of double crochet. Do they have different size swatches? We're sure they do.

Your gauge may also be affected by the weather, your mood, or the type of yarn you are using. Tense people crochet more tightly. If you are tired or sleepy, you may work more loosely. If your gauge isn't the same as the one given in your pattern, you will need to make some changes. When you learn how to determine your "Personal Stitch Profile," you will always be able to crochet to gauge…*your* gauge.

Your Personal Stitch Profile

We understand the excitement of starting a new project. However, when you're going to commit a significant amount of time, money, and energy to a project, you owe it to yourself to take the time to make sure it will fit properly. How many undone sweaters do you have that wouldn't even have been started if you had tried a small sample first?

If your pattern doesn't give specific instructions for working a preliminary swatch, start with the gauge suggested and crochet enough stitches to work *at least* a 4" x 4" (10-cm x 10-cm) piece of the pattern stitch. You may need to make a much larger swatch if your project has a large pattern repeat or calls for thick yarn.

Now compare your results to the stated gauge in your pattern. Are they the same? Probably not exactly. Decide if you are satisfied with the look and feel of the stitches. Work a new piece if you prefer it to be tighter or looser. Decrease your hook size to make it tighter or increase hook size if you want it looser. Keep changing hook sizes until you are satisfied.

If you are making a garment, it is especially important to make changes *now* since even a half stitch per inch difference can result in an ill-fitting garment. For example, if a sweater is 20" (50 cm) wide and the gauge given in the pattern is 4 sts = 1" (2.5 cm), the pattern would ask you to make the sweater 80 stitches wide. However, if your gauge were 3.5 stitches to the inch or 2.5 cm, but you hadn't checked it and just made the sweater 80 stitches wide, your sweater would be almost 23" (57.5 cm) wide. Together, your front and back would make the garment 6" (15 cm) bigger! If your row gauge were also different, you could end up with a sweater that was too long and too wide. Think of all the money and time you will waste if you don't make a gauge swatch.

Even if size isn't critical to your project, the amount of yarn you use will change if your gauge isn't the same as the one given in the pattern. How many times have you been one ball short or over on a project? Gauge differences may be the reason why.

> **TIP:** Since crochet is somewhat heavier, bulkier, and less elastic than knitting, it requires more precise shaping and contouring. As a rule, crocheted garments should not be too tight because they can warp and buckle around the body. A roomier cut, contrary to what many people think, gives a smooth and flattering line.
>
> *Contributed by Patricia Baron*

What if your gauge is different and you either like it that way or you've tried different hooks and still can't match the stated gauge? Just adjust the number of stitches and rows. In the example given above, instead of making your sweater 80 stitches wide, you would make it 70 stitches wide (3.5 x 20). If you are making a project that has a repeating pattern, you may have to adjust this number slightly up or down.

PART TWO
Learn-to-Crochet Afghan

The first part of this book provided all the basic information and techniques needed to make you a successful crocheter. If you are new to crochet, we hope you practiced those techniques and experimented with forming the stitches. Now it's time to put your newly found skills to practical use in the Learn-to-Crochet Afghan.

Whether you're an experienced crocheter or a beginner; a right- or left-hander; whether you like working from international symbols or following text directions, the afghan blocks are sure to provide you with hours of fun, inspiration, and education as they guide you through increasingly more intriguing stitches and techniques. For practical application of what you learn in each block, the stitches and techniques are used in projects later in the book. The projects are listed at the end of each block, along with design ideas for further inspiration.

Afghan Introduction

To help you crochet *your* way, each block is written in traditional step-by-step text and in international symbols. Many blocks have "In other words…" footnotes that refer you to additional explanations and instructions written especially for beginners and left-handers.

If you have not yet discovered how fast and easy it is to follow patterns using international symbols, we recommend that you take this opportunity to learn. A detailed explanation of international symbols can be found in "Beginnings and Basics" on pp. 8–63. When you learn to work from symbols, it will open up the fabulous world of international patterns. Unusual fashion designs from Japan, traditional multicolor work from Scandinavia and Europe, and wonderful dimensional lace from Ireland are just a few of the options that will be open to you when you learn international symbols.

General Information

Finished Size

Approx 56" x 70" (142 cm x 178 cm)

Each block will measure approximately 13" x 13" (33 cm x 33 cm) after light steaming, *before* any edging rows are added.

Materials You Will Need

The original models were made using Coats Patons Decor yarn 100 gr/210 yd/192 meters (25% wool, 75% Acrilan acrylic). In addition to color-coordinated solid colors, matching multicolored yarn was used to edge and seam all blocks, and as an accent on some blocks. The different stitches show off better when made in a variety of colors. We made two models, which are shown throughout the book. The predominately blue model was made by Gloria, a right-hander. The predominately rose model was made by Susan, a left-hander. Choose your colors based on personal preference.

Worsted-Weight Yarn
    4 skeins #1621 Country Blue or
#1626 Aubergine (A)
    7 skeins #1620 Pale Country Blue or
#1625 Pale Aubergine (B)
    5 skeins #1602 Aran (C)
    6 skeins #1695 Mountain Top Multi (D)
Crochet hook US size I/9 (5.5 mm)
Bobbins
Tapestry needle for finishing

Gauge

12 sts and 7 rows = 4" (10 cm) in dc st

The gauge given is what we got using an I/9 hook and Coats Paton *Decor*; it should be used as a general guideline. Since each block uses different stitches and techniques and varying numbers of stitches are used in each block, your gauge will vary based on the pattern in a particular block.

If you make your blocks from thicker or thinner yarn or use a larger or smaller hook, your blocks will be correspondingly larger or smaller when using the numbers given in these directions. This poses no problem as long as you consistently use the same yarn and hook throughout. For more information on gauge, see p. 63.

Finishing

Once you've crocheted all 20 blocks, they're ready to be joined into a fabulous afghan. We always love fin- ishing because that's when we see the bits and pieces come together to form a beautiful finished project. We've used an easy joining technique for the Learn-to-Crochet Afghan that will quickly ready your afghan for the admiration of your family and friends.

Finishing the Individual Blocks

Round 1: With RS facing and D, sc along ea side so sides rem flat, working 3 sc into ea corner.[1]

Round 2: Sc around working 40 sts along ea side and 3 sc into each corner, inc or dec along edge evenly as needed

Round 3: Beg in center corner st, ch 1, (sc, ch 2, sc into same st). One corner made, sc into next st, *ch 2, sk 1 st, sc in next st, rep from * 19 times ending with 20 2-ch spaces per side, rep ( ) sts for corner, continue working around all four sides.

In other words...

[1] Since each block has a different number of stitches based on the pattern, you may not want to work stitch for stitch along each side on the first single crochet round. Approximately 38 to 40 stitches will probably work for each side. You can make final adjustments to your count on Rounds 2 and 3. An easy way to help maintain an even number of stitches on each side is to place a marker in the center of the side, then divide each half into quarters and place a marker. If you want approximately 40 stitches per side, you will need to make 10 sc sts between each marker.

Assembling the Afghan

Following the arrangement shown on the "Afghan Assembly" chart below, join the bottom edges of the upper blocks to the top edges of the lower adjacent blocks in each of the four 5-block vertical strips as follows:

With right sides together and D, sl st yarn to front corner 2-ch sp, ch 1, sc, ch 2, sc in back corner 2-ch sp, *ch 2, sc in next front 2-ch sp, ch 2, sc in next back 2-ch sp, rep from * to corner, ch 2, sc in front corner 2-ch sp, ch 2, sc in back corner 2-ch sp. Fasten off.

Join the four 5-block strips as above, working the intersections as follows: sc into the front corner 2-ch sp, ch 2, sc into the back corner 2-ch sp, ch 2, sc around the ch 2 between the corners of the front piece, ch 2, sc around the ch 2 between the corners of the back piece, ch 2, sc into the front corner 2-ch space and cont as est.

Outside edging

Rnd 1: Work the *sc, ch 2* edging into the 2-ch sps of previous rnd, working corners as est.

Rnd 2: Work Rsc (crab stitch) into ea sc and 2-ch sp.

Fasten off.

Afghan Assembly			
9 Basketweave	13 Trebles & Aran Stitches	8 Chevrons	16 Multicolor Crochet
18 Three-Color Interlocking Blocks	20 Lace	11 Picots, Puffs, Popcorns, and Bobbles	10 Fans and Vees
4 Combination Stitches	2 Double Single Crochet and Variations	7 Twisted Loops	15 Waves
14 More Single Crochet Variations	5 Double Crochet and Variations	12 Filet Crochet	1 Single Crochet and Variations
19 Three-Color Post Stitch Variations	6 Woven Plaid	3 Half Double Crochet and Variations	17 Crosses and Bars

Afghan Block 1
Single Crochet and Variations

Single crochet is the perfect beginning because it is one of the most commonly used of all crochet stitches. It can be used alone as the body of a project; as a decorative join; as a one- or two-row edging; or as the base stitch for other edgings in crochet, knitting, or other types of needlework.

Additionally, in this block you'll learn three simple techniques that change the appearance of single crochet stitches. Three chains in the middle of every fourth stitch form a neat little picot bump; working into the back loop only of each stitch forms a little ledge or "front porch" across the front of the work; and working alternately into the back loop and front loop creates an interesting surface texture.

Although you're working every stitch in this block in a variation of single crochet, each of these variations can easily be used to create a similar effect when worked in another stitch.

Stitches you'll learn in this block

    Single crochet (see pp. 20–21)

    Front porch pattern (see p. 32)

    Picot single crochet (see p. 37)

    Alternating front and back
      porch pattern (see pp. 32–33)

Other stitches or techniques used

    Increases by working two single
      crochets into one stitch

    Decreases by working two
      single crochet stitches
      together

    Multiples

    Changing colors

    Carrying yarn along the side

Colors used

    A, B, C, D

New abbreviations

alt - alternate(ing)

ch(s) - chain(s)

dec(ing) - decrease(ing)

ea - each

est - established

hk - hook

inc - increase

lp(s) - loop(s)

pat st - pattern stitch

Psc - picot single crochet

rem - remain(ing)

rep - repeat

RS - right side

sc - single crochet

sc2tog - single crochet two together

sk - skip

sl st - slip stitch

st(s) - stitch(es)

tog - together

WS - wrong side

yo - yarn over

Projects that use single crochet and variations

Single crochet is used in every block and project. It is the only stitch used in the spectacular Reversible Jacket and Matching Shoulder Bag.

Alternating multicolors worked in simple single crochet, both straight and in reversed single crochet (crab stitch), give interest to the trim in the Tapestry Tabard and Matching Crusher Hat, various hats, and the Carry-All Shoulder Bag.

Picot single crochet and picots are used in the Aran Angles Pullover and Hat; Popcorns, Picots, and Puffs Pullover, and Hat; and Tasseled Shoulder Bag and Cloche Hat.

The front and back porch stitches are used in the Amelia Cuff-to-Center Jacket and Matching Beret and Furry Hooded Scarf and Mittens.

Afghan Block I
Step-by-Step Text Instructions

With A, ch 41 plus 1 for turn.

Row 1 (RS)[1]: Sc in 2nd ch from hk and in every ch across, turn—41 sc.[2]

Row 2: Ch 1, sc in ea sc across[3], turn.

Rows 3–8: Rep Row 2 for 6 more times, changing to D on last st of Row 8.[4] Do not cut yarn if desired. Carry up the side wrapping unused color(s) at the beg. of row.

Rows 9–10: Rep Row 2 twice.[5]

Rows 11–14: Work the **Psc** pattern Rows 2–5 once[6], changing to B in last st of Row 14.

Rows 15–22: Rep Rows 2 and 3 of **front porch** pattern 4 times, changing to C in last st of Row 22.

Row 23: Work Row 2 of **front porch** pattern once.

Row 24: Work Row 3 of the **alt back and front porch** pattern, turn.

Rows 25–30: Work Rows 2 and 3 of the **alt back and front porch** pattern 3 times, changing to B in last st of Row 30.

Rows 31–38: Rep Rows 2 and 3 of **front porch** pattern 4 times, changing to D in last st of Row 38.

Rows 39 and 40: Rep Rows 2 and 3 of **front porch** pattern.

Rows 41–44: Work the **Psc** pattern Rows 2–5 once, changing to A in last st of Row 44, turn.

Rows 45–52: Rep Row 2 changing to D in the last st of Row 52.

Finish block according to instructions in "Afghan Introduction" on p. 66.[7]

Fasten off.

In other words...

[1] Abbreviation for right side. Right side refers to the "public" side of the finished piece *not* necessarily the side facing you. Since this afghan block designates Row 1 as the right side, all odd-numbered rows will be right-side rows. You can use this

as a reference point to make sure you have the correct number of rows. If you are working an odd-numbered row and are on the wrong side of your work, you will know you have made an error. Place a safety pin or split-ring marker on the right side of your work to identify it.

[2] Skip one chain (this is the turning chain) and start the first single crochet in the second chain from the hook. Never count the loop that is on the hook. Continue to work a single crochet in each chain across for a total of 41 single crochets.

[3] In this block, the pattern directs you to start all rows in the first stitch. It is the personal preference of the authors when working in single crochet to make the turning chain, then start in the first stitch of single crochet. It forms a more attractive edge and one to which an edging is more easily applied.

[4] Refer to pp. 58–60 for information on how to change colors. Continue working in the new color until another color change is indicated.

[5] Refer to the directions for Row 2, which, in this case, are to work a row of single crochet. So, the directions mean to

work two more rows of single crochet. By writing the pattern in this manner, it shortens the text considerably, especially if the instructions for the row are long or complicated.

[6] Usually individual pattern stitches are located in a single chapter for easy reference. This also avoids repeating the same information over and over when patterns are used in various projects. Many crochet stitch patterns have a foundation row, which may be called the Base Row, Foundation Row, or Row 1. This first row is used only once to establish the pattern and is not repeated as part of the pattern. Since the Picot Single Crochet is used in the middle of the block, no foundation row is needed, therefore you repeat only Rows 2 through 5.

[7] We recommend that you edge each block as you finish it since it will make the final assembly go much faster!

DESIGN IDEAS

When making the three stitch variations in Block 1, don't think of them as techniques to be used only with single crochet stitches but as variations that you can use on all crochet stitches. They are tools you will tuck away in your crochet tool kit to use over and over any time you want that particular effect. Just as knowledge of many tools serves a carpenter, the more crochet tools you know how to use, the more likely you are to create a finished product that is exactly what you had in mind.

One or more rows of single crochet picots may be inserted as a decorative element with any stitch. A few rows make a great divider to separate broader bands of color or stitches. In this block, we separated the rows of picots with one row of single crochet, but you may use any stitch. For instance, you could broaden the stitch pattern by using a row of double single or half double stitches between the single crochet picot rows. Or you could form a lacy open effect by placing tall stitches between the rows.

Picot single crochet rows make an effective design feature at a cuff, neck, or hat band, or they may form an allover pattern. The picots may be offset by placing the loops of the second row of picots between the loops of the first row as we've designed on this block, or they may be placed above each other to form a grid effect. They may also be positioned more closely or spaced farther apart to achieve other effects.

This same variety is true of stitches worked into the front and back. They may be offset or formed in a grid, and you may work into the back or front loops of any stitch.

As you work the variations given for other stitches (such as the half double, double, or treble), don't forget that many of these variations may also be applied to single crochet. A few different crochet stitches, and a handful of variations, provide an almost limitless variety of fun and easy effects when used in different combinations.

Afghan Block 1

International Symbols

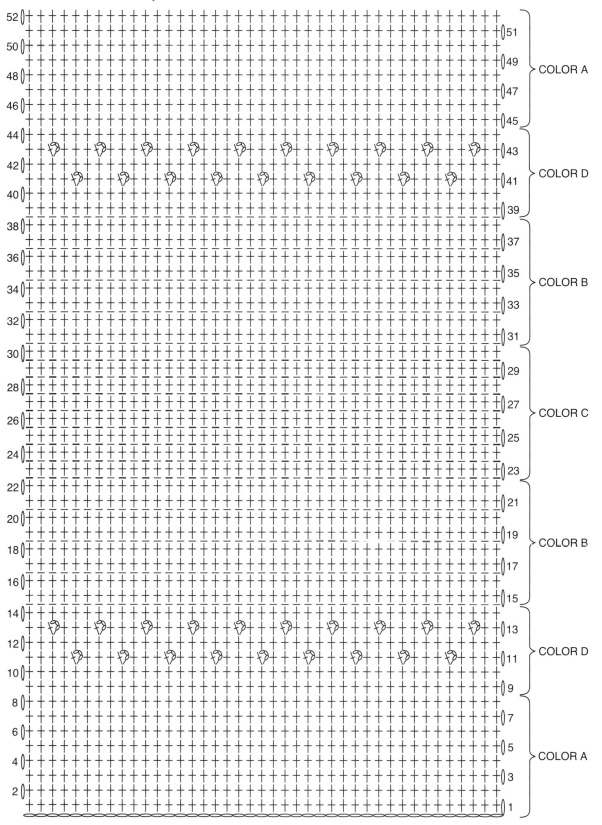

COLOR A

COLOR D

COLOR B

COLOR C

COLOR B

COLOR D

COLOR A

Afghan Block 2
Double Single Crochet and Variations

Double single crochet is a vastly underused stitch. It is similar to the single crochet, but with a chain worked before the stitch is completed. It is a handsome stitch, slightly more elongated than single crochet, yet not quite as high or as "bumpy" as the half double. It is the stitch we use when we want a simple, firm fabric with a little more "give" than single crochet. This is only the first of several nontraditional stitches you'll be learning.

Two variations on the double single stitch are used in this block. The grit stitch is one of several patterns formed by skipping a stitch, then working two stitches into one stitch. The comma pattern uses a type of spike stitch in which the hook is inserted one or more rows below the current row being worked.

Stitches you'll learn in this block
   Double single crochet (see pp. 21–22)
   Grit double single crochet stitch (see p. 45)
   Comma pattern (see p. 41)

Other stitches or techniques used
   Single crochet
   Changing colors

Colors used
   A, B, C, D

New abbreviations
   dsc - double single crochet
   tch - turning chain

Projects that use double single crochet and variations
   Convertible-Collar Classic Jacket and Toque Hat (Linked double single crochet)
   The Becoming Vest (grit double single crochet)
   Carry-All Shoulder Bag (comma pattern)

Afghan Block 2

Step-by-Step Text Instructions

With B, ch 39 plus 2 for turn.

Row 1: Starting in 3rd ch from hk, work 39 dsc[1] across, turn.

Row 2 (RS): Ch 2, dsc in 1st st and in every dsc across, turn. Mark front side of work.

Rows 3–7: Rep Row 2 five times, changing to A on last st of Row 7, turn.

Rows 8–10: Work Row 2 of **grit double single crochet,** changing to B on last st of Row 10.

Row 11: Rep Row 2 changing to A on last st.

Rows 12–25: Work rows 2–5 of **comma pattern,** changing colors at the ends of pattern rows 3 and 5 working two rows of each color as follows: A, C, D, C, D, C, A. Do not cut yarn when working with C and D until Row 23 is completed, changing to B on last st of Row 25, turn.[2]

Row 26: Work Row 4 of **comma pattern,** changing to A in last st.

Rows 27–29: Work Row 2 of **grit double single crochet** three times, changing to B on last st of Row 29.

Rows 30–35: Repeat Row 2 six times.

Finish block according to instructions in "Afghan Introduction" on p. 66.
Fasten off.

In other words...

[1] See pp. 21–22 for directions on how to form the Double single stitch.

[2] Patterns that change color are frequently written using shorthand such as this. If the colors are interchanged frequently, it is more convenient and you will have fewer ends to work in if you carry the nonworking color loosely up the side of your project. The row-by-row translation is given in the chart at top right.

Changing Colors (Rows 12 to 26)

Row #	Pat Row #	Color	
12	2	A	
13	3	A	Cut yarn
14	4	C	
15	5	C	
16	2	D	
17	3	D	
18	4	C	
19	5	C	
20	2	D	
21	3	D	Cut yarn
22	4	C	
23	5	C	Cut yarn
24	2	A	
25	3	A	Cut yarn
26	4	B	Cut yarn

DESIGN IDEAS

Spike stitches make a wonderful overall fabric when used with multicolors. You can substitute almost any stitch as the base stitch when making spikes. Experiment with lining them up in a grid pattern or offset them for a staggered pattern.

The spikes may also be varied in the same row by working a series of stitches, which reach down four, three, two, and then one row below the current row.

Try making the spikes closely spaced and then spread out.

A few rows of contrasting colored spikes inserted at the cuff, neck, or border may be just the amount of accent color needed.

Spiked stitches are also a good design technique to segue from one color block to another. The zigzag effect is more interesting than a flat, straight color change.

Afghan Block 2

International Symbols

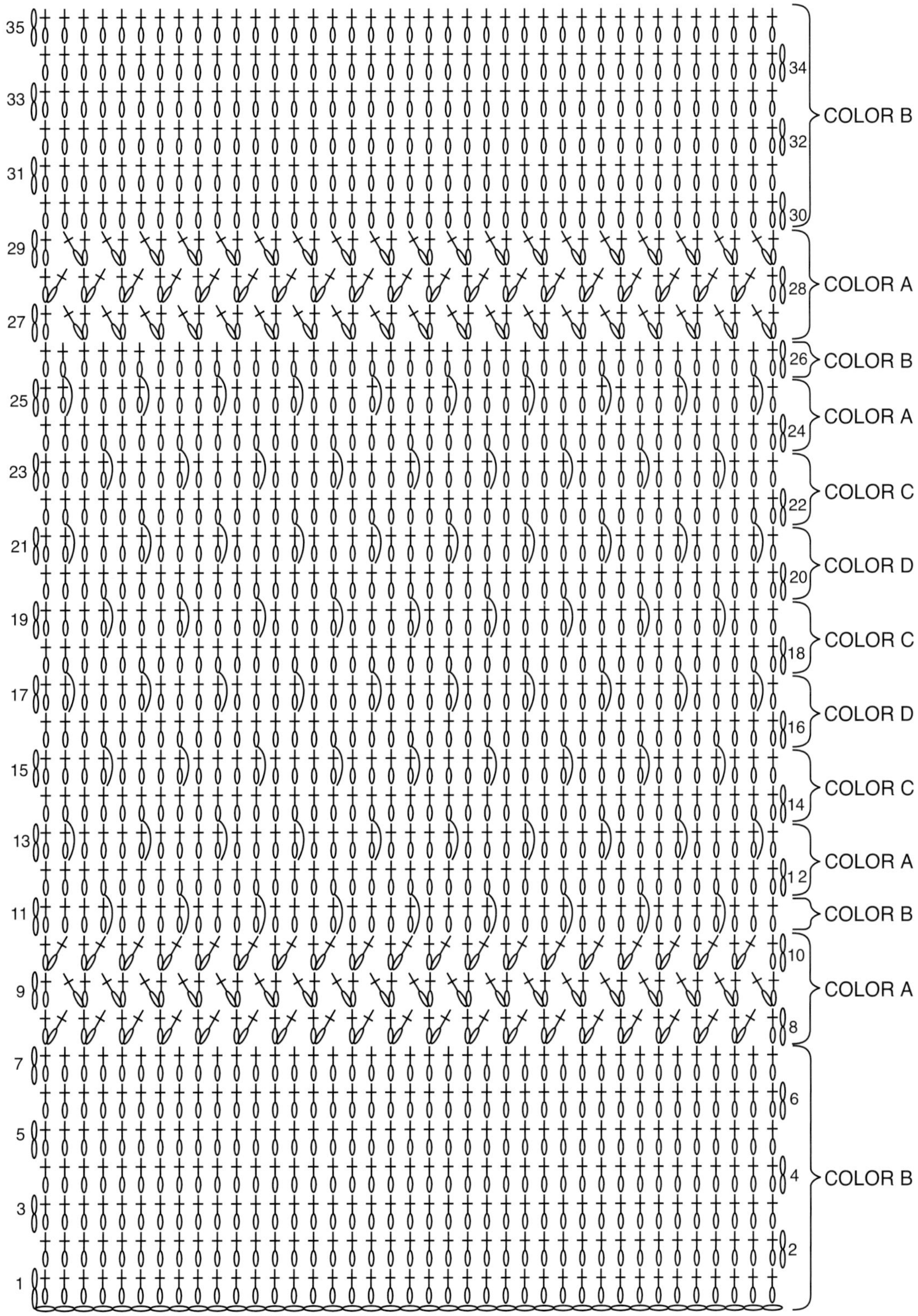

Afghan Block 3
Half Double Crochet and Variations

Half double crochet is the first stitch in which you yarn over before inserting the hook into the stitch. The purpose of this is to give you more yarn or thread loops to use to elongate the stitch. All of the new stitches you learn from now on will have one or more of these beginning yarn overs.

The two variations on half double crochet in this block are chained crosses and diagonal spikes. Both are formed by rotating the hook back in the direction just worked—back to the right for a right-hander and back to the left for a left-hander. These stitches are an example of how different a stitch may look when worked by a right-hander or left-hander.

The look of the right- and left-handed chained crosses varies only slightly: The only difference is which angled stitch lies on top. The diagonal spike is more distinctively different because the diagonal slant is clearly in the opposite direction. Notice that the two sides of your block slant in opposite directions.

Remember, both variations can be worked with other stitches.

Stitches you'll learn in this block
Half double crochet (see pp. 21–23)
Chained cross (see pp. 39–40)
Diagonal spike (see p. 43)

Other stitches or techniques used
Single crochet
Changing colors
Working into a space

Colors used
A, B

New abbreviations
hdc - half double crochet
ch sp - chain space
sp(s) - space(s)

Projects that use half double crochet and variations
Pretty Posies (half double crochet)
Convertible-Collar Classic Jacket and Toque Hat (diagonal spikes)

Afghan Block 3
Step-by-Step Text Instructions

With A, ch 42 plus one for turn.

Row 1: Starting in 2nd ch from hk, work 42 sc across[1], turn.

Row 2 (RS)[2]: Ch 2 (counts as hdc), hdc[3] in 2nd st and in every st across making last st in top of tch[4], turn. Mark front side of work.

Rows 3–5: Rep Row 2 for 3 times changing to B on last st of Row 5.

Rows 6 and 7: Work Row 2 of **chained cross** pattern two times changing to A on last st of Row 7.

Rows 8–11: Rep Row 2 for 4 times changing to B on last st of Row 11.

Rows 12–20: Work Rows 2 and 3 of the **diagonal spike** four times, then work Row 2 of diagonal spike pattern 1 more time changing to A in last st of Row 20.

Rows 21–24: Rep Row 2 for 4 times changing to B on last st of Row 24.

Rows 25–26: Rep Rows 6 and 7 changing to A on last st of Row 26.

Rows 27–30: Rep Row 2 for 4 times.

Row 31: Ch 1, work sc in ea st across.

Finish block according to instructions in "Afghan Introduction" on p. 66.

Fasten off.

In other words...

[1] This block begins and ends with a row of sc to make it the correct height. This method is often used to increase length a small amount.

[2] In this block, the even numbered rows are the right side.

[3] See pp. 21–23 for directions on how to form this stitch.

[4] See pp. 25 on the importance of the turning chain.

DESIGN IDEAS

The chained cross lends itself to many applications just by changing the length of the stitch used. Longer stitches produce a more airy look suitable for a shawl, stole, or little jacket. Shorter stitches make a firmer fabric.

When working the diagonal spike stitch with thick yarn or when several strands are held together, try a variation that uses a longer stitch to create a less dense fabric.

Diagonal spike stitches make "instant" buttonholes that form naturally because of the little holes in the stitch. Try weaving contrast-color yarn through the holes for a woven effect or use for the bands on a sweater for instant buttonholes.

Afghan Block 3
International Symbols

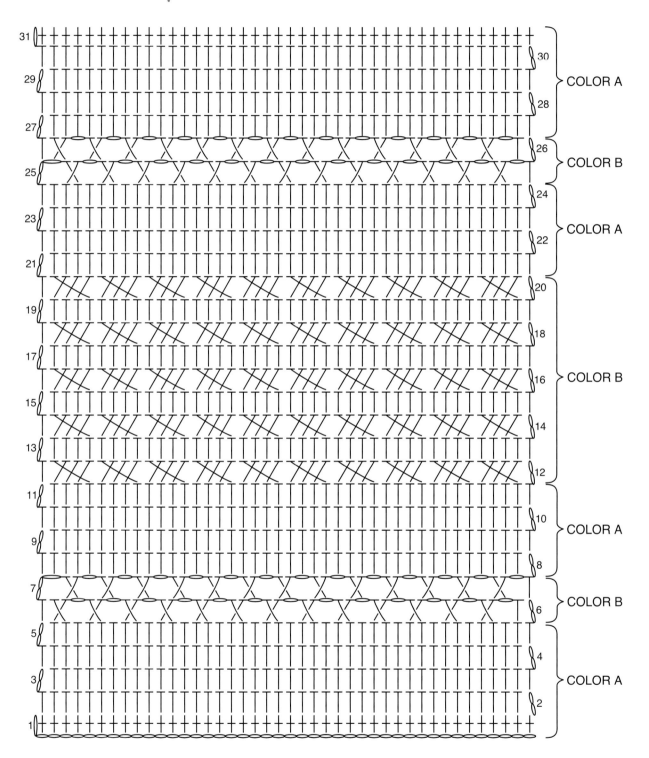

31
30
29 COLOR A
28
27
26 COLOR B
25
24
23 COLOR A
22
21
20
19
18
17
16 COLOR B
15
14
13
12
11
10
9 COLOR A
8
7
6 COLOR B
5
4
3 COLOR A
2
1

Afghan Block 4
Combination Stitches

In this block, you'll learn more variations you can apply to the three stitches we've already covered plus the ones yet to come. What these three patterns have in common is that they all alternately work a short stitch next to a taller stitch. This has the effect of scrunching up or compressing the taller stitch so that it protrudes and forms interesting surface texture on your fabric.

Remember, you can use this technique with many different stitch combinations.

Stitches you'll learn in this block
Crunch stitch (see p. 42)
Floret stitch (see p. 45)
Crumpled griddle stitch (see p. 42)
Other stitches or techniques used
Slip stitch
Single crochet
Half double crochet
Changing colors
Decreasing

Colors used
A, B, C, D
Projects that use combination stitches
Lacy Evening Wrap and Matching Juliet Cap (crumpled griddle stitch)
Convertible-Collar Classic Jacket and Toque Hat (crumpled griddle stitch)

Amelia Cuff-to-Center Jacket and Matching Beret (crunch stitch)
Carry-All Shoulder Bag (floret stitch)
The Becoming Vest (crunch stitch)

Afghan Block 4
Step-by-Step Text Instructions

With A, ch 41 plus 2 for turn.
Row 1: Work Row 1 of **crunch stitch.**

Rows 2–14: Work Row 2 of **crunch stitch** 13 times, changing to B on last st of Row 13. Do not cut yarn.

Rows 15–34: Work Rows 2 and 3 of **floret stitch,** dec 1 st in the 1st row by starting in the 2nd st and sk the tch—40 sts. Work in a B, D, A color sequence, changing colors every row and ending with D. Change to A in last st of Row 34. Do not cut yarn.

Rows 35–48: Work Row 2 of **crumpled griddle stitch.**

Finish block according to instructions in "Afghan Introduction" on p. 66.
Fasten off.

TIP: *If you are a beginning crocheter, count across as you finish each row to make sure that you have maintained the correct number of stitches. If you have come out incorrectly at the end of a row, first check the number of stitches in the preceding row. If the number of stitches is accurate, then carefully follow your work across each stitch on the topmost row to see if you have inadvertently skipped a stitch in the row below or have worked two stitches into one.*

Contributed by Barbara Thurber

DESIGN IDEAS

Crumpled, crunched, and compressed stitches offer an infinite variety of easy and interesting surface textures. Short stitches can be placed directly above the short stitches of the row below, or the appearance can be changed by offsetting the same stitch combination—place the short stitches above the tall stitches of the row below.

Because these patterns don't have wide repeats and have a shallow row gauge, designing with them is very flexible because you can stop and start the pattern pieces where you want rather than having to be concerned with beginning or ending repeats evenly.

Crumpled griddle stitch worked from the back as an edging makes a nice variation to the more commonly used crab stitch and is not as awkward to work.

Easy to work; easy to design with; easily applied to a variety of stitches; can be offset or gridded—what more can you want! These stitches merit some design play.

Afghan Block 4

International Symbols

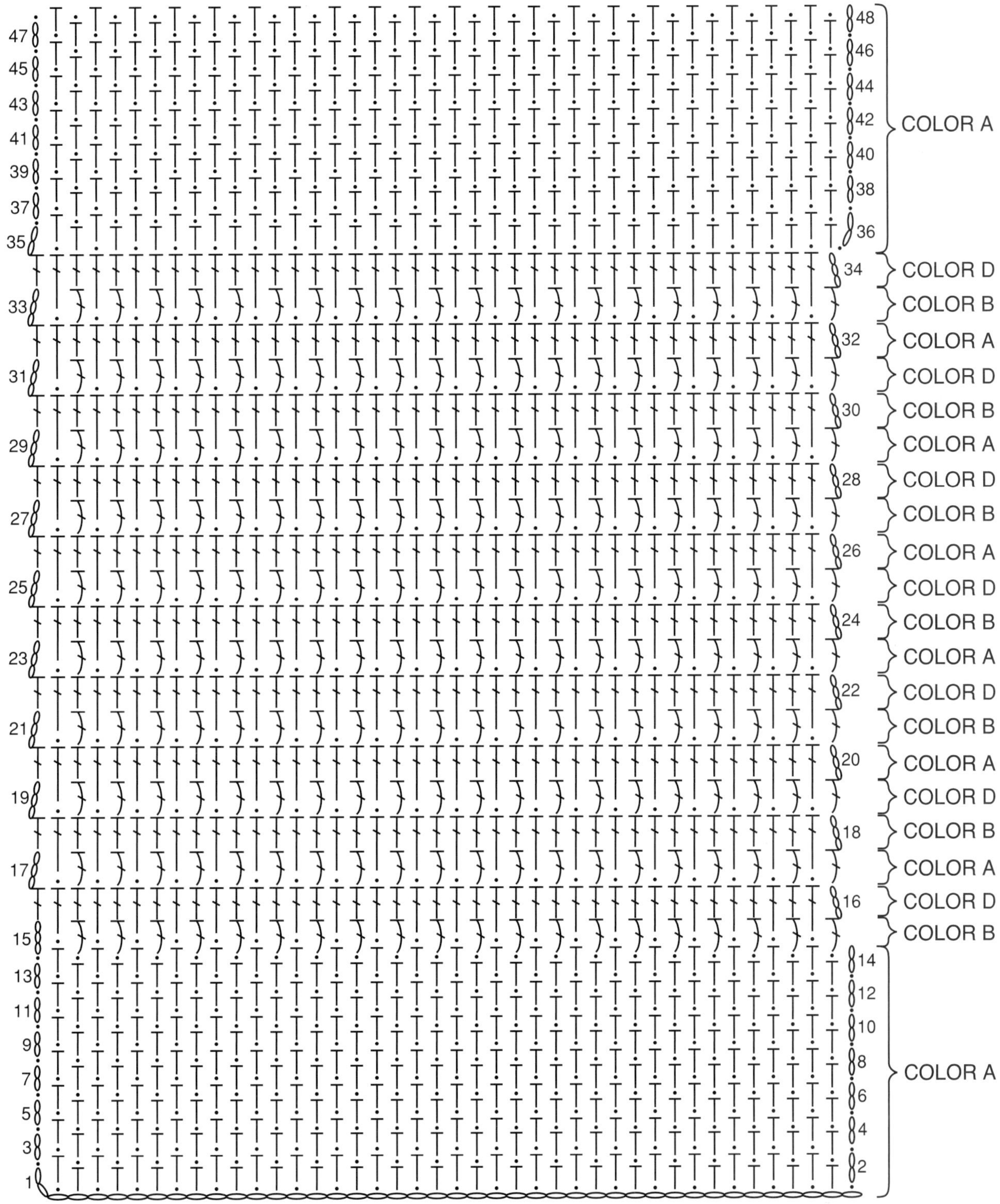

47
45
43
41
39
37
35
33
31
29
27
25
23
21
19
17
15
13
11
9
7
5
3
1
48
46
44
42
40
38
36
34
32
30
28
26
24
22
20
18
16
14
12
10
8
6
4
2
COLOR A
COLOR D
COLOR B
COLOR A
COLOR D
COLOR B
COLOR A
COLOR D
COLOR B
COLOR A
COLOR D
COLOR B
COLOR A
COLOR D
COLOR B
COLOR A
COLOR D
COLOR B
COLOR A
COLOR D
COLOR B
COLOR A

Afghan Block 5
Double Crochet and Variations

In this block, you'll learn the stitch that is probably the second most popular crochet stitch—the double crochet.

Jack-o'-lantern teeth uses short chains as a base for the double crochet stitches worked on the following row.

Linked double crochet is a handy technique for joining stitches together, and it can make long, usually open stitches into a solid fabric.

In the squares variation, the pattern is formed by working a three-stitch double crochet cluster alternated with a chain. In the variation in this block, they are lined up in a grid to form a neat little pattern, hence their name; however, they would look equally well offset.

Stitches you'll learn in this block
    Double crochet (see pp. 23–24)
    Linked double crochet (see
      p. 33)
    Squares (see p. 48)
    Jack-o-lantern teeth (see p. 46)
Other stitches or techniques used
    Single crochet
    Changing colors
    Increasing and decreasing
    Working into chain space

Colors used
    A, B, C
New abbreviations
    dc - double crochet
    Ldc - linked double crochet
Projects that use double crochet and variations
    Pretty Posies
      (double crochet)
    Summer One-Button Jacket
      (Jack-o-lantern teeth and
      linked double crochet)

Shawl-Collared Jacket (linked
    double crochet and squares)
Convertible-Collar Classic
    Jacket and Toque Hat
    (linked double crochet)

Afghan Block 5
Step-by-Step Text Instructions

With B, ch 41 plus 1 for turn.

Row 1: Starting in 2nd ch from hk, work sc across, turn—41 sts.

Row 2 (RS): Ch 3 (counts as dc), dc in 2nd st and in every st across, mark front side of work, turn.

Row 3: Rep Row 2 changing to A on last st, turn.

Row 4: Ch 1, sc in 1st 2 dc, * ch 2, sk 2 dc, sc in next dc, rep from * across changing to C in last st, turn. Do not cut yarn.

Rows 5–9: Starting with Row 2 of pattern, work 5 rows of **Jack-o-lantern teeth** in the following color sequence: C C (do not cut), A A (cut A), C, ending with Row 2.

Row 10: Ch 1, sc in 1st st, sk ch-1 sp, *sc in next 3 dc, sk ch-1 sp, rep from * across, sc in 3rd ch of tch changing to B in this st, turn.

Rows 11 and 12: Work 2 rows of **linked double crochet,** dec 1 st, changing to A on last st of Row 12, turn—40 sts.

Rows 13–20: Work 8 rows of **squares,** changing to B in last st of Row 20, turn (do not cut A).

Rows 21 and 22: Work 2 rows of **linked double crochet,** changing to A on last st of Row 22.

Rows 23–28: Rep Rows 4–9, inc 1st in Row 23 and changing to B on last st of Row 28—41 sts.

Row 29: Rep Row 10.

Rows 30 and 31: Rep Rows 2 and 3 but do not change color at the end of Row 31.

Row 32: Ch 1, sc in ea st to end.

Finish block according to instructions in "Afghan Introduction" on p. 66.

Fasten off.

DESIGN IDEAS

Linking stitches is a technique you'll wonder how you got along without. For example, linking the end stitches on rows of tall stitches makes them much easier to seam.

Linked stitches make a smaller stitch gauge, so linking the stitches in the yoke of a garment would automatically narrow a shoulder area.

Linked stitches are perfect for edges and bands because they are firm. They are also opaque so you could use them where you want a solid fabric.

Linking stitches enables you to use a longer stitch and still maintain a firm fabric. And it's quick to work.

Jack-o-lantern teeth is also a good pattern for multicolor work since it reaches down into the row below. It is a good pattern to use up leftovers since every two rows form a distinctive pattern. Three repeats of "teeth" worked in a contrast color would look well at the bottom edge and cuffs of a cardigan. Choose a neutral color such as black or white then pick out various colored leftovers of equal value. For a fun, small-scale project such as a vest, keep the main color neutral and randomly change the colors of the teeth. Or, if you're feeling ambitious and have lots of leftovers, it would make a fabulous colorful afghan.

The neat gridded version of the easy squares stitch pattern makes a wonderful trim. An offset variation would make a nice all-over surface texture for a wearable or for home decor.

Afghan Block 5
International Symbols

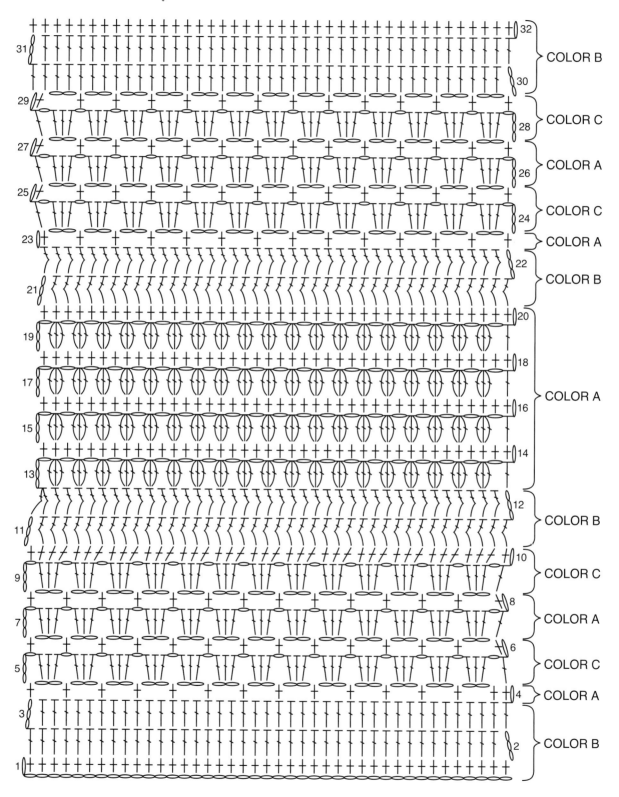

Afghan Block 6
Woven Plaid

In this block, using just basic stitches—single crochet, double crochet and chain stitches—you'll learn how to create a mesh base, and then how to thread crocheted chains vertically through the holes to create plaid fabric. It's an easy technique that shows how even simple stitches can be used to create unusual and interesting results.

Stitches you'll learn in this block
    Single crochet (see pp. 20–21)
    Double crochet (see pp. 23–24)
    Chains (see pp. 15–17)
    Woven plaid (see p. 50)
Other stitches or techniques used
    Changing colors
    Weaving

Colors used
    A, B, C
Projects that use woven plaid
    Traditional Plaid Afghan and
    Pillow

Afghan Block 6

Step-by-Step Text Instructions

With A, ch 44 plus 4 for 1st dc and ch 1.

Work 25 rows of **woven plaid** pattern in the following color order: A 1, C 3, B 2, C 3, A 1, B 5, A 1, C 3, B 2, C 3, A 1. Piece will have 23 eyelets across.

For vertical stripes: Make 22 chs 44 sts long in the following color quantities: A 2, B 8, C 12. Beginning at the lower-right-hand corner, lace chains vertically under and over striped rows, filling alt sps of ea row. Starting at side, work the following color sequence: C 3, B 2, C 3, A 1, B 4, A 1, C 3, B 2, C 3.

Chs should be pulled firmly so there is no slack, but not too tightly or fabric may pucker. Weave ends of chs into WS of block or catch in when working the border.

Finish block according to instructions in "Afghan Introduction" on p. 66.

Fasten off.

> **TIP:** Inserting the hook from back to front from the center of the stitch is not "normal," but it is what gives this stitch its unique characteristics. Break rules! Have Fun!
>
> *Contributed by Jamie Webster*

Afghan Block 6
International Symbols

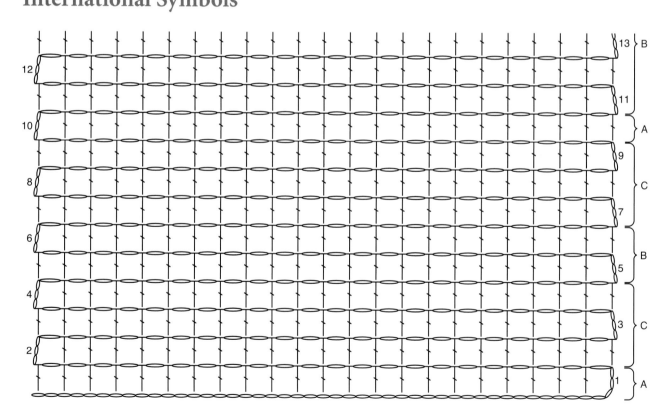

Afghan Block 7
Twisted Loops

This stitch is like a long-haired cat—fat and fluffy on the outside, but lean and lank on the inside. The fluff is made from spiraled chains attached to the front loop of a mesh of stitches. We've chosen half doubles for our stitch and chain-sevens for our loops, but you could vary this for a smaller or larger project.

We enjoyed the challenge of working out this variation of the Astrakhan stitch. We wanted a technique that would cause the chains to spiral instead of scallop, but not require the awkward manipulation of working backward every other row. We also wanted directions that would be the same for both a right-hander and left-hander. We managed to do it and hope you enjoy our twisted loop stitch.

Stitches you'll learn in this block
Twisted loops (see p. 50)

Other stitches or techniques used
Double crochet
Slip stitch
Chains
Changing colors

Colors used
A, B, C

Projects that use twisted loops
Loopy Bath Mat and Lid Cover
Furry Hooded Scarf and
  Mittens
Lacy Evening Wrap and
  Matching Juliet Cap

Afghan Block 7
Step-by-Step Text Instructions

With B, ch 35 plus 3 for turn.
Row 1 (WS): Work Row 1 of **twisted loops** pattern.

Rows 2–43: Rep rows 2 and 3 of **twisted loops** pattern for a total of 21 rows of lps in the following 2-row rep color sequence: 7B, 1C, 5A, 1C, 7B, always changing color after Row 2.

Finish block according to instructions in "Afghan Introduction" on p. 66.
Fasten off.

Afghan Block 7
International Symbols

Afghan Block 8
Chevrons

The wavy or chevron shaping on the body of this block is created by working stitches that gradually ascend and then descend in height. Three stitches are worked into one stitch at the highest peak of the pattern, and three stitches are decreased into one at the lowest point.

Stitches you'll learn in this block
- sc3tog
- dc3tog

Other stitches or techniques used
- Single crochet
- Double single crochet
- Half double crochet
- Rotating colors (see pp. 54–56)
- Double crochet
- Clusters

Colors used
- A, B, C, D

New abbreviations
- sc3tog - single crochet 3 together
- dc3tog - double crochet 3 together

Projects that use chevrons
- Chevrons Cap-Sleeved Tee Top or Long-Sleeved Tunic

Afghan Block 8
Step-by-Step Text Instructions

With A, ch 37 plus 1 for turn.
Work Foundation Row then 7 rep of **Chevrons,**
   Version #1 in the following color sequence: A,
B, D, C, changing color every 2 rows beginning
after Row 1[1]. End final rep with Row 5.

In other words...

[1] Since the pattern repeat is six rows and you are using four
colors, the colors will rotate and give the effect of a random
repeat. Only the first and fifth repeat, second and sixth, and
third and seventh will have the same rows worked in the same
colors.

Afghan Block 8
International Symbols

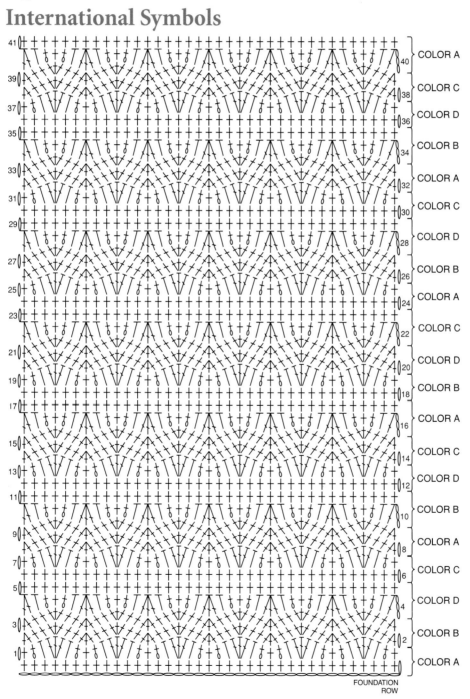

COLOR A
COLOR C
COLOR D
COLOR B
COLOR A
COLOR C
COLOR D
COLOR B
COLOR A
COLOR C
COLOR D
COLOR B
COLOR A
COLOR C
COLOR D
COLOR B
COLOR A
COLOR C
COLOR D
COLOR B
COLOR A

FOUNDATION
ROW

Afghan Block 9
Basketweave

In this block, you'll learn the front post, or relief stitch, a technique that can be applied for a variety of effects. In the two-color basketweave stitch, we alternated blocks of post stitches, which give a vertical appearance, with rows of single crochet, which have a distinct horizontal look. The juxtaposition created by changing color and stitches produces the basketweave effect.

Stitches you'll learn in this block
Front post double crochet stitch (see pp. 34–35)
Two-color basketweave blocks (see p. 50)

Other stitches or techniques used
Single crochet
Changing colors
Carrying colors

Colors used
B, C

Special abbreviation
FPdc - front post double crochet—yo hk, from front side, insert hk from right to left around post of the st in the row below, yo and draw through lp, then complete as for a dc.

Projects that use basketweave pattern
Comfy Casual Tunic

Afghan Block 9

Step-by-Step Text Instructions

With C, ch 41 plus 1 for turn.

Work the 2 foundation rows of **two-color bas-ketweave blocks,** changing to color B on last st of the 2nd row.

Afghan Block 9
International Symbols

Rows 1–50: Work 2 reps of pattern, then Rows 1–10 one more time, changing color every 2 rows.[1]

Finish block according to instructions in "Afghan Introduction" on p. 66.
Fasten off.

In other words...
[1] Since the explanations are all in the pattern stitch itself, the directions for the block require very little written text. This is typical of many projects that have little or no shaping.

Afghan Block 10
Fans and Vees

In this block, you'll learn only three of the almost infinite variety of stitch patterns that can be formed by using fans and vees. Both fans, often called shells, and vees are formed by working multiple stitches into the same base stitch.

The FanCee vees in our block are formed by separating each shell with a chain. Our solid shells are made by working sets of five double crochet stitches into the same base stitch separated by a single crochet, which serves to spread the fan open. In the open shells pattern, the fans are given a more open look by working five double crochet stitches into a chain-three space.

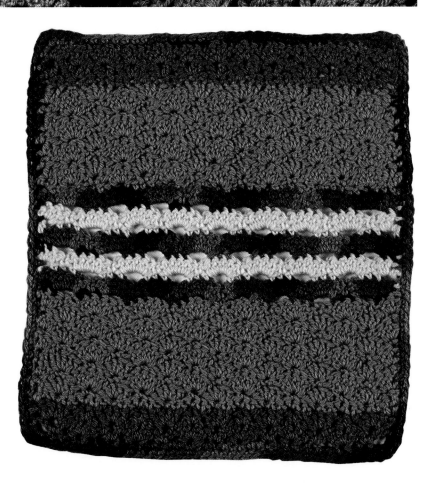

Stitches you'll learn in this block
  FanCee vees (see p. 45)
  Solid shells (see p. 48)
  Open shells (see p. 46)

Other stitches or techniques used
  Single crochet
  Double crochet
  Chains
  Changing colors
  Increases and decreases

Colors used
  A, B, C, D

Projects that use the fans and vees
  Fans and Vees Tunic and
    Juliet Hat

Afghan Block 10
Step-by-Step Text Instructions

With A, ch 40 plus 2 for turn.

Row 1 (WS): Work Row 1 of **FanCee vees** pattern.

Row 2: Work Row 2 of **FanCee vees** pattern, changing to B on last st.

Row 3: Ch 1, sc into st and ch sp across, turn—43 sts.

Row 4: Ch 1, sc, *sk 2 sc, 5 dc into next st, sk 2 sc, sc into next st; rep from * ending last rep with sc into top of tch, turn.

Rows 5–11: Work Rows 2 and 3 of **solid shells** pattern 3 times, then rep Row 2 of **solid shells** pattern 1 time, changing to D on last st of Row 11.

Row 12: Ch 1, sk 1 st, 2 sc, *ch 3, sk 2 sts, 3 sc, rep from * ending 2 sc, turn—49 sts.

Row 13: Work Row 2 of **open shells** pattern, changing to C on last st.

Rows 14 and 15: Work Rows 3 and 4 of **Open Shells** pattern, changing to D on last st of Row 15.

Rows 16 and 17: Work Rows 5 and 2 of **open shells** pattern, changing to C on last st of Row 17.

Rows 18 and 19: Rep Rows 14 and 15, changing to D on last st of Row 19.

Rows 20 and 21: Rep Rows 16 and 17, changing to B on last st of Row 21.

Row 22: Ch 1, sc, sk 1 st, *5 sc, sk 1 st, rep from * ending last rep 7 sc, turn—43 sts.

Rows 23–29: Work Rows 2 and 3 of **solid shells** pattern 3 times, then rep Row 2 of **solid shells** pattern 1 time, changing to A on last st of Row 29.

Row 30: Sc across row dec 2 sts evenly—41 sts.

Row 31: Ch 3, sk 1 st, *2 dc into next st, ch 1, 2 dc into same st, sk 2 sts, dc, ch 1, dc into same st, sk 2 st, rep from * to last 2 sts, sk 1 st, dc, turn.

Row 32: Work Row 3 of **FanCee vees** pattern.

Finish block according to instructions in "Afghan Introduction" on p. 66.

Fasten off.

DESIGN IDEAS

This versatile stitch technique has been a favorite of crocheters for years. It is handsome as an allover pattern in both home decor and wearables and equally popular as an edging.

The height of the row repeat in fans, shells, and vees patterns may be controlled by the choice of stitch used.

As you work in Fans and Vees tunic, try varying the number of stitches on each side of the center chain.

TIP: When multiple stitches are worked into one stitch, an even row count is maintained by skipping stitches in a number equal to the number of stitches being added.

Afghan Block 10
International Symbols

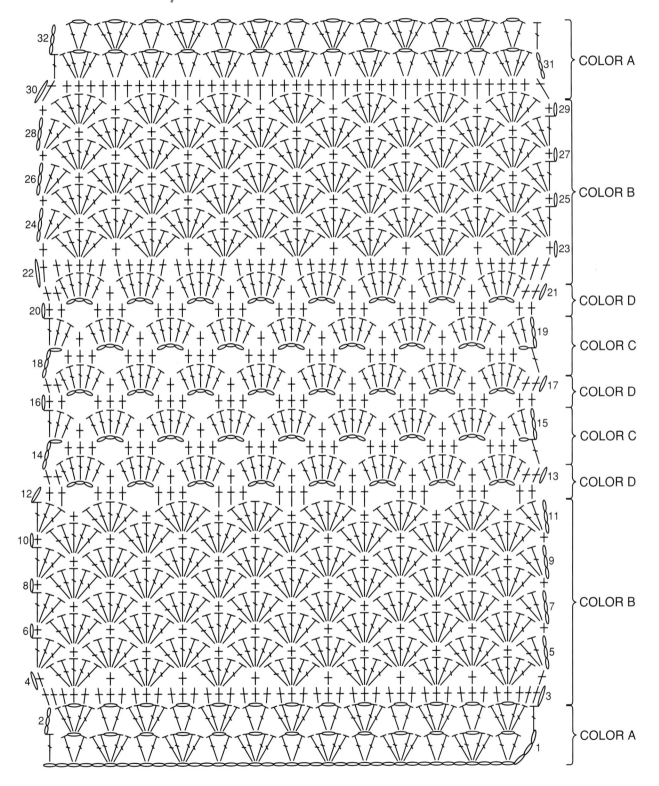

COLOR A

COLOR B

COLOR D

COLOR C

COLOR D

COLOR C

COLOR D

COLOR B

COLOR A

Afghan Block 11
Picots, Puffs, Popcorns, and Bobbles

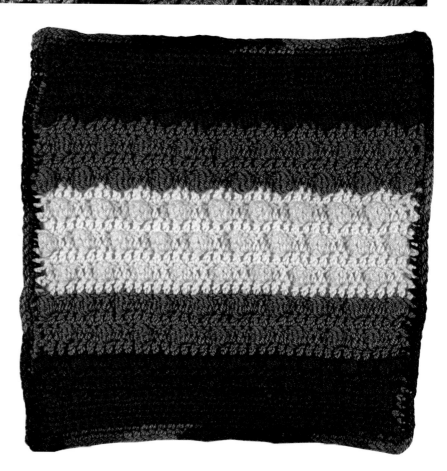

Gathering stitches together to form bumps of varying size gives interesting surface texture to your work. Although the stitches look complicated, they are quite easy and satisfying to work.

You first learned about picots in the single crochet block. Bobbles, popcorns, and puffs are other types of bumps made of multistitches, but they usually have their base in the same stitch, space, or chain.

As you'll see as you work this block, there are no specifics for the number of stitches that are used to make these interesting stitches. As with so much in crochet, personal preference can make each project unique.

Stitches you'll learn in this block
Puffs (see p. 38)
Popcorns (see p. 38)
Bobbles (see p. 36)
Other stitches or techniques used
Single crochet
Half double crochet
Double crochet
Picots

Colors used
A, B, C

Projects that use picots, puffs, popcorns, and bobbles
Popcorns, Picots, and Puffs
Pullover and Hat (puffs, popcorns, and picots)
Aran Angles Pullover and Hat (picots)
Tasseled Shoulder Bag and Cloche Hat (picots)

Afghan Block 11
Step-by-Step Text Instructions

With A, ch 39 plus 1 for turn.

Row 1: Starting in 2nd ch from hk, work 39 sc, turn.

Row 2 (RS): Ch 1, sc in ea st across, turn.

Rows 3 and 4: Work Rows 4 and 5 of **picot single crochet** pattern, turn.

Rows 5 and 6: Work Rows 2 and 3 of **puff** pattern, drawing yarn through 4 times for ea puff.

Row 7: Work Row 4 of **puff** pattern, drawing yarn through 5 times for ea puff, changing to B on last st.[1]

Row 8: Ch 3, dc in ea st across, turn.

Rows 9 and 10: Work Rows 2 and 3 of **bobble** pattern, working 4 legs into ea bobble st.

Row 11: Work Row 4 of **bobble** pattern, working 5 legs into ea bobble st, changing to C on last st.

Row 12: Rep Row 8.

Rows 13 and 14: Work Rows 2 and 3 of **popcorn** pattern, working 3 legs into ea popcorn.

Rows 15 and 16: Work Rows 4 and 5 of **popcorn** pattern, working 4 legs into ea popcorn.

Rows 17 and 18: Work Rows 2 and 3 of **popcorn** pattern, working 5 legs into ea popcorn, changing to B on last st of Row 18.

Rows 19–22: Rep Rows 11–8[2], working row of 5-leg bobbles and then a row of 4-leg bobbles, changing to A on last st of Row 22.

Rows 23–29: Rep Rows 7–1, drawing yarn through 5 times on 1st row of puffs and 4 times on 2nd row of puffs.

Finish block according to instructions in "Afghan Introduction" on p. 66.

Fasten off.

In other words...

[1] Each pattern stitch in this block is done in progressively larger sizes to the middle of the block.

[2] You are now working the first half of the block backwards so the second half mirrors the first half.

DESIGN IDEAS

Experiment with adding bumps and bobbles to any existing pattern that looks a little flat. The additional surface interest will change the entire look of your project.

Bobbles and popcorns can easily be attached to the surface of purchased item or to a finished handmade crocheted or knitted garment. If the gauge is too tight to insert your crochet hook, simply embroider a line of stem stitches where you want your bumps and insert your hook into these stitches.

Experiment with other stitches and the number of legs to see what other variations are possible.

A group of bumps could become balloons with embroidered strings on a child's afghan or sweater.

On an adult project, a group of bumps could become a cluster of grapes or cherries with crocheted or embroidered leaves.

Afghan Block 11
International Symbols

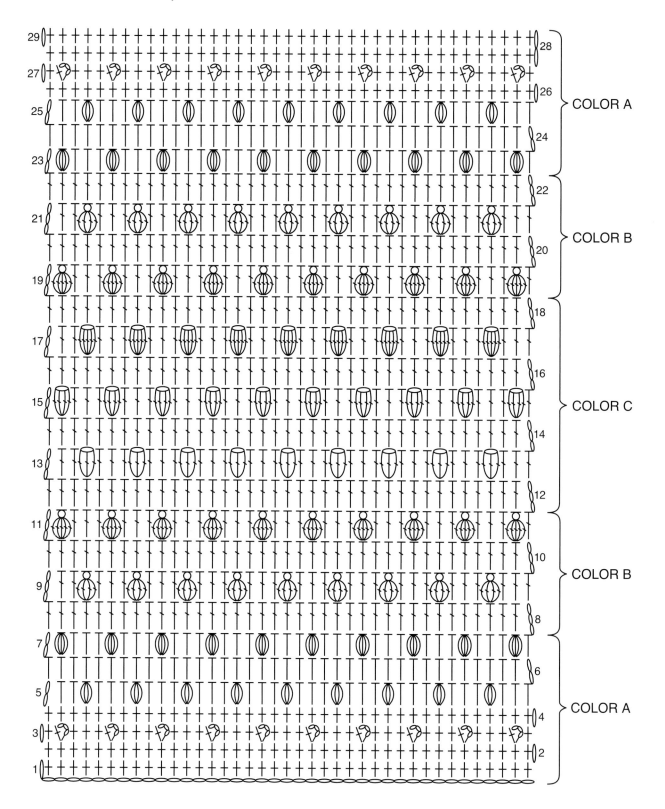

COLOR A

COLOR B

COLOR C

COLOR B

COLOR A

Afghan Block 12
Filet Crochet

Filet crochet is a type of crochet that deserves much more space than we are able to give it in this format. However, we wanted to include this small sample to give you just a taste.

Filet crochet is worked from a chart. In a nutshell, each square on the chart equals 3 stitches in width. This means that our 15-square chart is really 45 stitches wide plus one more for the final edge stitch. You'll find a detailed explanation of how filet crochet is worked in "Unique Techniques" (pp. 51–57). Read the information and get ready to enjoy a sampling of this wonderful technique.

Stitches you'll learn in this block
Filet crochet (see pp. 52–54)

Other stitches or techniques used
Chains
Double crochet

Colors used
B

Afghan Block 12

Step-by-Step Text Instructions

With B, ch 46 plus 4 for tch and 1st ch.

Beginning in the 4th ch from hk, follow the filet crochet graph below. The tch will count as the 1st edge st.

(If you are not sure how to do filet crochet, refer to pp. 52–54.)

Finish block according to instructions in "Afghan Introduction" on p. 66.

Fasten off.

Filet Crochet

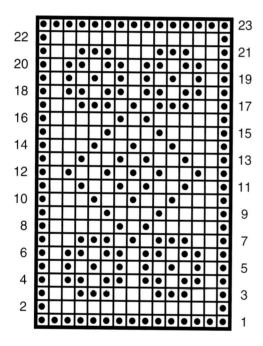

STITCH KEY

Afghan Block 13
Trebles and Aran Stitches

This is the first time you'll yarn over twice before inserting the hook into the stitch. Two yarn overs give you enough yarn to be able to work through two loops three times; the stitch is called a treble crochet. This block also combines several maneuvers used elsewhere to form the highly textured Aran surface. Treble crochet front post stitches form a picket fence stitch. Pairs of trebles, angled to the right and left then decreased into one, f orm diamonds in the dots and diamonds stitch. The dots are formed by the versatile three-chain picot.

Stitches you'll learn in this block
>   Treble crochet (see pp. 24–25)
>   Post treble crochet (see p. 46)
>   Dots and diamonds (see p. 44)
>   Post stitches (see pp. 34–35)
>   Picket fences (see p. 46)

Other stitches or techniques used
>   Single crochet
>   Picot single crochet

Colors used
>   A, B

New abbreviations
>   tr - treble crochet
>   FPtr - front post treble
>   crochet
>   FPtr2tog - front post treble
>   crochet 2 together

Projects that use trebles and Aran stitches
>   Pretty Posies (treble crochet)
>   Aran Angles Pullover and Hat
>   (dots and diamonds)
>   Convertible-Collar Classic
>   Jacket and Toque Hat (front
>   and back post stitches)

Afghan Block 13
Step-by-Step Text Instructions

With B, ch 39 plus 1 for turn.

Row 1: Starting in 2nd ch from hk, work 39 sc across, turn.

Rows 2 (RS) and 3: Ch 1, sc in ea st across, turn.

Row 4: Ch 4 (counts as 1 tr), sk 1 sc, 1 tr in ea sc across, ending last tr in top of tch, turn.

Rows 5–7: Rep Row 2, changing to A on last st of Row 7.

Rows 8–13: Work Rows 2–5 of **picket fences** 1 time, then Rows 2–3 of **picket fences**, again changing color every 2 rows using sequence ABA, changing to B at the end of Row 13.

Row 14: Ch 1, sc into 1st 3 sts, *Psc, sc into ea of next 3 sts, rep from * to end.

Rows 15–20: Work Rows 2–7 of **dots and diamonds** pattern.

Rows 21–27: Rep Rows 4–7 of **Dots and Diamonds** pattern 1 time then Rows 4–6 of **dots and diamonds** 1 more time, changing to A on last st of Row 27.

Rows 28–33: Work Rows 8–13 as before, making the tr/rf sts in the 1st row alternately around the tops of the raised clusters and the Pscs 2 rows below and changing to B in the last st of Row 33.

Rows 34–35: Ch 1, sc in ea st across, turn.

Row 36: Rep Row 4.

Rows 37–38: Rep Rows 34–35.

Finish block according to instructions in "Afghan Introduction" on p. 66.
Fasten off.

DESIGN IDEA

The dots and diamonds pattern would make a great cozy afghan.

Panels of dots and diamonds would be an effective insert in the body of a plain fabric.

The picket fence stitch suggests a border, cuff, or bottom band. The vertical appearance of this pattern would also be great combined with a horizontal pattern to break up the space in an interesting fashion.

Post stitches alternately worked into the front and back make a handsome ribbing for any traditional sweater.

Afghan Block 13
International Symbols

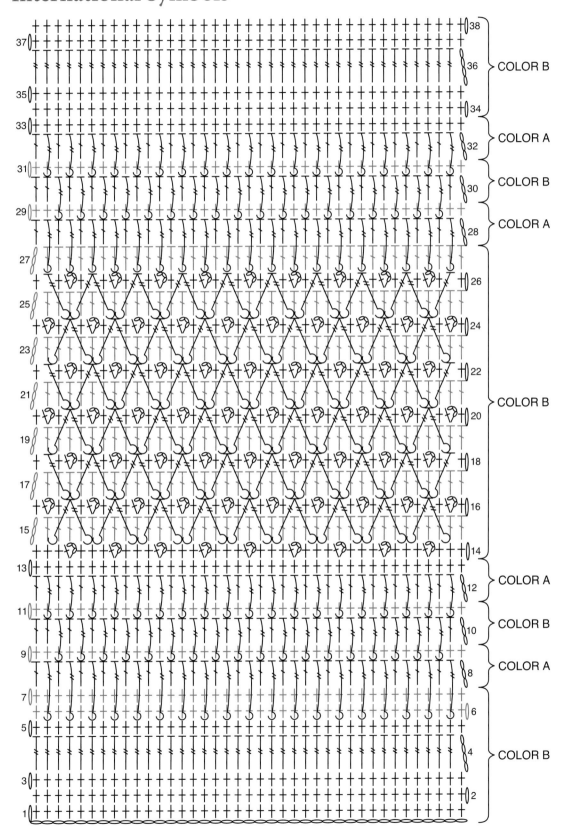

COLOR B

COLOR A

COLOR B

COLOR A

COLOR B

COLOR A

COLOR B

COLOR A

COLOR B

Afghan Block 14
More Single Crochet Variations

We couldn't resist giving you three more easy variations to add to your crochet tool kit. They will give your projects interest and variety. Remember, they can each be used with the other stitches you are learning as you progress through the blocks.

The granite pattern is a one-row pattern that alternates single crochets and chains. It is fast and easy and gives an almost woven effect.

The trinity pattern is formed by working three single crochet stitches together with the outside legs sharing the same base stitch.

Triple tucks are formed by folding a row of treble stitches in half and working a row of single crochet to join them.

Stitches you'll learn in this block
   Granite pattern (see p. 45)
   Trinity pattern (see p. 49)
   Triple tucks (see p. 49)

Other stitches or techniques used
   Single crochet
   Working in the back loop
   Working in the chain space

Colors used
   B, C, D

Projects that use more single crochet variations
   Carry-All Shoulder Bag
      (granite pattern, trinity
      pattern)
   Aran Angles Pullover and
      Hat (triple tucks)

Afghan Block 14
Step-by-Step Text Instructions

With B, ch 43 plus 1 for turn.

Row 1 (RS): Starting in 2nd ch from hk, work Row 1 of **granite pattern**.

Rows 2–12: Work Row 2 of **granite pattern**, changing to D on last st of Row 12.

Row 13: Work Row 2 of **trinity pattern**, inserting hk into ch sp and sc of previous row of granite pattern.

Rows 14–18: Rep Row 3 of **trinity pattern**, changing to C on last st of Row 18.

Row 19: Work Row 2 of **triple tucks** and dec 3 sts evenly across row—40 sts.

Rows 20–22: Work Rows 3–5 of **triple tucks.**

Rows 23–30: Work 2 more reps of Rows 2–5 of **triple tucks,** inc 3 sts in last row and changing to D on last st—43 sts.

Rows 31–38: Rep Row 2 of **granite pattern**, changing to B on last st of row 38.

Row 39: Work Row 2 of **trinity pattern**, inserting hk into ch sp and sc of previous row of granite pattern.

Rows 40–47: Rep Row 3 of **trinity pattern.**

Finish block according to instructions in "Afghan Introduction" on p. 66.

Fasten off.

Afghan Block 14
International Symbols

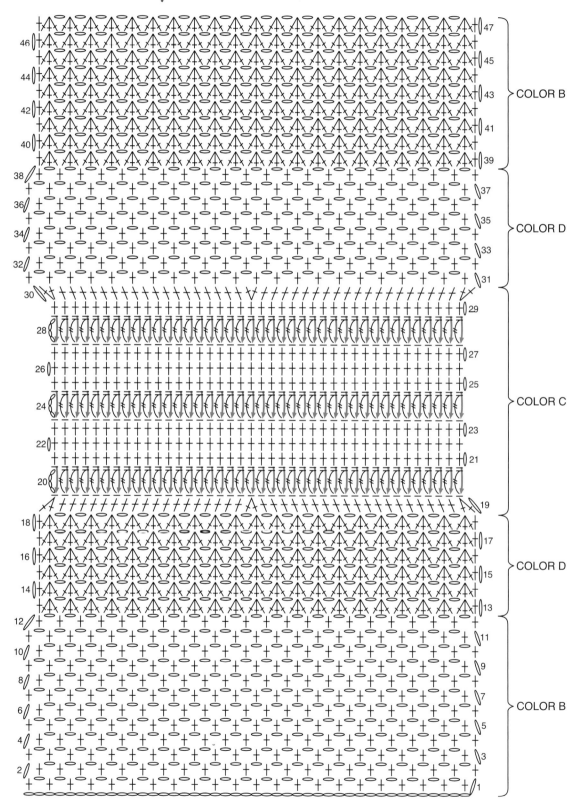

COLOR B

COLOR D

COLOR C

COLOR D

COLOR B

Afghan Block 15
Waves

This pattern uses five innovative stitches cataloged by Bill Elmore. Elmore stitches fall in height between the traditional stitches. Like the half tones or black keys on a piano, these stitches give you more control in creating gradual curves, such as when shaping an underarm or anywhere gentle curves are desirable.

If you aren't familiar with these stitches, follow the step-by-step directions given in the "EZ Reference Crochet Shorthand Chart" (p. 213) and in the "Half-Step Stitches" section (pp. 27–31).

Stitches you'll learn in this block

   Half Elmore (see p. 27)

   Elmore (see p. 27)

   Double Elmore (see p. 28)

   Elmore treble (see p. 29)

   Elmore double treble (see p. 30)

Other stitches or techniques used

   Changing colors

   Single crochet worked three rows below

Colors used

   A, B, C, D

New Abbreviations

   dE - double Elmore

   E - Elmore

   Edtr - Elmore double treble

   Etr - Elmore treble

   hE - half Elmore

Projects that use waves

   Gentle Waves Baby Afghan

Afghan Block 15
Step-by-Step Text Instructions

With D ch 40 plus 1 for turn.

Row 1 (RS): Sc in the 2nd ch from hk and in every ch across, turn.

Row 2: Ch 1, sc into 1st 6 sc, *sc into next sc, hE into next 2 sc, E into next sc, dE into next sc, E tr into next sc, E d tr into next 2 sc, E tr into next sc, dE into next sc, E into next sc, hE into next 2 sc, sc into next sc, rep from * once, sc into ea of last 6 sts, turn.

Rows 3 and 4: Ch 1, sc in ea st across, changing to C in last st of Row 4, turn. Do not cut D.

Row 5: Ch 2, (counts as hE), sk 1st sc, hE into next sc, E into next sc, dE into next sc, E tr into next sc, E d tr into next 2 sc, E tr into next sc, dE into next sc, E into next sc, hE into next 2 sc, *ch 2, sk 2 sc, hE into next 2 sc, E into next sc, dE into next sc, E tr into next sc, E d tr into next 2 sc, E tr into next sc, dE into next sc, E into next sc, hE into next 2 sc, rep from * to end, turn.

Row 6: Ch 2, sk 1st st, work 1 hE into next st, 1 E into next st, dE into next st, E tr into next st, E d tr into ea of next 2 sts, E tr into next st, dE into next st, E into next st, hE into ea of next 2 sts, *ch 2, sk 2 sts, work hE into ea of next 2 hE, E into next E, dE into next st, E tr into next st, E d tr into ea of next 2 sts, E tr into next st, dE into next st, E into next st, hE into each of next 2 sts, rep from * to end working last hE into top of tch and changing to D in last st, turn. Cut C.

Row 7: Ch 1, work sc into 1st 12 stitches, (inserting hk from front of work, work sc into sc 3 rows below), rep between ( ), sc into next 12 sts, rep from * end, 1 sc into top of tch, turn.

Row 8: Rep Row 3, changing to B in last st. Do not cut D.

Row 9: Ch 5, work E tr into 1st st, dE into next st, E into next st, hE into next 2 sts, *ch 2, sk 2 sts, hE into next 2 st, E into next st, dE into next st, E tr into next st, E d tr into next 2 sts, E tr into next st, dE into next st, E into next st, hE into ea of next 2 sts, rep from * to last 7 sts, ch 2, sk 2 sts, hE into next 2 sts, E into next st, dE into next st, E tr into last st, turn.

Row 10: Ch 5, *E tr into next st, dE into next st, E into next st, hE into next 2 sts, *ch 2, sk 2 sts, hE into next 2 sts, E into next st, dE into next st, E tr into next st, E d tr into next 2 sts, E tr into st, dE into next st, E into next st, hE into next 2 sts, rep from * to last 7 sts, ch 2, sk 2 sts, hE into next 2 sts, E into next st, dE into next st, E tr into next st, changing to D in last st, turn.

Row 11: Ch 1, sc into 1st 7 sts, (inserting hk from front of work, work sc into sc 3 rows below), rep between ( ), sc to last 7 sts, rep between ( ) 2 times, sc to end, turn.

Row 12: Rep Row 8, changing to A in last st.

Rows 13 and 14: Rep Rows 5 and 6, changing to D in last st of Row 14.

Rows 15 and 16: Rep Rows 7 and 8, changing to B in last st of Row 16.

Rows 17 and 18: Rep Rows 9 and 10, changing to D in last st of Row 18.

Rows 19 and 20: Rep Rows 11 and 12 changing to C in last st of Row 20.

Rows 21 and 22: Rep Rows 5 and 6 changing to D in last st of Row 22.

Rows 23 and 24: Rep Rows 7 and 8 without changing color.

Row 25: Rep Row 2 without changing color.

Row 26: Rep Row 3 without changing color.

Finish block according to instructions in "Afghan Introduction" on p. 66.

Fasten off.

Afghan Block 15
International Symbols

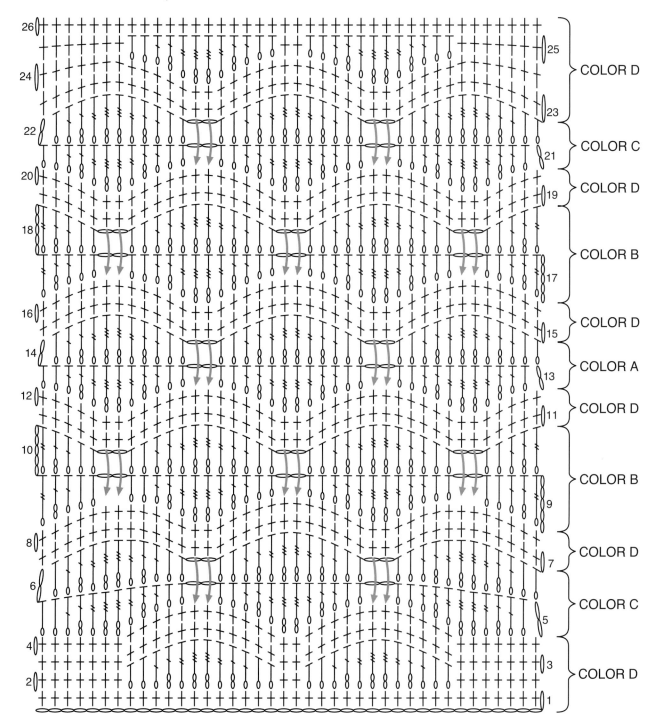

COLOR D

COLOR C

COLOR D

COLOR B

COLOR D

COLOR A

COLOR D

COLOR B

COLOR D

COLOR C

COLOR D

Afghan Block 16
Multicolor Crochet

Taking a little bit of time to learn how to work with multicolors in the same row brings a big payoff, and it's probably much easier than you imagined! It will also bring variety and interest to your work, open up a whole new world of patterns, allow you to use up lots of leftovers, and be incredibly satisfying. There are two main techniques used when working with multicolors in the same row: stranding and intarsia.

Stranding is when both colors are carried across the row, one being used and one being stranded, floated, or carried along at the back of the work. This technique is most often used when two colors are regularly alternated across the whole width of the piece.

Intarsia is Italian for "inlay." This technique is used when many colors are used in one row or when the colors are separated by more stitches than it would be practical to strand across. Both techniques are explained in detail in "Unique Techniques" (pp. 51–57).

Stitches you'll learn in this block
No new stitches! Just single crochet worked in multicolors.

Other stitches or techniques used
Stranding
Intarsia

Colors used
A, B, C, D

Projects that use multicolor crochet
Reversible Jacket and Matching Shoulder Bag (stranding, intarsia)

Afghan Block 16
Step-by-Step Text Instructions

With A, ch 48 plus 1 for turn.

Follow chart working entire block in sc. Work first section in stranding technique, second multicolor section in intarsia, and third section in your choice of techniques. (Third section of model was worked in stranding.) Refer to "Unique Techniques" for detailed information on how to work stranding and intarsia techniques.[1]

Finish block according to instructions in "Afghan Introduction" on p. 66.

Fasten off.

In other words...

[1] The diagram for the block shows it from a right-handed perspective, beginning at the lower-right corner of the block. If you are left-handed and start at the lower-left corner, all color placements will be reversed, or mirrored. Left-handers who want their block to look exactly like the photo will need to follow the color sequence as given for right-handers.

Afghan Block 16
Multicolor Chart

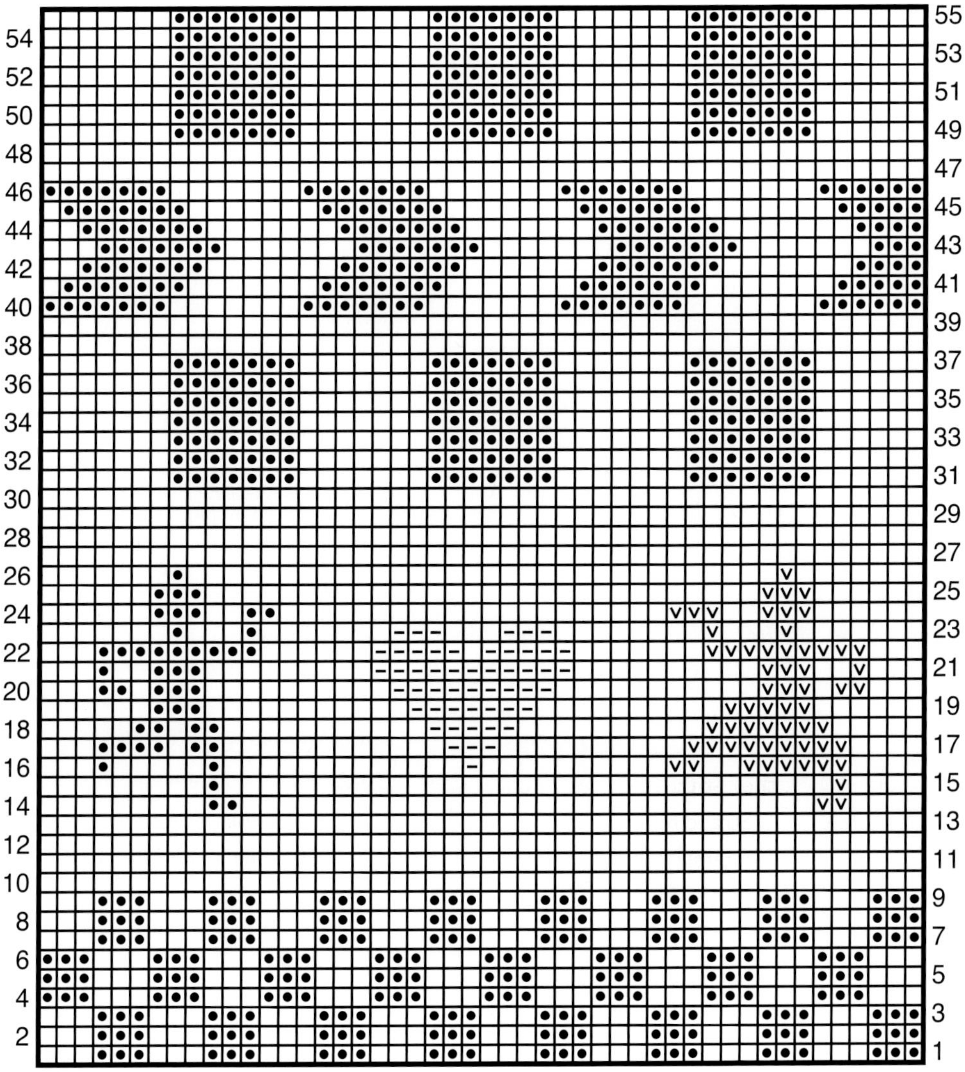

Afghan Block 16
Chart Key

CHART KEY
- ● = COLOR A
- V = COLOR B
- □ = COLOR C
- – = COLOR D

Afghan Block 17
Crosses and Bars

In this pattern, you're asked to yarn over three times before inserting the hook into the stitch, which gives you enough yarn to draw through two loops four different times. This makes a stitch long enough to form the long-legged Xs across the solid bars of this good-looking pattern. Longer stitches may look leggy when they aren't combined with other techniques; however, in this block we've taken advantage of the plus side of long stitches, which allows interesting stitch manipulations.

Stitches you'll learn in this block
 Double treble crochet (see
  p. 26)
 Crosses and bars in two colors
  (see p. 42)

Colors used
 A, B, C

New abbreviations
 dtr - double treble crochet

Other stitches or techniques used
 Single crochet
 Double crochet
 Crossed stitches

Projects that use crosses and bars
 Tapestry Tabard and Matching
  Crusher Hat

Afghan Block 17
Step-by-Step Text Instructions

Use color C for main color throughout.[1]

With C, ch 40 plus 1 for turn.

Row 1: Sc in 2nd ch from hk and every ch across, turn.

Rows 2 (RS)–9: Work Rows 2–9 of **crosses and bars in two colors,** using A as CC.

Rows 10–13: Repeat Rows 2–5 of pattern using B as CC.

Rows 14–29: Continue in pattern using A as CC.

Rows 30–33: Continue in pattern using B as CC.

Rows 34–41: Continue in pattern using A as CC.

Finish block according to instructions in "Afghan Introduction" on p. 66.

Fasten off.

In other words...

[1] This pattern is described in the pattern stitches section as a two-color pattern. In this block you will use three colors.

Afghan Block 17
International Symbols

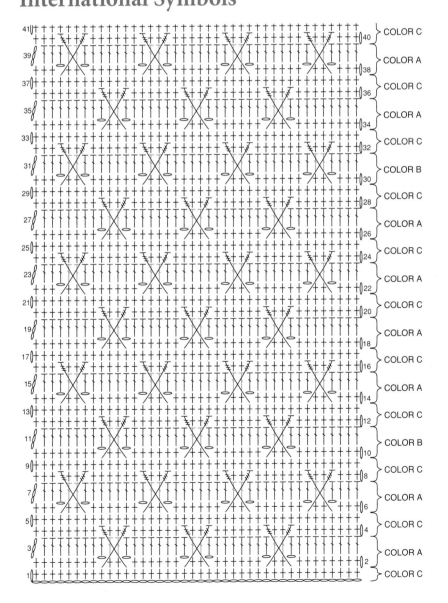

COLOR C
COLOR A
COLOR C
COLOR A
COLOR C
COLOR B
COLOR C
COLOR A
COLOR C
COLOR A
COLOR C
COLOR A
COLOR C
COLOR A
COLOR C
COLOR B
COLOR C
COLOR A
COLOR C
COLOR A
COLOR C

Afghan Block 18
Three-Color Interlocking Blocks

This block is one of those clever ideas that looks more difficult than it really is. It is made up of stitches you've already learned—chains, double crochet and spikes—but they are combined in unique ways. The challenge in this stitch pattern is to make sure to keep all the chains hidden on the wrong side. Once you master this, it is a fun, easy-to-work pattern that gives lots of satisfaction.

Stitches you'll learn in this block
Spike double crochet (see pp. 35–36)
Three-color interlocking blocks (see p. 48)

Other stitches or techniques used
Single crochet
Double crochet
Rotating colors

Colors used
B, C, D

New abbreviations
Sdc - spike double crochet

Afghan Block 18
Step-by-Step Text Instructions

With B, ch 44 plus 3 for turn.

Work 1 row of ea color throughout while carrying other colors along side.

Row 1: With B, work Row 1 of **three-color interlocking blocks** changing to C in last st.

Rep Rows 2–3 of **three-color interlocking blocks,** changing color at the end of every row until block measures 13 in.[1]

Finish block according to instructions in "Afghan Introduction" on p. 66.

Fasten off.

In other words…

[1] It is important to end this block after a Row 3 so that each column of squares has the same number.

Afghan Block 18
International Symbols

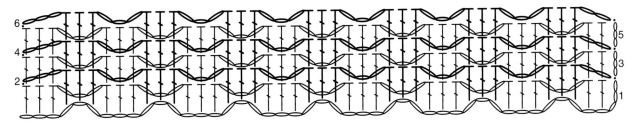

DESIGN IDEAS

Since the interlocking blocks pattern has such a cushy feel, it is perfect for seat covers or rugs. It would make a great bath rug, floor pad for baby, or a cozy afghan worked loosely with an extra large hook and chunky yarn.

This pattern is most effective when used with three or more colors. To make sure the colors appear to be random, always use an odd number of colors.

If you used a constant neutral such as black, white, or even red for every third row, it would be a wonderful way to use leftover colors of matching values.

If using up leftovers is your goal, try making small items like hot pads or coasters out of this pattern.

Afghan Block 19
Three-Color Post Stitch Variations

This block features another intriguing use of multicolors. In the chart on the facing page, you can see the six ways the three colors can be combined. You'll be working all six combinations in this block. We hope you'll enjoy the challenge.

Notice how much subtler the colors appear in the lower-right and upper-left sections of this block when the vertical post stitches are the low contrast A and B colors. The center-left section, where the vertical post stitches are the two highest contrast colors, appears most dramatic of all.

This pattern stitch looks quite different on the reverse side where the horizontal stripes have equal merit.

Stitches you'll learn in this block
   Back post treble crochet (see pp. 48–49)

Other stitches or techniques used
   Single crochet
   Front post treble crochet
   Changing colors
   How alternating the order in which colors are used changes the appearance of the finished piece

Colors used
   A, B, C, D

New abbreviations
   BPtr - back post treble crochet

Projects that use three-color post stitch variations
   Reversible Chenille Scarf and Hat

In order to write the instructions for working the block using colors A, B, and C in six different sequences, we used X, Y, and Z to indicate when each of the colors is used (see the chart below). The vertical color arrangement in the pattern is two rows of X, one row of Y, then two rows of Z and one of Y, etc., which allows the needed color to be always waiting on the correct side of the work.

The block is 44 stitches wide by 55 rows long and is divided into six sections: two vertical sections and three horizontal sections. The two vertical sections are worked at the same time, *working X across both sections and changing colors at the midpoint on the Y and Z rows.* The color changes can clearly be seen in the photo of the back side of the block.

The diagram for the block shows it from a right-handed perspective, beginning at the lower-right corner of the block. If you are left-handed and start at the lower-left corner, all color placements will be reversed, or mirrored. Left-handers who want their block to look exactly like the photo will need to follow the color sequence as given for right-handers. This can be a bit tricky since you will be working from left to right, but following the color placements from right to left.

Color Chart for Block 19

(22sts)			(22sts)		
X	Y	Z	X	Y	Z
A	C	B	A	B	C
C	B	A	C	A	B
B	A	C	B	C	A

Because of the way this block uses the yarn colors, we've written a special version of the three-color post stitch pattern. Use this version for the block and use the one in three-color post stitch (pp. 48–49) to make the chenille scarf and other projects that don't require color changes in mid-row.

Three-Color Post Stitch for Mid-Row Color Changes

Multiple of 3+2 plus 1 for turn.

This pattern uses three colors: X, Y, and Z

Special abbreviations

BPtr (back post treble crochet): placing hk in back of work, yo 2 times, insert hk around the post of the st as directed, yo and draw through lp, then complete as a regular tr.

FPtr (front post treble crochet): keeping hk in front of work, yo 2 times, insert hk around the post of the st as directed, yo and draw through lp, then complete as a regular tr.

Pattern stitch

Row 1 (WS): Starting in 3rd ch from hk, with X, sc in ea ch across, turn.

Row 2: Ch 1, sc across changing to Y on last st, turn.

Row 3: Working ea 22-st section in its respective color Y, rep Row 2 changing to Z on last st, turn.

Row 4: Ch 1, sc into 1st and 2nd sts, *FPtr on next st, sc into ea of next 2 sc, rep from * to end changing color after ea 22-st section as indicated, turn.

Row 5: Rep Row 2, changing to Y on last st, turn.

Row 6: Rep Row 2, changing to X on last st, turn.

Row 7: Ch 1, sc into 1st and 2nd sts, *BPtr on next st working around the tr/rb 2 rows below, sc into ea of next 2 sc, rep from * to end, turn.

Row 8: Rep row 2, changing to Y on last st, turn.

Rep Rows 3–8 for pattern.

Afghan Block 19
Step-by-Step Text Instructions

With B, ch 44 sts plus 2 for turn.

Rows 1 and 2: Work Rows 1 and 2 of **three-color post stitch** pattern as given on previous page.

Rows 3–8: Work Rows 3–8 of the pat st working ea area in the color indicated in the color chart.

Rows 9–17: Rep Rows 3–8 then rep Rows 3–5, changing to B in the last st of Row 17.

Row 18: Ch 1, sc in ea st across, changing to C in last st, turn.

Rows 19 and 20: Ch 1, sc across, changing to the appropriate Y color for center section on the last st of Row 20, turn.

Rows 21–35: Rep Rows 3–8 twice then Rows 3–5 once more, maintaining correct color for ea center section as indicated on the color chart, changing to C on the last st of Row 35.

Row 36: Ch 1, sc in ea st across, changing to A on last st, turn.

Rows 37 and 38: Rep Rows 19 and 20, changing to the appropriate Y color for top section on the last st of Row 38.

Rows 39–53: Rep Rows 3–8 twice then Rows 3–5 once more, maintaining correct color for ea top section as indicated on the color chart, changing to A on the last st of Row 53.

Rows 54 and 55: Ch 1, sc in ea st across, turn.

Finish block according to instructions in "Afghan Introduction" on p. 66.

Fasten off.

DESIGN IDEAS

This pattern is a good one to use to experiment with color.

Try using five or seven analogous or monochromatic colors for an even more intricate look.

Keep a one-row accent color in black and then use all different deep jewel tones for the verticals.

Use two or four colors for a checkered effect.

Make an interesting shawl collar for a jacket by folding a long strip in half. As the collar extends down the front of your jacket, the opposite side will show.

TIP: *In order to minimize cutting yarn, try working from both ends of the pull skein, or use a separate skein for each section.*

Afghan Block 19
International Symbols

COLOR A	55
COLOR B	53
COLOR C	51
COLOR A	49
COLOR C	
COLOR B	47
COLOR C	45
COLOR A	43
COLOR C	
COLOR B	41
COLOR C	39
COLOR A	37
COLOR C	
COLOR A	35
COLOR B	33
COLOR C	31
COLOR B	
COLOR A	29
COLOR B	27
COLOR C	25
COLOR B	
COLOR A	23
COLOR B	21
COLOR C	19
COLOR B	
COLOR C	17
COLOR A	15
COLOR B	13
COLOR A	
COLOR C	11
COLOR A	9
COLOR B	7
COLOR A	
COLOR C	5
COLOR A	3
COLOR B	1

54	COLOR A
52	COLOR C
	COLOR B
50	COLOR A
48	COLOR B
46	COLOR C
	COLOR B
44	COLOR A
42	COLOR B
	COLOR C
40	COLOR B
38	COLOR A
	COLOR C
36	COLOR C
	COLOR B
34	COLOR A
32	COLOR C
	COLOR A
30	COLOR B
28	COLOR A
26	COLOR C
	COLOR A
24	COLOR B
22	COLOR A
20	COLOR C
18	COLOR B
16	COLOR A
	COLOR C
14	COLOR B
12	COLOR C
10	COLOR A
	COLOR C
8	COLOR B
6	COLOR C
4	COLOR A
2	COLOR C
	COLOR B

Afghan Block 20
Lace

There are probably more patterns written for lacework than for any other kind of crochet. We bring you this block only as an introduction to a few of the ways in which you can create open areas in your work; perhaps you'll be motivated to read and experiment further with the many variations of lace crochet. The pattern for our block was adapted with permission from a Bernat Baby Yarns crocheted crib cover.

Stitches you'll learn in this block
 Diamond Lace (see pp. 43–44)
Other stitches or techniques used
 Chains
 Single crochet
 Double crochet
 Arches

Colors used
 A
Projects that use lace
 Lacy Evening Wrap and
 Matching Juliet Cap

Afghan Block 20
Step-by-Step Text Instructions

With A, ch 37 plus 1 for turn.
Row 1: Work Row 1 of **diamond lace** pattern.

Rows 2–17: Rep Rows 2–9 twice.

Row 18: Sc into ea st across.

Finish block according to instructions in "Afghan Introduction" on p. 66.
Fasten off.

Afghan Block 20
International Symbols

PART THREE
Creative Projects

You learned many different crochet techniques and stitches in the first part of this book. You applied those stitches and techniques in the Learn-to-Crochet Afghan blocks. Now take your skills one step further and combine what you've learned to make over 40 great projects. To continue the theme of *Crochet Your Way*, we created a wide variety of projects and used yarns in a broad range of fiber and price. In two instances, we made a pair of models from the same basic pattern: one in an economical, easy-care Acrilan acrylic fiber, the other in luxury designer yarns.

Availability of yarn, your budget and the intended use of the project will all influence what fibers you ultimately choose. In the materials list for each project we've included the yarn(s) we've used; a materials source list is presented on p. 212. Feel free to substitute any yarn or combination of yarns that produces the same gauge. By taking a few minutes to work a swatch, you'll know what size your finished project will be, you'll determine if you like working with the yarn you've chosen, you'll be able to practice the stitch or technique, and you'll even be able try out other yarns.

That's a lot of information for a small investment of time. If your combination of hook and yarn is producing something other than the gauge given, or a different drape than desired, change your hook size or yarn combination. For more information about fit and gauge, see pp. 61–63.

Designed by Susan Levin

Aran Angles Pullover and Hat

There's something about the wonderful depth and texture of Aran stitches that just makes us want to crunch them in our hands, turn them into marvelous sweaters, and hope for cool days to wear them. Unfortunately, many crocheted Arans are so stiff and thick they don't provide that tactile experience. The combination of hook size, yarn weight, and stitch is critical to producing a supple finished product. Using too small a hook or too heavy a yarn results in a stiff fabric. This combination of traditional off-white worsted wool yarn and interesting textured patterns results in a classic that is sure to please every man and woman in your life.

Sizes

Finished Chest Measurements: 35½ (42, 48½, 53, 57, 61)"

Finished Length: 25 (25½, 26, 26½, 27, 27½)"

Hat: 20¼" circumference

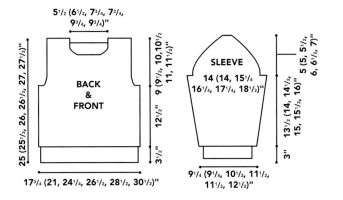

5½ (6½, 7¾, 7¾, 9¾, 9¾)"

BACK & FRONT

25 (25½, 26, 26½, 27, 27½)"

12½"

3½"

9 (9½, 10, 10½, 11, 11½)"

17¾ (21, 24¼, 26½, 28½, 30½)"

SLEEVE

14 (14, 15¼, 16¼, 17¼, 18½)"

13½ (14, 14½, 15, 15½, 16)"

3"

5 (5, 5½, 6, 6½, 7)"

9¼ (9¼, 10½, 11½, 11½, 12½)"

Materials

Knit One, Crochet Too *Parfait Solids,* 100 g/
210 yd/192 m (100% wool worsted weight)
12 (13, 15, 17, 19, 20) skeins #1101 Ivory
Crochet hook US size I/9 (5.5 mm)

Gauge

In dots and diamonds pattern, 15 sts and 12 rows = 4"
In triple tucks in rds pattern, 13 sts = 4"

Stitches and Patterns Used

Chain, slip stitch, single crochet, double crochet,
treble crochet, sc2tog
Dots and diamonds (Block #13)
Triple Tucks (Block #14)

Dots and Diamonds *(see p. 44)*

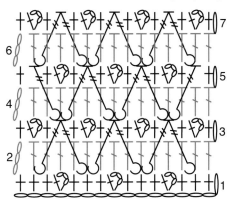

Triple Tucks *(see p. 49)*

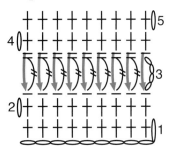

Triple Tucks in the Rnd

(any number of sts)

Rnd 1: Sc in ea ch around; sl st in 1st sc.

Rnd 2: Ch 1, sc in ea st around; sl st in 1st sc.

Rnd 3: Ch 4 (counts as 1st tr), tr in front lp of next
sc and ea sc around; sl st in top of ch-4.

Rnd 4: Ch 1, sc through (back lp of ea tr and front
lp of ea sc on row below) around; sl st in 1st sc.

Rnd 5: Ch 1, sc in ea st around; sl st in 1st sc.

Rep Rnds 2–5 for triple tucks in rnds pat.

Directions for Pullover

BACK

Ribbing (worked sideways): Ch 12 + 1 for turn.
Work in triple tucks (see p. 49) for approx 16¾
(20, 23¼, 25½, 27½, 29½)", ending after Row 5.
Fasten off.

Back: Working on long edge of ribbing and with
WS facing, work 67 (79, 91, 99, 107, 115) sc
evenly across; turn. With RS facing, begin working dots and diamonds pattern, working Row 1
sts into the sc sts along top of ribbing. Cont in
pattern rep for 16" from beg including ribbing,
ending with a RS row.

Armhole Shaping: Sl st across 4 sts, work in pattern
to last 4 sts, turn leaving rem sts unworked.
Then, keeping in pattern, dec 1 st ea end eor
4 times—51 (63, 75, 83, 91, 99) sts.

Work even until 8½ (9, 9½, 10, 10½, 11)" above armhole, ending with a RS row.

Neck Shaping: In pattern, work across 15 (19, 23, 27, 27, 31) sts, turn leaving rem sts unworked. Work 1 more row in pattern. Fasten off.

To complete other side, leave center 21 (25, 29, 29, 37, 37) sts unworked, attach yarn in next st and work on rem sts to match 1st side. Fasten off.

FRONT

Work as for Back until 22½ (23, 23½, 24 , 24½, 25)" from beg.

Neck Shaping: In pattern, work across 19 (23, 27, 31, 31, 35) sts; turn leaving rem sts unworked. Cont dec 1 st at neck edge every row 4 times—15 (19, 23, 27, 27, 31) sts. Work even until same length as Back to shoulder. Fasten off.

To complete other side, leave center 13 (17, 21, 21, 29, 29) sts unworked, attach yarn in next st, and work on rem sts to match 1st side. Fasten off.

SLEEVE (make two)

Ribbing (worked sideways): Ch 10 + 1 for turn. Work in triple tucks pattern until approximately 8 (8, 8½, 8½, 9, 9)", ending after Row 5. Fasten off.

Upper Sleeve: Working on long edge of ribbing and with WS facing, work 35 (35, 39, 43, 43, 47) sc evenly across; turn. With RS facing, begin working dots and diamonds pattern, working Row 1 as follows: Ch 1, sc in ea sc across. Cont with pattern rep for rest of Sleeve, while at the same time, inc 1 st ea end every 4th row 9 (8, 7, 6, 11, 11) times, then every 6th row 0 (1, 2, 3, 0, 0) times working pattern on new sts—53 (53, 57, 61, 65, 69) sts. Work even until 16½ (17, 17½, 18, 18½, 19)" from beg including ribbing, ending after a RS row.

Armhole and Cap Shaping: Sl st across 4 sts, work in pattern to last 4 sts, turn leaving rem sts unworked. Then, keeping in pattern, dec 1 st ea

end eor 4 (4, 5, 5, 6, 6) times—37 (37, 39, 43, 45, 49) sts.

Next Dec Row: Sl st across 2 sts, work in pattern to last 2 sts, turn leaving rem 2 sts unworked—33 (33, 35, 39, 41, 45) sts. Rep this row 5 (5, 5, 6, 6, 7) more times—13 (13, 15, 15, 17, 17) sts. Fasten off.

FINISHING

Sew shoulder seams. Set in top of sleeves at armhole edge easing in as needed. Sew underarm and side seams.

Collar (worked sideways): Ch 10 + 1 for turn. Work in triple tucks pattern until band is long enough to fit around neck opening, slightly stretched, ending with Row 5. Fasten off.

Sew short ends tog to form a continuous band. Sew long edge of band to neck edge.

Directions for Hat

Ch 66; sl st in 1st ch to form a ring. Work triple tucks in rnds pattern for 5 reps, ending after Rnd 4.

Dec Rnd 1: Ch 1, * sc in 2 sts, sc2tog; rep from * around, end sc2tog; sl st in 1st sc—49 sts.

Work 3 rnds even in pattern.

Dec Rnd 2: Ch 1, sc in 1 st, * sc in 2 sts, sc2tog; rep from * around; sl st in 1st sc—37 sts.

Work 3 rnds even in pattern.

Dec Rnd 3: Rep Dec Rnd 2—28 sts.

Work 3 rnds even in pattern.

Dec Rnd 4: Ch 1, * sc in 2 sts, sc2tog; rep from * around; sl st in 1st sc—21 sts.

Work 3 rnds even in pattern.

Dec Rnd 5: Rep Dec Rnd 2—16 sts. Fasten off.

Weave yarn tail in and out of rem sts and pull tightly to close. Weave in end.

Designed by Gloria Tracy

Reversible Jacket and Matching Shoulder Bag

A sophisticated use of color turns this traditional classic V-neck cardigan into a beautiful fashion statement. Twelve colors, six each in two different values, zigzag their way across a soft fabric made of wonderful 100% merino wool. The trim is a stark black and white stranded arrow motif, a dramatic counterpoint to the softly muted squares in the intarsia body.

A serendipitous design feature emerged from the 25" strands of yarn used to make the three-stitch by four-row squares of single crochet. Rather than working in all the tails or weaving them all in afterwards with a yarn needle, we trimmed the ends and allowed them to hang free—and the reversible jacket made its debut!

Sizes

Finished Bust Measurements: 38 (43, 48)"
Finished Length: 21½ (22, 22¾)"
Bag: Unfolded, approximately 9" x 17"

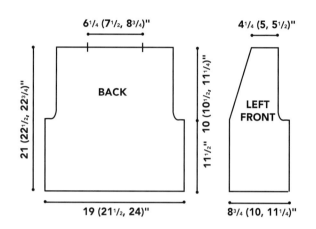

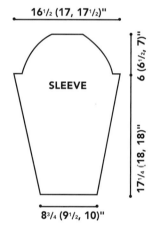

Materials

Knit One, Crochet Too *Crème Brulee* DK 50 g/
   131 yd/120 m (100% Merino superwash wool)
   2 (2, 3) balls each color
     #849 Adobe (A)
     #299 Deep Blush (a)
     #893 Camel (B)
     #420 Sunshine (b)
     #555 Pine (C)

#527 Kiwi (c)
#539 Deep Seafoam (D)
#510 Seafoam (d)
#659 Seaport (E)
#683 Soft Sky (e)
#226 Wine (F)
#789 Violet (f)
#909 Jet (G)
#101 Ivory (H)
Crochet hook US size G/6 (4 mm)
Five JHB Buttons #14034, ⅜" black knot buttons
   for smooth side
Five JHB Buttons #20289, ¾" flapper buttons for
   fringe side
One large 2-hole button for fringe side of bag

Gauge

In sc, 19 sts and 24 rows = 4"

Stitches and Patterns Used

Chain, slip stitch, single crochet, sc2tog
Stranding and intarsia (Block #16)

Notes

1. Jacket, worked in single crochet, uses 12 colors, 6 in a darker value, and 6 in a lighter value, plus black and white.
2. Color blocks are worked intarsia-style from 25" lengths.
3. Precut the 25" lengths ahead of time in lots of 25 to 30.
4. Black and white trim is worked in stranding, consistently picking up the black from under white and picking white over the black so the pattern on the reverse side is consistent and so that skeins do not become tangled.
5. To change color, insert hook in next stitch and pull up loop with current color, yarn over with next color and pull through two loops on hook.
6. When changing colors, do not work over ends. These will be trimmed neatly during finishing and used as a decorative element to create a "Flapper" reversible side.

7. When working from Chart 2, work across first four rows of color pattern with darker values (shown as upper case letters), and across next four rows with lighter values (shown as lowercase letters).

CHART 1

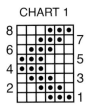

CHART 2

Color Pattern

Each square on Chart 2 is worked over 3 sts and 4 rows. Work chart from right to left rep 6-color 3-st rep across. Keep colors aligned correctly as you work up the 12-color 4-row rep.

Directions for Reversible Jacket

BACK

With G, ch 90 (102, 114) + 1 for turn.

Border: Starting in 2nd ch from hk, * sc 3 G, sc 3 H; rep from * to end.

Next Row: Following Row 2 of Chart 1 for color placement, ch 1 with 1st color, and sc in ea sc across; turn.

Cont through Row 8 of Chart 1 for Border.

Begin with A, work Chart 2 across, and cont in sc for fifteen 4-row reps above Chart 1.

Armhole Shaping: While keeping in est pattern, sl st across 1st 5 sts, work across to last 5 sts; turn leaving rem sts unworked—80 (92, 104) sts. Then, work sc2tog at beg and end of ea row 4 times—72 (84, 96) sts.

Work even until you have worked 15 (16, 17) 4-row rep from beg of armhole shaping. Fasten off.

LEFT FRONT

With G, ch 42 (48, 54) + 1 for turn. Work Border as for Back.

Begin with A, work Chart 2 across, and cont in sc for fifteen 4-row reps above Chart 1.

Armhole Shaping: While keeping in est pattern, sl st across 1st 5 sts, work across to last 2 sts, sc2tog—36 (42, 48) sts. Cont shaping at armhole edge to match Back, while at the same time dec 1 st at neck edge as est every 4 (3, 3) rows 12 (14, 17) more times—20 (24, 27) sts. Work even until same length as Back to shoulder. Fasten off.

RIGHT FRONT

Work as for Left Front through end of Border. Then cont matching Left Front, reversing color placement, armhole, and neck shaping.

SLEEVE (make two)

With G, ch 42 (45, 48) + 1 for turn.

Border: Starting in 2nd ch from hk, * sc 3 G, sc 3 H; rep from * across, end sc 0 (3, 0) G.

Next Row: Following Row 2 of Chart 1 for color placement, ch 1 with 1st color, and sc in ea sc across; turn.

Cont through Row 8 of Chart 1 for Border.

Begin with E, work Chart 2 across, and cont in sc for 24 (25, 26) 4-row rep above Chart 1, while at the same time, inc 1 st ea end every 5 rows 18 (16, 14) times, then every 6th row 0 (2, 4) times, working Chart 2 on new sts—78 (81, 84) sts.

Armhole and Cap Shaping: Row 1: Sl st across 5 sts, work across to last 5 sts; turn, leaving rem sts unworked—68 (71, 74) sts.

Work 1 row even.

Dec Row: Ch 1, sc2tog, work to last 2 sts, sc2tog; turn—66 (69, 72) sts.

Rep last 2 rows 6 (7, 8) more times—54 (55, 56) sts.

Rep Dec Row every row 14 (15, 16) times—26 (25, 24) sts.

Dec Row 2: Ch 1, sc2tog twice, work across; turn—24 (23, 22) sts.

Rep this row 5 more times—14 (13, 12) sts. Fasten off.

FINISHING

Sew shoulder seams. Set in top of sleeves at armhole opening. Sew underarm and side seams, taking care not to catch yarn ends in seams.

Right Front Band: With RS facing, beg at lower edge of Right Front, and working Chart 1, work alt 3 sc G and 3 sc H along front edge to shoulder seam, working 3 sc for every 4-row rep on vertical edge; turn.

Work through Row 4 of Chart 1.

Buttonhole Row: Keeping in est pattern, work to 1st set of 3 G sc, sc in 1st G sc, * ch 1, sk next sc, sc on 10 sc; rep from * until you have worked a total of 5 buttonholes, then complete row.

Next Row: Work Row 6 of Chart working in ea sc and ch across.

Complete Chart 1. Fasten off.

Left Front Band: Work as for Right Front Band, beg at shoulder seam and reversing color pattern.

Sew black knot buttons opposite buttonholes on RS, and flapper buttons on WS opposite knot buttons. Knot buttons are used to fasten garment. Flapper buttons are decorative only.

Edging: With RS facing and G, work 1 rnd sl st along entire body edge and lower sleeve edges.

Turn garment to WS side and trim all ends to a uniform 2" to 2½" length. You will achieve the best results by slipping ends between fingers and cutting as you would hair. Trim lowest row carefully so as not to hide border.

Directions for Shoulder Bag

Note: Bag is worked in one piece and folded over to create flap.

With G, ch 42 + 1 for turn.

Border: Starting in 2nd ch from hk, * sc 3 G, sc 3 H; rep from * to end.

Next Row: Following Row 2 of Chart 1 for color placement, ch 1 with 1st color, and sc in ea sc across; turn.

Cont through Row 8 of Chart 1 for Border.

Begin with A, work Chart 2 across, and cont in sc for fourteen 4-row reps above Chart 1. Place markers ea end of row. Cont as est until 24 4-row reps above Chart 1. Fasten off.

Finishing

Fold back with WS tog on marked row and sew side seams.

With RS facing and G, work 1 rnd sc around upper edge of back and flap, working a ch-6 button loop at center of flap; sl st in 1st sc. Fasten off.

Crochet Ball Button: Work in rnds without turning.

With G and leaving a 12" tail, ch 3 and sl st in 1st ch to form ring.

Rnd 1: Ch 1, work 8 sc in ring; sl st in 1st st.

Rnd 2: Ch 1, work 2 sc in each st around; sl st in 1st st—16 sc.

Rnd 3: Ch 1, 2 sc in 1st st, sc in next st, * 2 sc in next st, sc in next sc; rep from * around; sl st in 1stt sc—24 sc.

Cont working inc 8 sts evenly in ea rnd until desired diameter. Work 1 rnd even.

Dec Rnd: Ch 1, * sc2tog, sc in next sc; rep from * around.

Fill button with stuffing material, then rep Dec Rnd. Fasten off leaving a 12" tail. Weave yarn end through rem sts and pull tightly to close opening. Sew button on smooth side of work using tail ends. On flapper side, sew a large 2-hole button.

Braided Shoulder Strap: Cut twenty-four 60" lengths of each G and H. Divide H into two 12" strand groups and place on either side of the G group. Knot these leaving a 6" tail, and braid together. Knot end leaving a 6" tail. Sew back of knots to each side at fold. Trim tassel ends evenly. Turn bag to WS and trim ends to a uniform 2" to 2½" length.

Designed by Gloria Tracy

Amelia Cuff-to-Center Jacket and Matching Beret

Cuff-to-cuff and cuff-to-center horizontally worked shaping has long been a favorite with crocheters because of the ease in working and finishing. This technique also adapts to any size and produces flattering vertical lines. On-seam pockets can be included, as we did in our model, when sewing up the side seams.

We chose a variety of yarns and used them singly and held together in various parts of the jacket. By making a longer coat length, adding a collar, or changing the stitches and yarn, you can easily alter this basic design technique. We used our leftover yarn to make a matching beret worked in a variety of the jacket stitches.

Sizes

Finished Bust Measurements: 42 (44, 46, 48, 50)"
Finished Length: 22"
Beret: 11" in diameter

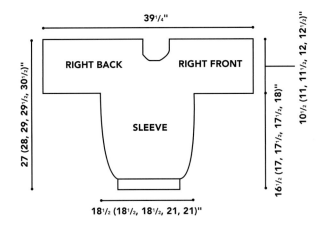

Materials

Knit One, Crochet Too *Parfait Solids* 100 g/
210 yd/192 m (100% worsted weight wool)
2 (2, 3, 3, 3) skeins #1539 Deep Seafoam (A)
2 (2, 3, 3, 3) skeins #1500 Seafoam (B)
2 (2, 3, 3, 3) skeins #2811 Cocoa Heather (C)
2 (2, 3, 3, 3) skeins #2822 Fawn Heather(F)
Mousse 50 g/112 yd/102 m (74% brushed mohair,
22% wool, 5% nylon)
4 (4, 5, 5, 5) skeins #6222 Spumoni (D)
Soufflé 50 g/104 yd/95 m (70% cotton, 30%
viscose)
5 (5, 6, 6, 7) skeins #7222 Spumoni (E)
Crochet hooks US sizes H/8, and I/9, and J/10 (5,
5.5, and 6 mm)
Yarn needle (optional)
Six buttons
Small snap

Gauge

In ribbing pattern with I hk and A, 13 sts and 17
rows = 4" (10 cm)
In alt dc with J hk and B, 16 sts and 7 rows = 4"
(10 cm)
In dsc with J hk and D, 11 sts and 8 rows = 4"
(10 cm)
In crunch stitch with I hk and one strand ea E and F
held tog, 12 sts and 7 rows = 4" (10 cm)

Stitches and Patterns Used

Single crochet, double single crochet, half double
crochet, half Elmore, double crochet
Crunch stitch (Block #4)
Front porch/back porch (Block# 1)

Special Stitches Used
sc dec: Pull up lp in next 2 sts, yo, draw through 2
lps on hk.

Ribbing Pattern
(any number of sts)

Row 1: Sc in 2nd ch from hk and in ea ch across;
turn.

Row 2: Ch 1, sc in back lp of ea st across.

Rep Row 2 for ribbing pattern.

Alternating Front & Back Porch Pattern

(odd number of sts)

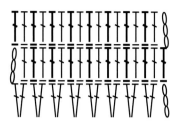

Row 1: Ch 3 (counts as 1st dc), * alt dc in back lp of next st, dc in front lp of next st; rep from * across.

Rep this row for pattern.

Crunch Stitch Pattern

(even number of sts)

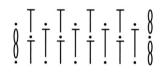

Row 1: Ch 2 (counts as 1st st), * sl st in next st, hdc in next st; rep from * across, sl st in last st, turn.

Row 2: Ch 2, * sl st in next hdc, hdc in next sl st; rep from * across, end with sl st in top of ch-2, turn.

Rep Row 2 for crunch stitch.

Notes for Jacket

1. It is imperative to work a gauge swatch in each of the individual stitches used.

2. Change hook size throughout garment as indicated in instructions. Work from cuff to center for each side.

Directions for Jacket

RIGHT HALF

Right Cuff: With smaller hk and A, ch 38 (38, 38, 41, 41). Work in ribbing pattern on 37 (37, 37, 40, 40) sts for 2". Fasten off.

Lower Sleeve, Right Half: With larger hk and B, ch 3 (counts as 1st dc), beg with next st, work 2 dc in ea st across; turn—73 (73, 73, 79, 79) sts. Work in back and front hE until 10½ (11, 11, 11½, 11½)" from beg. Fasten off.

Divider: Row 1 (RS): With A and larger hk, ch 1, sc in ea sc across; do not turn.

Row 2: Work crab stitch (reverse single crochet) across; turn. Fasten off.

Upper Sleeve, Right Half: With D and larger hk, work across in dsc evenly dec 26 (26, 26, 24, 24) sts in 1st row—47 (47, 47, 55, 55) sts. Work even in dsc inc 1 st ea end every 4th row 3 times—53 (53, 53, 61, 61) sts. Work even until 16½ (17, 17½, 17½, 18)" from beg of cuff.

Body: With D, ch 30 (30, 30, 26, 26). Fasten off and set aside to be used later for 1st row of Body. Ch 30 (30, 30, 26, 36) + 1 for turn. Beg in 2nd ch from hk, work in dsc across these ch for 1st side of Body, across top of sleeve sts, across ch set aside earlier for 2nd side of Body—113 sts. Work even until 3 (3½, 4, 4½, 5)" from start of Body, ending after a WS row. Work Divider Rows 1 and 2.

Center Right Half: With smaller hk and holding 1 strand each E and F, work in crunch stitch inc 11 sts evenly in 1st row—124 sts. Work even in crunch stitch until 24 (25, 26, 26, 27)" from beg of cuff, or 3 (3, 3, 3½, 3½)" less then desired length to center back. Mark center of row.

Right Back: Work in pattern to marker, turn leaving rem sts unworked—62 sts. Working on this side only, dec 1 st at neck edge every other row twice—60 sts. Work even until 27 (28, 29, 29½, 30½)" from beg of cuff. Fasten off.

Right Front: Leave 1st 6 sts free at neck edge, attach yarn in next st, then beg with this same st, work across in crunch stitch to end of row; turn—56 sts. Cont neck shaping by dec 1 st at neck edge every row 6 times—50 sts. Work even until ¾" less then total Right Back length. Fasten off.

LEFT HALF

Work as for Right Half, substituting C for B for Lower Sleeve, and reversing neck shaping.

FINISHING

Steam edges lightly through wet toweling. Join center backs. Sew sleeve and side seams as follows: Beg at lower edge of sides, sew 1", leave next 6" free for pocket opening, complete seam.

Bottom Band: Row 1 (RS): With smaller hk and A, beg at left front corner and evenly sl st 98 (104, 108, 114, 118) along lower edge of Body, turn.

Row 2: Ch 1, sc in front lp of ea sl st across, turn.

Row 3: Ch 1, sc in back lp of ea sc across, turn.

Row 4: Ch 1, sc in both lps of ea sc across, turn.

Rep Rows 3 and 4 until 1½" from beg. Fasten off.

Buttonhole Band: Row 1 (RS): With smaller hk and A, beg at lower right front edge and evenly work 60 sc to neck edge, turn.

Rows 2–4: Work as for Rows 2–4 of Bottom Band.

Row 5: Mark 6 evenly spaced buttonholes; ch 1, (sc in back lp of ea sc to marker, ch 2, sk 2 sts) 6 times, sc in back lp of ea sc to end of row, turn.

Row 6: Ch 1, sc in both lps of ea sc and work 2 sc in ea ch-2 sp across, turn.

Row 7: Rep Row 3. Fasten off.

Buttonband: Work as for Buttonband on opposite side, omitting buttonholes. Sew buttons opposite buttonholes.

Neckband: Row 1 (WS): With smaller hk and A, beg left neck edge and evenly work 70 sc to opposite edge, turn.

Work Rows 2–7 of Buttonband. Fasten off. Sew small snap at upper right corner of band.

Outer Pocket Facing: With RS facing, larger hk and D, beg at front side of opening and evenly work 16 sc across; turn. Work in sc until facing is ¾" wide. Fasten off. Sew each short end to RS of back.

Pocket Lining, Right Pocket: Row 1 (RS): With larger hk and D, ch 5, sc in 2nd ch from hk and in next 3 ch, work 16 sc along back side of opening, turn—20 sc.

Row 2: Ch 1, sc dec, sc across, turn.

Cont in this manner, dec 1 st at top of pocket every 4th row, until approximately 7" from beg. Fasten off. Sew in place to WS of front.

Pocket Lining, Left Pocket: Row 1 (RS): With larger hk and D, work 16 sc along back side of opening, turn.

Row 2: Ch 5, sc in 2nd ch from hk and in next 3 ch, work across to last 2 sc, sc dec; turn—19 sc.

Complete to match first pocket.

Directions for Beret

Notes for Beret

1. Turning chains are counted as stitches.

2. The first nine rounds are worked in the round with WS facing.

Ch 3, sl st into 1st ch to form a ring.

Rnd 1: With strand ea of D and E, ch 1, sc 8 into ring, sl st to top of 1st st—8 sts.

Rnd 2: Ch 1, sc into same st, 2 sc into ea sc, sl st to top of beg ch—16 sts.

Rnd 3: Ch 3, sl st into same st, *hdc, sl st into next st, rep from * around, sl st to top of beg ch changing color to strand ea of C and E on sl st—32 sts.

Rnd 4: Ch 3, working into front lp, *hE into next st, rep from * around, sl st into top of beg ch, changing color to strand ea of A and E on sl st—32 sts.

Rnd 5: Ch 3, sl st into same st, *hdc, sl st into next st, rep from * around, sl st to top of beg ch changing color to strand ea of B and E on sl st—64 sts.

Rnd 6: Ch 3, *hE into next st, rep from * around, sl st into top of beg ch, changing color to strand ea of A and E on sl st—64 sts.

Rnd 7: Ch 3, hE into same st, working into front lp, *hE into each of next 6 sts, 2 hE into next st, rep from * around, sl st into top of beg ch, changing color to strand ea of C and E on sl st—72 sts.

Rnd 8: Ch 3, hE into same st, working into front lp, *hE into ea of next 7 sts, 2 hE into next st, rep from * around, sl st into top of beg ch, changing color to strand ea of D and E on sl st—80 sts.

Rnd 9: Ch 3, sl st into same st, *hdc, sl st into next st, sk 1 st, hdc, sl st into next st, rep from * to last st, hdc, sl st, sl st to top of beg ch changing color to 1 strand C on sl st—108 sts. Turn.

Rnd 10: With RS facing, ch 3, *dc behind the knot of the next st and into back lp of the next st, rep from * around, ending sl st to top of beg ch changing color to 1 strand A on st—108 sts.

Rnd 11: Ch 3, *dc into back lp of the next st, dc into front lp of the next st, rep from * around, ending sl st to top of beg ch changing color to 1 strand B on sl st—108 sts.

Rnd 12: Ch 3, *dc into front lp of the next st, dc into back lp of the next st, rep from * around, ending sl st to top of beg ch changing color to 1 strand A on sl st—108 sts.

Rnd 13: Ch 3, keeping in the alt back lp/front lp pattern as est, *pattern into ea of the next 7 sts, dc2tog, rep from * around, ending sl st to top of beg ch changing color to 1 strand C on st—96 sts.

Rnd 14: Ch 3, keeping in the alt front lp/back lp pattern as est, *pattern into ea of the next 6 sts, dc2tog, rep from * around, ending sl st to top of beg ch changing color to 1 strand D on st—84 sts.

Rnd 15: Ch 3, keeping in the alt back lp/front lp pattern as est, *pattern into ea of the next 5 sts, dc2tog, rep from * around, ending sl st to top of beg ch changing color to 1 strand A on st—72 sts.

Rnd 16: Ch 3, keeping in the alt front lp/back lp pattern as est, *pattern into each of the next 4 sts, dc2tog, rep from * around, ending sl st to top of beg ch—60 sts.

Rnds 17-20: Ch 1, sc into same st, sc into back lp around.

Fasten off.

Designed by Gloria Tracy

Convertible-Collar Classic Jacket and Toque Hat

This classic jacket is another example of a basic, traditional shape given style by changing the design details. Lying flat, the convertible collar appears to be a traditional polo style; turned up and fastened with its tab flap, it makes a cozy turtleneck closure. Adding the toque-styled hat will make this set one of your fall favorites.

Sizes

Finished Bust Measurements: 39¼ (45¼, 50¾, 56¼, 61½, 67¼)"
Finished Length: 20½ (21½, 22, 23, 23½, 24½)"
Hat: 21¾" circumference

6¼ (6¼, 7, 7½, 8¼, 9)"
BACK
18 (19, 19½, 20½, 21, 22)"
9 (9, 10, 10, 11, 11)"
9 (10, 9½, 10½, 10, 11)"
20 (23, 25¾, 28½, 31¼, 34)"
5½ (7, 8, 9, 10, 11)"
LEFT FRONT
9 (10½, 11¾, 13¼, 14½, 16)"
16 (16, 17¼, 17¼, 18¾, 18¾)"
SLEEVE
5½ (5½, 6½, 6½, 7¼, 7¼)"
17"
9 (9, 10½, 10½, 11¾, 11¾)"

Materials

Knit One, Crochet Too *BonBon boucle mohair*
50 g/100 yd/ 91 m
9 (11, 12, 14, 16, 18) skeins #5777 Blackberry Cobbler (A)
Parfait Solids 100% worsted wool (100 g/ 218 yd/199 m)
5 (6, 7, 8, 9, 10) #1730 Eggplant (B)
Crochet hooks US sizes H/8, I/9, and K/10.5 (5, 5.5, and 6.5 mm)
Yarn needle (optional)
Eight buttons

Gauge

In diagonal spike pattern with largest hk and 1 strand ea A and B held tog, 11.5 sts and 5 rows = 4"
With B only, smallest hk and working (hdc, sl st) in ea st, 9 sts = 4"

Stitches and Patterns Used

Chain, slip stitch, single crochet, double crochet, front post double crochet, back post double crochet, linked double singles, reverse single crochet (crab stitch)
Diagonal spike (Block #3)
Linked double crochet (Block #5)

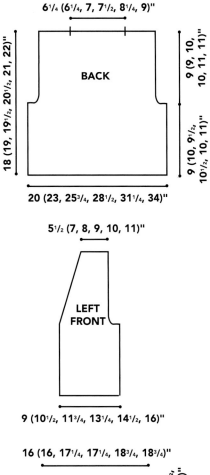

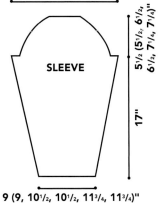

Special Stitches Used

Dc dec: Keeping last lp of ea on hk, work dc in next 2 sts, yo, draw through 4 lps on hk.

Diagonal spike (DS): Yo, insert hk from front to back into sk st before 3-dc group, pull up lp to same height as current row, (yo, draw through 2 lps on hk) twice.

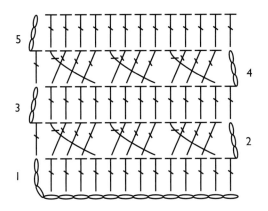

Diagonal Spike Pattern

(multiple of 4 sts + 2)

Row 1: Dc in 4th ch from hk and in ea ch across, turn.

Row 2: Ch 3 (counts as dc), * sk next st, dc in next 3 sts, ds in sk st; rep from * across, dc in last st, turn.

Row 3: Ch 3 (counts as dc), dc in next and every st across, turn.

Rep Rows 2 and 3 for diagonal spike pattern.

Diagonal Spike Pattern in the Rnds

(multiple of 4 sts)

Rnd 1: Ch 3 (counts as 1st dc), dc in next and every st around, sl st in top of ch-3.

Rnd 2: Ch 3 (does not count as dc), * sk next st, dc in next 3 sts, work ds in sk st, rep from * around, sl st in top of ch-3.

Rep Rnds 1 and 2 for diagonal spike pattern in the rnds.

Ribbing Pattern

(even number of sts)

Row 1: Ch 2 (counts as 1st st), * BPdc in next st, Fpdc in next st, rep from * across, BPdc in last st, turn.

Rep this row for ribbing pattern.

Notes

1. Work the Jacket first since the hat is worked from the remaining yarn. Use one strand each A and B held together with the larger hook throughout main sections of garment and hat.
2. Use one strand B and the smaller hook for all ribbings only.

Directions for Jacket

BACK

With largest hk, and A and B tog, ch 58 (66, 74, 82, 90, 98) + 2 for turn. Work even in diagonal spike pattern until 9 (10, 9½, 10½, 10, 11)" from beg, ending after a rep of Row 1.

Armhole Shaping: Sl st across 1st 2 sts, work in pat st to last 2 sts, turn leaving rem 2 sts unworked—54 (62, 70, 78, 86, 94) sts. Dec 1 st ea end at beg of next 2 rows—50 (58, 66, 74, 82, 90) sts. Work even until 9 (9, 10, 10, 11, 11)" above armhole—18 (19, 19½, 20½, 21, 22)" from beg. Fasten off.

LEFT FRONT

With largest hk, and A and B tog, ch 26 (30, 34, 38, 42, 46) + 2 for turn. Work as for Back to armhole shaping.

Armhole Shaping: Sl st across 1st 2 sts, work in pattern to end of row, turn—24 (28, 32, 36, 40, 44) sts. Dec 1 st at armhole edge every row twice—22 (26, 30, 34, 38, 42) sts. Work even until 16¼ (17¼, 17¾, 18¾, 19¼, 20¼)" from beg, ending after a WS row.

Neck Shaping: Work in pattern to last 4 (4, 5, 6, 7, 8) sts, turn leaving rem sts unworked—18 (22, 25, 28, 31, 34) sts. Dec 1 st at same edge every row twice—16 (20, 23, 26, 29, 32) sts. Work even until same length as Back to shoulder. Fasten off.

RIGHT FRONT

Work as for Left Front to neck shaping.

Neck Shaping: Sl st across 1st 4 (4, 5, 6, 7, 8) sts, beg in next st, work in pattern to end of row. Complete to match Left Front.

SLEEVE (make two)

With largest hk, and A and B tog, ch 26 (26, 30, 30, 34, 34) + 2 for turn. Work in diagonal spike pattern, while at the same time, inc 1 st ea end eor 10 times, working in pattern on new sts as number will allow—46 (46, 50, 50, 54, 54) sts. Work even until 17" from beg.

Armhole and Cap Shaping: Sl st across 1st 2 sts, work in pattern st to last 2 sts, turn leaving rem 2 sts unworked—42 (42, 46, 46, 50, 50) sts.

Rep this row until 18 sts rem—7 (7, 8, 8, 9, 9) rows total. Fasten off.

FINISHING

Pocket Lining (make two): With A only and largest hk, ch 18 + 2 for turn. Work in dc on 18 sts for 7". Fasten off.

Sleeve Cuff (make two): With RS facing, B and medium-sized hk, work along bottom edge of sleeve as follows: Ch 1, 2 sc in 1 (1, 0, 0, 0, 0) st, * sc in next 4 sts, 2 sc in next sc, rep from * across, end sc in last 0 (0, 0, 0, 4, 4) sts, turn— 32 (32, 36, 36, 40, 40) sts. Work in ribbing pattern for 2½". Fasten off.

Sew shoulder seams. Set in top of sleeve at armhole opening. Sew underarm sleeve seams. Sew side seams leaving a 6" opening at 1" from lower edge for pocket. Sew side of pocket to back side of opening. Sew rem 3 sides of pocket to WS of front.

Lower Body Edging: With RS facing, B and medium-sized hk, work along bottom edge of Body as follows: Ch 1, * sc in 4 sts, 2 sc in next st, rep from * across working 1 st in side seams, adjusting sts to obtain an even number, turn. Work in ribbing pattern for 2½". Fasten off.

Front Band (work on both sides of front): With RS facing, B and medium-sized hk, evenly sc along left front edge, beg at neck, and working a multiple of 4 + 2 sts across, turn.

Row 1 (WS): Ch 2 (counts as hdc), hdc in next and every sc across, turn.

Row 2: Ch 2 (counts as hdc), * sk next st, hdc in next 3 sts, dse in sk st, rep from * across, hdc in last st, turn.

Row 3: Ch 1, work Ldc across linking through bottom lp of st just completed. Fasten off.

Sew buttons planning to use space created by dsc on opposite band as buttonholes.

Collar: With RS facing, B and medium-sized hk, begin at right front edge, ch 1, work 6 sl st on side of front band, ch 3 (counts as dc), keeping work flat and tension even, work 6 Ldc on side of neck, add A and holding both B and A tog, work 10 more dc to shoulder seam, work 12 (12, 14, 16, 18, 20) dc across back of neck, 10 dc on side of neck, then with B only, work 7 Lsc to side of front band, 6 sl st on side of band. Fasten off.

Reattach B in top of 1st Ldc, ch 3 (counts as dc), Ldc in next 6 sts, make 2 dc with both strands in next st, work in dc to last 2-strand st, 2 dc in next st, with B only, Ldc on next 7 sts, turn.

Cont in this manner inc 1 st on ea side of collar at beg and end of 2-strand section until 9" from beg. Then beg ea row with ch 3 (counts as dc), work in Ldc across entire row with 1 strand B only for 1½". Fasten off.

Fold collar in half to outside. Invisibly sl st front edge tog through both layers using B.

Tab: With 1 strand B and medium-sized hk, ch 18 + 2 for turn.

Row 1: Ch 3 (counts as dc), Ldc in 4th ch from hk and every ch across, turn—18 sts.

Row 2: Ch 3 (counts as dc), Ldc in next st, dc in next st for buttonhole, Ldc in next 12 sts, dc in next st for buttonhole, Ldc on last 2 sts; turn.

Row 3: Ch 3 (counts as dc), Ldc in next and every st across; do not turn.

Work crab stitch around tab working 3 sts at ea corner. Fasten off.

Sew button on each side of collar where B edge meets center of collar. Attach tab.

Directions for Toque Hat

With largest hk and A and B held tog, ch 4, sl st in 1st ch to form ring.

Rnd 1: Ch 1, work 8 sc in ring, sl st in 1st sc.

Rnd 2: Ch 3 (counts as 1st dc), dc in same st, 2 dc in ea rem sc around, sl st in top of ch-3—16 sts.

Rnd 3: Ch 1, sc in 1st st, * 2 sc in next st, sc in next st; rep from * to last st, 2 sc in last st, sl st in 1st sc—24 sts.

Rnd 4: Ch 3 (counts as 1st dc), dc in same st, dc in next 2 sts; * 2 dc in next st, dc in next 2 sts, rep from * around, sl st in top of ch-3—32 sts.

Cont in this manner inc 8 sts every rnd and alt sc and dc rnds until 56 sts are obtained, ending with a sc rnd.

Drop A and turn.

WS Rnd 1: With B only and smallest hk, ch 2 (counts as 1st hdc), sl st in same st, * (hdc, sl st) in next st, rep from * around; sl st in top of ch-2.

Add A and turn.

Next Rnd (RS): With largest hk and A and B held tog, work diagonal spike pattern in rnds for Rnds 1 (working in hdc only) and 2 twice, then Rnd 1 once more.

Drop A and turn.

WS Rnd 2: Rep WS Rnd 1 sk every 8th st—49 sts. Fasten off.

Designed by Susan Levin

Shawl-Collared Jacket

Quick-to-crochet using a P hook, this soft luxurious jacket could easily be a weekend project. The color for the trim was inspired by the garnet flecks in the unusual tweedy chenille. We liked the contrast between the soft linked double crochet stitches in the body and the precision of the squares stitch made of shiny ribbon. For an even quicker variation, you could leave off the sleeves and use the pattern as a vest. Another interesting experiment would be to use multistrands of lighter-weight yarns to achieve the same gauge and create your own tweedy look.

Sizes

Finished Bust Measurements: 37 (42½, 47¾, 49, 54¼)"

Finished Length: 23 (24, 24, 25, 25)"

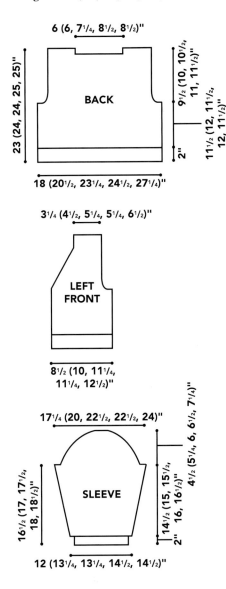

6 (6, 7¼, 8½, 8½)"

23 (24, 24, 25, 25)"

BACK

9½ (10, 10½, 11, 11½)"

11½ (12, 11½, 12, 11½)"

2"

18 (20½, 23¼, 24½, 27¼)"

3¼ (4½, 5¼, 5¼, 6½)"

LEFT FRONT

8½ (10, 11¼, 11¼, 12½)"

17¼ (20, 22½, 22½, 24)"

16½ (17, 17½, 18, 18½)"

SLEEVE

4½ (5¼, 6, 6½, 7¼)"

14½ (15, 15½, 16, 16½)"

2"

12 (13¼, 13¼, 14½, 14½)"

Materials

Body: Trendsetter *Brava*, 100 g/66 yd/60 m (90% acrylic, 10% polyester)
7 (8, 10, 10, 11) hanks #1209 (A)

Trim: Trendsetter *Piatina*, 50 g/66 yd/60 m (100% viscose)
10 (10, 11, 12, 12) balls #303 (B)

Crochet hooks US sizes H/8, I/9, J/10, P/16 (5, 5.5, 6, and 15 mm)

Four buttons: K1C2 CH36 Abalone

Gauge

In Ldc, color A and P hk, 6 sts and 6 rows = 4"
In squares pattern, color B and I hk, 14 sts = 4"

Stitches and Patterns Used

Chain, slip stitch, single crochet, double crochet, linked double crochet
Squares (Block #5)

Directions for Jacket

BACK

With largest hk and A, ch 27 (31, 35, 37, 41) + 2 for turn. Work in Ldc for rest of Back. Work even until 11½ (12, 11½, 12, 11½)" from beg.

Armhole Shaping: Sl st across 1st 2 sts, work in pat st to last 2 sts, turn leaving rem 2 sts unworked—23 (27, 31, 33, 37) sts. Dec 1 st ea end at beg of next 2 rows—19 (23, 27, 29, 33) sts. Work even until 9 (9½, 10, 10½, 11)" above armhole.

Shoulder Shaping: Work across 3 (5, 6, 6, 8) sts, work next 2 dc tog, Ldc in next st—5 (7, 8, 8, 10) sts. Fasten off. Leave center 7 (7, 9, 11, 11) sts unworked. Attach yarn in next st, ch 3 (counts as 1st dc), work next 2 dc tog, work to end of row—5 (7, 8, 8, 10) sts. Fasten off.

LEFT FRONT

With largest hk and A, ch 13 (15, 17, 17, 19) + 2 for turn. Work as for Back to armhole shaping.

Armhole and Neck Shaping: Sl st across 1st 2 sts, work in pattern to last 2 sts, work 2 dc tog, turn—10 (12, 14, 14, 16) sts. Dec 1 st at armhole edge every row twice, and dec 1 st at neck edge every 2" 3 (3, 4, 4, 4) more times—5 (7, 8, 8, 10) sts. Work even until same length as Back to shoulder. Fasten off.

RIGHT FRONT

Work as for Left Front reversing armhole and neck shaping.

SLEEVE (make two)

With largest hk and A, ch 18 (20, 20, 22, 22) + 2 for turn. Work in Ldc, while at the same time, inc 1 st ea end every 3½ (2¾, 2, 2½, 2¼)" 4 (5, 7, 6, 7) times—26 (30, 34, 34, 36) sts. Work even until 14½ (15, 15½, 16, 16½)" from beg.

Armhole and Cap Shaping: Sl st across 1st 2 sts, work in pat st to last 2 sts, turn leaving rem 2 sts unworked—22 (26, 30, 30, 32) sts. Dec 1 st ea end every row 6 (7, 8, 9, 10) times—10 (12, 14, 12, 12) sts. Fasten off.

FINISHING

Pocket Lining (make two): With A and largest hk, ch 9 + 2 for turn. Work in Ldc for 7". Fasten off. Lining is worked from side to side. Sl st in place to inside having beg edge even with front side edge and placing lower edge of lining even with 2nd row of front.

Sew shoulder seams. Sew side seams down to Pocket Lining. Leave front edge free and instead sew edge of Pocket Lining to back. Join last row of front to last row of back.

Pocket Trim: With I hk, RS facing and B, work 20 sc evenly across front edge of pocket, turn. Work Rows 1 and 2 of squares. Fasten off. Fold trim to right side and sl st in place.

Armhole Opening Trim: With I hk, RS facing and B, beg at armhole edge and evenly work 80 (84, 88, 90, 94) sc along armhole opening ending at opposite armhole edge, turn. Work Rows 1 and 2 of squares twice. Fasten off.

Cuff: With H hk, RS facing, and B, work 36 (38, 38, 40, 40) sc evenly along lower edge of sleeve. Work Rows 1 and 2 of squares 3 times. Fasten off. Sew underarm sleeve seams. Sew in top of sleeves at armhole opening.

Body Lower Edge Trim: With I hk, RS facing and B, work 122 (140, 160, 164, 182) sc along lower edge of body. Work Rows 1 and 2 of squares 3 times. Fasten off.

Front Band (work on each side): With I hk, RS facing and B, work 48 (50, 48, 50, 48) sc evenly bet lower edge and point where neck shaping begins. Work Rows 1 and 2 of squares 3 times. Fasten off. Sew buttons on left band and use sp between squares as buttonholes.

Collar: Row 1: With H hk, RS facing and B, work 106 (110, 118, 126, 130) sc evenly around neck beg and ending where neck shaping begins.

Row 2: Ch 1, sc across, turn.

Row 3: Work squares Row 1.

Row 4: With H hk, ch 1, * sc in ch-1 sp, sc in square; rep from * across, turn leaving last st unworked—104 (108, 116, 124, 128) sts.

Row 5: Ch 3 (counts as dc), sk next sc, * square in next sc, ch-1, sk next sc, rep from * across to last 4 sc, square in next sc, sk next sc, ch 1, dc in next dc, turn leaving rem st unworked—102 (106, 114, 122, 126) sts.

Row 6: Rep Row 4—100 (104, 112, 120, 124) sts.

Row 7: Rep Row 5   98 (102, 110, 118, 122) sts.

Row 8: Rep Row 4—96 (100, 108, 116, 120) sts.

Row 9: With J hk, rep Row 5 and 4—92 (96, 104, 112, 116) sts.

Row 10: Ch 1, sc in ea st across. Fasten off.

With RS facing and J hk, attach B at left edge of Row 1 of Collar and work 1 row sc evenly around entire edge of Collar. Fasten off.

Summer One-Button Jacket

This jacket will be a timeless, classic addition to your wardrobe for many years to come. The body is worked in the slightly open Jack-o-lantern teeth pattern. The collar, pockets, and edges are worked in linked doubles for stability. The triangular points on the collar are repeated as flaps on the patch pockets, and an oversized abalone shell button adds a final design touch.

Sizes

Finished Bust Measurements: 36¼ (40½, 44, 48¼, 52½)"
Finished Length: 22 (22½, 23, 23½, 24)"

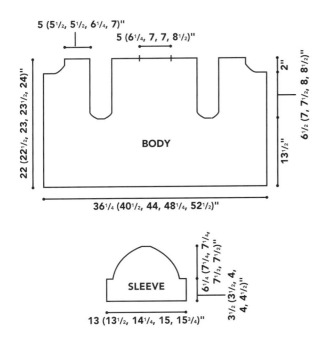

Materials

Knit One, Crochet Too *Richesse et Soie* 25 g/
146 yd/133 m (65% cashmere, 35% silk)
9 (10, 11, 12, 13) balls #9100 Snow (A)
Trendsetter *Flora Eyelash*, 20 g/70 yd/64 m (76%
viscose, 24% polyamide)
17 (20, 22, 25, 27) balls #166 color (B)
Crochet hook US size I/9 (5.5 mm)
Two ⅞" buttons
One 1⅜" button

Gauge

In pat st and 1 strand ea A and B held tog, 17 sts
and 9 rows = 4" (10 cm)

Stitches and Patterns Used

Chain, slip stitch, single crochet, double crochet,
linked double crochet
Jack-o-lantern teeth (Block #5)

Special Stitches

2-sc dec: Pull up lp in 3 sts, yo, draw through 4 lps
on hk.

Jack-o-Lantern Body Pattern Stitch

(multiple of 3 sts)

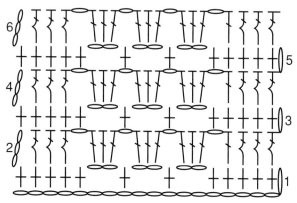

Row 1 (RS): Ch 1, sc in 5 ch, * ch 2, sk 2 ch, sc in
next ch; rep from * to last 4 chs, sc in last 4 chs;
turn.

Row 2: Ch 3 (counts as 1st 1 dc), sk 1st Ldc in next
3 sts, * ch 1, 3 dc in next ch-2 sp; rep from *

across to last 4 sts, ch 1, Ldc in next st, 1
Ldc in last 3 sts; turn.

Row 3: Ch 1, sc in 4 sts, * sc in next ch-1 sp, ch 2;
rep from * across, sc in last ch-1 sp, sc in last 4
sts; turn.

Rep Rows 2 and 3 for pat st.

Jack-o-Lantern Sleeve Pattern Stitch

(multiple of 3 sts + 1)

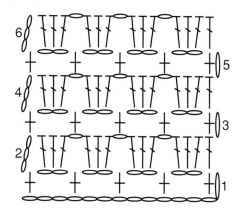

Row 1 (RS): Ch 1, sc in 1st ch, * ch 2, sk 2 ch, sc
in next ch; rep from * across; turn.

Row 2: Ch 3 (counts as 1st dc), * 3 dc in next ch-2
sp, ch 1; rep from * across to last ch-2 sp, 3 dc in
ch-2 sp, dc in last sc; turn.

Row 3: Ch 1, sc in 1st dc, * ch 2, sc in next ch-1 sp;
rep from * across ending last sc in top of turning
ch-3; turn.

Rep Rows 2 and 3 for sleeve pat st.

Notes

1. Use one strand each A and B held together
   throughout the entire garment.

2. The body is worked in one piece to armhole, then
   the fronts and back are worked separately to
   shoulders.

Directions for Jacket

BODY

With A and B tog, ch 154 (172, 187, 205, 223) + 1
for turn.

Row 1 (RS): Sc in 2nd ch from hk and in ea ch across; turn—154 (172, 187, 205, 223) sts.

Row 2: Ch 3 (counts as 1st dc), 1 Ldc in next and ea sc across; turn.

Row 3: Ch 1, sc in ea 1 Ldc across; turn.

Row 4: Rep Row 2.

Work pat st Rows 1–3, working Pat row 1 into sts of previous row, then rep Rows 2 and 3 for rest of piece—49 (55, 60, 66, 72) 3-dc groups across. Work even until 13½" from beg, ending after a WS row.

Dividing Row (RS): Ch 1, sc in 4 sts, (sc in next ch-1 sp, ch 2) 12 (13, 14, 16, 17) times, (sc in next ch-1 sp, sc in next 3 sts) 1 (1, 2, 2, 2) times for underarm, (sc in next ch-1 sp, ch 2) 23 (27, 28, 30, 34) times, (sc in next ch-1 sp, sc in next 3 sts) 1 (1, 2, 2, 2) times for underarm, (sc in next ch-1 sp, ch 2) 12 (13, 14, 16, 17) times, sc in next ch-1 sp, sc in last 4 sts; turn.

LEFT FRONT

Row 1 (WS): Work in est pat st to last ch-2 sp before underarm, work 2 dc in next ch-2 sp; turn.

Row 2: Ch 1, sc in first dc, sk next dc, sc in next ch-1 sp, cont in est pat st to end of row; turn.

Row 3: Work in est pat st through last ch-2 sp, Ldc in next sc; turn.

Row 4: Ch 1, sc in 1st dc, cont in est pat st to end of row; turn—11 (12, 13, 15, 16) 3-dc groups across.

Rep Rows 3 and 4 for rest of Left Front. Work even until 6½ (7, 7½, 8, 8½)" above armhole, ending after a WS row.

Neck Shaping: Row 1 (RS): Work in pattern to last 2 (2, 3, 4, 4) 3-dc groups; turn leaving rem sts unworked—9 (10, 10, 11, 12) 3-dc groups.

Row 2: Sl st in 1st ch-2 sp, ch 3, work 3 dc in next ch-2 sp, complete row in est pat st; turn—8 (9, 9, 10, 11) 3-dc groups.

Row 3: Work in pat st, ending with sc in turning ch-3; turn.

Row 4: Rep Row 2—7 (8, 8, 9, 10) 3-dc groups; turn.

Resume working even in pat st until 8½ (9, 9½, 10, 10½)" above armhole, ending after a WS row. Fasten off.

RIGHT FRONT

Row 1: With WS facing, attach yarn in 1st ch-2 sp after underarm, ch 3 (counts as dc), dc in same ch-2 sp, work in pat st to end of row; turn.

Row 2: Work in pat st ending with sc in last ch-2 sp; turn.

Row 3: Ch 3 (counts as 1st dc), work 3-dc in next ch-2 sp, complete in pat st.

Row 4: Work in pat st across ending with sc in top of tch-3; turn.

Rep Rows 3 and 4 for rest of Right Front until 2 rows before same row as Left Front to begin Neck Shaping.

Buttonhole Row: Ch 1, sc in 1st st, ch 3, sc in next ch-1 sp, complete row.

Next Row: Work across in est pattern to ch-3 sp at end of row, work 3 1 dc in ch-3 sp, 1 dc in sc; turn.

Neck Shaping: Row 1 (RS): Sl st across to 3rd (3rd, 4th, 5th, 5th) ch-1 sp, ch 1, sc in same sp, complete row in pat st; turn.

Row 2: Work in pat st ending with 1 dc in last ch-2 sp; turn.

Row 3: Ch 1, sc in 1st dc, complete row in Pat St.

Row 4: Rep Row 2.

Rep Rows 3 and 4 until same length as Left Front to shoulder. Fasten off.

UPPER BACK

Row 1: With WS facing, attach yarn in 1st ch-2 sp after underarm and complete armhole shaping at this end as for Right Front, and on opposite end as for Left Front—21 (25, 26, 28, 32) 3-dc groups. Work even until same length as Fronts to shoulder. Fasten off.

SLEEVE (make two)

With A and B tog, ch 55 (58, 61, 64, 67) + 1 for turn. Work Body Rows 1–4, then work sleeve pat st Rows 1–3, then rep Rows 2 and 3 until 3½ (3½, 4, 4, 4½)" from beg, ending after a WS row—18 (19, 20, 21, 22) 3-dc groups.

Armhole and Cap Shaping: Row 1 (RS): Sl st to 1st (1st, 2nd, 2nd, 2nd) ch-1 sp, ch 1, sc in ch-1 sp, work in pattern across to last 1 (1, 2, 2, 2) ch-1 sp, sc in ch-1 sp; turn leaving rem sts unworked.

Row 2: Sl st in 1st ch-2 sp, ch 3 (counts as dc), 3 dc in next ch-2 sp, work in pattern to last ch-2 sp, dc in last sp; turn.

Row 3: Ch 1, sc in first dc, work in pattern to tch-3, sc in tch-3; turn.

Rep Rows 2 and 3 until 2 (3, 4, 5, 2) 3-dc groups rem.

Sizes Extra-small and Extra-large: Fasten off.

Size Small: Work even for 2 more rows. Fasten off.

Size Medium: Work even for 2 more rows, then rep Rows 2 and 3 once—two 3-dc groups rem. Fasten off.

Size Large: Work even for 2 more rows, rep Rows 2 and 3 once—three 3-dc groups rem. Work even for 2 more rows. Fasten off.

FINISHING

Collar: With RS facing, sk 4 sts at front band and attach yarn at that point.

Row 1: Ch 1, work 60 (72, 78, 78, 90) sc evenly along neck edge ending before front band; turn.

Row 2: Ch 1, sc across; turn.

Row 3: Ch 3 (counts as 1 Ldc), [1 Ldc in next 8 (10, 11, 11, 13) sc, 2 Ldc in next sc] 6 times, Ldc to end of row; turn—66 (78, 84, 84, 96) sts.

Row 4: Rep Row 2.

Row 5: Ch 3 (counts as 1 Ldc), [1 Ldc in next 9 (11, 12, 12, 14) sc, 2 Ldc in next sc] 6 times, Ldc to end of row; turn—72 (84, 90, 90, 102) sts.

Row 6: Rep Row 2.

Row 7: Ch 3 (counts as 1 Ldc), [1 Ldc in next 10 (12, 13, 13, 15) sc, 2 Ldc in next sc] 6 times, Ldc to end of row; turn—78 (90, 96, 96, 108) sts.

Row 8: Rep Row 2. Fasten off.

Pocket (make two): With A and B tog, ch 21 (21, 23, 25, 25) + 1 for turn. Work rows 1 and 2 of Body until 5 (5, 5½, 5½, 6)" from beg, ending after a WS row.

Shaping: Row 1 (RS): Ch 1, 2-sc dec, sc to last 3 sts, 2-sc dec; turn—17 (17, 19, 21, 21) sts.

Next Row: Work even.

Rep these 2 rows 4 (4, 4, 5, 5) more times—1 (1, 3, 1, 1) st(s) rem. Fasten off.

Fold flap over to RS and sew small button in place at point. Center pockets on each front, placing 1" from lower edge and sew in place.

Sew large button opposite buttonhole. Sew underarm sleeve seams. Set in top of sleeves at armhole opening.

Designed by Susan Levin

Popcorns, Picots, and Puffs Pullover and Hat

This easy-to-wear unisex pullover is quick to crochet and will definitely perfect your ability to make "bumps." The rolled neck was a serendipitous design feature that is inherent when crocheting in the front loop only of single crochet in the round. The neck and cuff just naturally form an attractive rolled edge.

Sizes

Finished Bust Measurements: 40½ (45, 49½, 54)"
Finished Length: 25½ (26, 26½, 27)"
Hat: 23¼" circumference

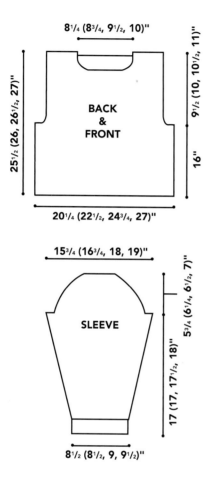

8¼ (8¾, 9½, 10)"

9½ (10, 10½, 11)"

25½ (26, 26½, 27)"

BACK & FRONT

16"

20¼ (22½, 24¾, 27)"

15¾ (16¾, 18, 19)"

SLEEVE

5¾ (6¼, 6½, 7)"

17 (17, 17½, 18)"

8½ (8½, 9, 9½)"

Materials

Plymouth Yarns *Cleckheaton Country 8 ply Tweed*,
50 g/106 yd/96 m (85% wool, 10% acrylic, 5%
rayon)
11 (12, 13, 14) #1812 Navy Tweed (A)
7 (7, 8, 9) #1809 Slate Blue Tweed (B)
5 (5, 5, 6, 6) #1808 Dusty Teal Tweed (C)
Crochet hook US size H/8 (5 mm)

Gauge

In picot single crochet pattern, 15 sts and
16 rows = 4"
In puffs pattern, 14 sts and 11 rows = 4"
In popcorn pattern, 14 sts and 9 rows = 4"

Stitches and Patterns Used

Chain, slip stitch, single crochet, half double cro-
chet, double crochet, sc2tog, hdc2tog, dc2tog
Picots, puffs, and popcorns (Block #11)
Picot single crochet pattern

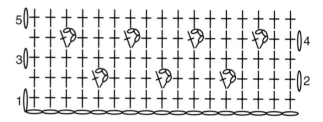

Puffs pattern (drawing through 4 times for each puff)

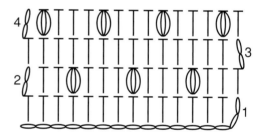

Popcorn pattern (working 5 dc for each DcPopcorn)

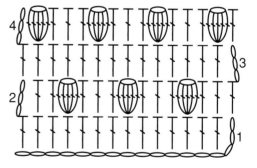

Directions for Pullover

BACK

With A, ch 75 (83, 91, 99) + 1 for turn. Work in picot single crochet pattern for 12", ending with a sc row, and dec 4 sts evenly in last row—71 (79, 87, 95) sts. With A, work in puffs pattern for 2" ending after an hdc row. Fasten off A. With B, cont in puffs pattern for 2" more, ending after an hdc row.

Armhole Shaping: Sl st across 1st 4 sts, work in pattern to last 4 sts, turn leaving rem sts unworked—63 (71, 79, 87) sts.

Hdc Dec Row: Ch 2, hdc2tog in next 2 sts, hdc to last 3 sts, hdc2tog in next 2 sts, hdc in last st; turn—61 (69, 77, 85) sts.

Work 1 row even, placing puffs across to cont est placement.

Rep these 2 rows 3 more times—55 (63, 71, 79) sts. Work 1 more Hdc Row—3½" above armhole shaping.

With B, work in popcorn pattern for 2", ending after a dc row. Fasten off B.

With C, cont in popcorn pattern for 3½ (4, 4½, 5)", ending after a dc row.

Neck Shaping: Work in pattern across 13 (16, 19, 22) sts, turn leaving rem sts unworked. Work 1 more row. Fasten off.

To complete other side, leave center 29 (31, 33, 35) sts unworked for back of neck, attach yarn in next st and complete to match 1st side.

FRONT

Work as for Back until you have worked ½ (1, 1½, 2)" in popcorn pattern with C.

Neck Shaping: Work in pattern across 18 (21, 24, 27) sts, turn leaving rem sts unworked.

Dec Row 1: Ch 3, work dc2tog in next 2 sts, complete row in pattern—17 (20, 23, 26) sts.

Dec Row 2: Work in pattern to last 3 sts, dc2tog in next 2 sts, dc in last st; turn—16 (19, 22, 25) sts.

Rep these 2 rows until 13 (16, 19, 22) sts rem. Complete to match Back. Fasten off.

To complete other side, leave center 19 (21, 23, 25) sts unworked, attach yarn in next st and complete to match 1st side.

SLEEVE (make two)

With A, ch 35 (35, 39, 43) + 1 for turn.

Color Sequence for Sleeve (work at the same time as working shaping given below)**:** Work in picot single crochet pattern for 10 (10, 10½, 11)" ending with a sc row. With A, work in puffs pattern for 2" ending with an hdc row. Fasten off A. With B, cont in puffs pattern for 2"—ready to shape armhole at this point.

Sleeve Shaping: While working in above stated color sequence, inc 1 st ea end every 1¼" 3 (12, 12, 12) times, then every 1½" 7 (0, 0, 0) times—55 (59, 63, 67) sts. Work to 17 (17, 17½, 18)" from beg, ending with an hdc row.

Armhole Shaping: Cont in puffs pattern with B, sl st across 1st 4 sts, work in pattern to last 4 sts, turn leaving rem sts unworked—47 (51, 55, 59) sts. While cont in puffs pattern, work shaping by following Hdc Dec Row from Back Armhole Shaping every row for 9 rows, end with a hdc row—29 (33, 37, 41) sts.

Dc Dec Row: With B and beg with popcorn pattern popcorn row, ch 3, dc3tog in next 3 sts, in pattern to last 4 sts, dc3tog in next 3 sts, dc in last st; turn—25 (29, 33, 37) sts.

Work Dc Dec Row every row, while cont in popcorn pattern for 2 more rows B, fasten off B—17 (21, 25, 29) sts. Cont Dc Dec Row in popcorn pattern for 1 (2, 3, 4) rows C—13 sts. Fasten off.

FINISHING

Sew shoulder seams.

Neckband: With RS facing and C, start at left shoulder seam, and evenly work 82 (86, 90, 94) sc through the flo around neck opening. Mark start of 1st rnd and cont in sc through the flo rnds until 3¼" from beg, ending above marker. Sl st in next st. Fasten off.

Set in top of sleeves at armhole opening matching colors. Sew underarm and side seams matching colors and leaving lower 2½" on ea side of front and back open for side slits.

Cuffs: With RS facing and A, start at seam and evenly work 32 (32, 34, 36) sc through flo around opening. Mark beg of 1st rnd and cont in sc rnds through flo until 2" complete, ending at marker. Sl st in next st. Fasten off and allow cuff to roll.

Lower edge: With RS facing and A, start at side seam and evenly work 1 row of sc around bottom and side slits. Fasten off.

Directions for Hat

MAIN SECTION

With C, ch 88; sl st in 1st ch to form ring.

Rnd 1: Ch 1, sc in 1st 3 sc, * psc in next sc **, sc in next 3 sc; rep from * around, ending at **; sl st in 1st sc.

Rnd 2: Ch 1, sc in ea sc around; sl st in 1st st.

Rnd 3: Ch 1, sc in 1st sc, * Psc in next sc, sc in next 3 sc; rep from * around to last 3 sts, Psc in next sc, sc in last 2 sc; sl st in 1st sc.

Rnd 4: Rep Rnd 2.

Rep these 4 rnds 3 more times. Fasten off C.

CROWN

Attach B in 1st st.

Rnd 1: With B, rep Main Section Rnd 1.

Rnd 2: Ch 1, * sc2tog in 2 sts, sc in next 3 sts, sc2tog in next 2 sts, sc in next 4 sts; rep from * around, sl st in 1st st—72 sts.

Rnd 3: Rep Main Section Rnd 3.

Rnd 4: Ch 1, * sc2tog in 2 sts, sc in next 4 sts; rep from * around; sl st in 1st st—60 sts.

Rnds 5, 7, 9, 11, and 13: Rep Rnd 3.

Rnd 6: Ch 1, * sc2tog in 2 sts, sc in next 3 sts; rep from * around; sl st in 1st st—48 sts.

Rnd 8: Ch 1, * sc2tog in 2 sts, sc in next 2 sts; rep from * around; sl st in 1st st—36 sts.

Rnd 10: Ch 1, * sc2tog in 2 sts, sc in next 1 st; rep from * around; sl st in 1st st—24 sts.

Rnd 12: Ch 1, sc2tog around; sl st in 1st st—12 sts.

Rnd 14: Rep Rnd 12—6 sts. Fasten off leaving a 12" tail. Weave tail through rem sts and pull tightly to close opening. Weave in end.

BRIM

With RS facing and A, sc in ea st around. Join. Mark beg of 1st rnd and cont in rnds, working all sc in flo. Work even for 2½", ending above marker. Sl st in next st. Fasten off.

Designed by Susan Levin

Comfy Casual Tunic

Two earthy colors make an effective design for the basketweave pattern in this unisex pullover. The project is not only easy to work but is also easy-wear and easy-care. The body of the pullover uses just the post stitch portion of the two-color basketweave pattern for flattering vertical lines. The shoulders and yoke were worked horizontally from cuff to center in the full basketweave pattern. The side slits and button-back V-neck add designerly touches and are easy to work. Make one tunic for yourself and one for your favorite companion.

Sizes

Finished Chest Measurements: 36½ (41½, 47, 52½)"

Finished Length: 25 (25½, 26⅜, 27⅝)"

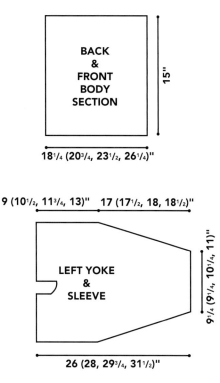

BACK
&
FRONT
BODY
SECTION

15"

18¼ (20¾, 23½, 26¼)"

9 (10½, 11¾, 13)"   17 (17½, 18, 18½)"

LEFT YOKE
&
SLEEVE

9¼ (9¼, 10¼, 11)"

26 (28, 29¾, 31½)"

Materials

Lion Brand *Homespun*, 6 oz/170 g 185 yd/169 m
   (98% acrylic, 2% polyester)
   3 (4, 5, 6) skeins #319 Adirondack (A)
   3 (3, 4, 5) skein #311 Rococo (B)
Crochet hook US size K/10.5 (6.5 mm)
Two 1" buttons
Two ¾" buttons

Gauge

In body pattern, 9 sts and 10 rows = 4"
In two-color basketweave pattern, 10 sts and 12 rows = 4"

Stitches and Patterns Used

Chain, slip stitch, single crochet, front post double crochet (FPdc)

Two-Color Basketweave Pattern

Two-color basketweave blocks (Block #9)
(*multiple of 16 sts + 9*)

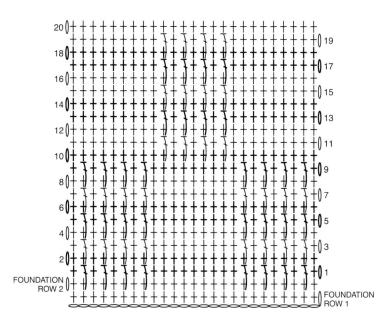

Body Pat
(*multiple of 2 sts + 1*)

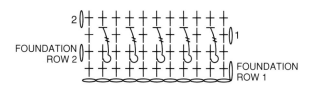

Foundation Row 1: With A, sc in 2nd ch from hk and in ea ch across; turn.

Foundation Row 2: Ch 1, sc across; turn.

Row 1 (RS): With B, ch 1, sc in 1st sc, * FPdc in next st 2 rows below, sc in next sc; rep from * across; turn.

Row 2: Ch 1, sc in ea st across; turn.

Rep Rows 1 and 2 for body pattern alt A and B eor.

Notes

1. Back and Front body sections are worked from the top down.

2. Sleeves and yoke are worked in one piece each for the right and front from the cuff to the center of the body.

Directions for Tunic

FRONT AND BACK LOWER BODY (make two)

With A, ch 41 (47, 53, 59) + 1 for turn. Work in body pattern until 15" from beg, ending after 2 rows of B.

Next Row: With A, ch 1, sc across. Fasten off.

LEFT SLEEVE AND YOKE

Sleeve: With A, ch 21 (21, 23, 25) + 1 for turn. Work in body pattern for 12 rows inc 2 (2, 1, 0) st(s) on ea end of last row—25 sts. Then, work in two-color basketweave pattern for rest of Sleeve, while at the same time, inc 1 st ea end every 1 (1, ¾,/4)" 12 (13, 16, 19) times, working est pattern on new sts—49 (51, 57, 63) sts. Work even until 17 (17½, 18, 18½)" from beg. Place yarn markers on ea end of row for underarm.

Yoke: Work even for 6 (7¼, 8, 8¾)", ending after a WS row.

Divide for Neck: Work across 25 (26, 29, 32) sts, turn leaving rem sts unworked. Work even on this side for 3 (3¼, 3¾, 4¼)". Fasten off.

To complete other side, attach yarn in next st and work across rem 24 (25, 28, 31) sts dec 1 st at neck edge every row 4 (4, 5, 6) times—20 (21, 23, 25) sts. Work even until same length as 1st side. Fasten off.

RIGHT SLEEVE AND YOKE

Work as for Left Sleeve reversing dividing row and neck shaping.

FINISHING

Sew left yoke to right yoke at center back. Sew top of Back Body Section to Back Yoke between yarn markers. Rep for Front Body Section having ea half of Yoke meet at center. Sew underarm and side seams leaving lower 3" open for side slit.

Neck Trim: Work 1 row Rsc with B around neck opening, working a ch-4 button lp at ea corner.

Frog Closure: With A, ch 18; sl st in 1st ch to form a ring.

Next Rnd: Ch 1, sc in 8 ch, insert hk in next and 18th ch and work sc, sc in rem 8 sc; sl st in 1st sc. Fasten off.

Sew largest buttons about 3" up from center front on ea side of yoke. Use frog closure to fasten.

Fold back ea corner to create a collar and sew smaller buttons opposite lps at corners.

Designed by Gloria Tracy and Ruthie Marks

Chevrons Long-Sleeved Tunic or Cap-Sleeved Tee Top

Here's an example of one basic pattern that inspired two totally different finished projects. Both projects are based on the pattern from Block #8 in the Learn-to-Crochet Afghan. For this use, the pattern was rewritten to form a lovely scalloped edge.

Long-Sleeved Tunic

The wide color selection available in this versatile acrylic yarn was the inspiration for this version of our chevrons top. We chose bright fiesta colors for our model, but other color combinations give quite a different look.

In the long-sleeved version, we gave the body of the tunic A-line shaping by decreasing the size of the hook as we worked up. We gave the sleeves V-line shaping by increasing the size of the hook as we worked upward.

Although the time investment for both versions would be almost the same, the cost and look of each top could be very different. Your choice depends on your pocketbook, yarn availability, and intended use.

Cap-Sleeved Tee Top

The cap-sleeved version is made of a shiny luxury yarn in wonderful shades of blues, green, and violet. The body is worked straight up to the underarm, then increased on each side to form a cap sleeve. The neckline was stopped at a row that would produce an upward scalloped edge. A couple of pattern rows form the scalloped edge of the sleeve cap complete the elegant tee.

Stitches and Patterns Used for Both Versions

Chain, slip stitch, single crochet, half double crochet, double crochet, treble crochet, sc3tog, tr2tog, tr3tog
Chevrons, version #1 (Block #8)

Wave and Chevron Pattern

(multiple of 8 sts + 1; rep of 6 rows):

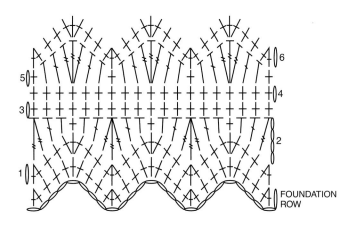

Note: Pat dec by 2 sts for each rep on Row 2 and inc back to original number of sts on row 5.

Foundation Row: Sc2tog in 2nd and 3rd ch from hk, sc in next 2 ch, * 3 sc in next ch, sc in next 2 ch **, sc3tog in next 3 ch, sc in next 2 ch; rep from * across ending last rep at **, sc2tog in last 2 ch; turn.

Row 1: Ch 1, sc2tog in 1st 2 sts, sc in next 2 sts, * 3 sc in next st, sc in next 2 sts **, sc3tog in next 3 sts, sc in next 2 sts; rep from * across ending last rep at **, sc2tog in last 2 sts; turn.

Row 2: Ch 4, tr in next st (counts as tr2tog), * dc in next st, hdc in next st, sc in next st, hdc in next st, dc in next st **, tr3tog in next 3 sts; rep from * across ending last rep at **, tr2tog in last 2 sts; turn.

Row 3: Ch 1, sc in each st across sk ch-4 at end of row; turn.

Row 4: Ch 1, sc in ea st across; turn.

Row 5: Ch 1, sc in 1st st, * hdc in next st, dc in next st, 3 tr in next st, dc in next st, hdc in next st, sc in next st; rep from * across, turn.

Row 6: Rep Row 1.

Rep Rows 1–6 for wave and chevron pattern.

VERSION #1
Long-Sleeved Tunic
Designed by Gloria Tracy

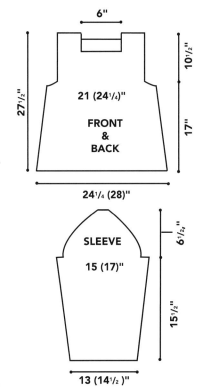

Sizes

Finished Bust Measurements: 42 (48½)"
Finished Length: 27½"

Materials

Herrschners *2-ply Yarn*, 56 g/200 yd/182 m (100% Acrilan acrylic)
    2 skeins each
    #047 Dark English Rose (A)
    #056 Dark Apricot (B)
    #342 Dark Gold (C)
    #055 Dark Carib (D)
    #084 Green (E)
    #039 Porcelain Blue (F)
    #126 Purple (G)
Crochet hooks US sizes G/6, H/8, and I/9 (4, 5, and 6 mm)

Gauge

In chevron pattern and with G hk, measuring across a sc row, 15 sts and 13 rows = 4"

In chevron pattern st Row 4 and I hk, measuring across a sc row, 13 sts and 11 rows = 4"

Color Pattern Sequence

Alt 2 rows ea A, B, C, D, E, F, and G

Notes

1. For Back and Front, work from the bottom, beginning with the largest hook, and changing to smaller hooks where indicated as you work up. This gives the body an A-line.

2. The sleeves are worked from the bottom, beginning with the smallest hook, and changing to the largest hook where indicated as you work up. This works as increases for sleeve shaping.

Directions for Long-Sleeved Tunic

BACK

With largest hk and A, ch 105 (121) + 1 for turn.

Note: When working chevron pattern, you will have 79 (91) sc on pattern Rows 3 and 4. Work in chevron pattern in color pattern sequence for 20 rows with largest hk, ending with pattern st Row 1, 20 rows with medium-sized hk, ending pattern st with Row 3, and 5 rows with smallest hk, ending pattern st with Row 3—46 rows from beg. Work rest of Back with smallest hk.

Armhole Shaping: Row 1: Sl st across 12 sts, ch 1, sc across center 55 (67) sts; turn leaving rem 12 sts unworked—73 (89) sts; 55 (67) sc.

Work even in pat st for 33 more rows, ending after Row 1. Mark center 23 sts for back of neck.

Neck Shaping: Work in pattern across to 1st marker, turn leaving rem sts unworked. Work on this side only for 1 more row. Fasten off.

To complete other side, leave marked sts unworked, attach yarn in next st and complete to match 1st side.

FRONT

Work as Back until 19 more rows after Armhole Shaping, ending after Row 1.

Shape neck as for Back, then work even until same row as Back to shoulder. Fasten off. Complete other side to match.

SLEEVE (make two)

With smallest hk and A, ch 65 (73) + 1 for turn.

Note: When working chevron pattern, you will have 49 (55) sc on pattern Rows 3 and 4. Work in chevron pattern in color pattern sequence for 10 rows with smallest hook, ending with pattern st Row 3, 18 rows with medium-sized hk, ending pattern st with Row 3, and 12 rows with largest hk, ending pattern st with Row 3—40 rows from beg. Work rest of Sleeve with largest hk.

Cap: Row 1: Sl st across 6 sts, ch 1, (sc, ch 1) 36 (42) times across, sc in next st; turn leaving rem 6 sts unworked.

Row 2: Work pattern Row 5 in sc only (sk all ch-1 sps)—49 (57) sts; 37 (43) sc on pattern Rows 3 and 4.

Rows 3–5: Work pattern Rows 6, 1, and 2.

Rows 6 and 7: Ch 1, sc2tog in 1st 2 sts, sc to last 2 sts, sc2tog in last 2 sts; turn—33 (39) sc at end of Row 7.

Row 8: Ch 3 (counts as dc), 2 tr in next st, dc in next st, hdc in next st, sc in next st; rep from * on pattern Row 5 to last 4 sts, hdc in next st, dc in next st, 2 tr in next st, dc in last st; turn—43 (51) sts.

Row 9: Sk 1st st, sl st in next st, sc in next 2 sts, sc3tog in next 3 sts, sc in next 2 sts; rep from * on pattern Row 1 to last 2 sts; turn, leaving last 2 sts unworked—37 (45) sts.

Row 10: Ch 1, sc in 1st st, sc3tog in next 3 sts, sc in next 2 sts; rep from * on pattern Row 1 across, ending last rep with sc in 1 st instead of 2; turn—35 (43) sts.

Row 11: Ch 3 (do no count as dc), tr2tog in next 2 sts; rep from * on pattern Row 2 across; turn—25 (31) sts.

Rows 12 and 13: Rep Sleeve Cap Row 6—21 (27) sc at end of Row 13.

Row 14: Rep Row 8—27 (35) sts.

Rows 15 and 16: Rep Rows 9 and 10—19 (27) sts.

Row 17: Rep Row 11—13 (19) sts.

Row 18—For Size S/M Only: Rep Sleeve Cap Row 6—11 sc.

Row 18—For Size L/XL Only: Ch 1, (sc2tog in 2 sts) 3 times, sc to last 6 sts, (sc2tog in next 2 sts) 3 times; turn—13 sc. Fasten off.

FINISHING

Sew shoulder seams. Set in top of sleeve at opening easing as needed. Sew underarm and side seams matching colors.

VERSION #2
Cap Sleeve Tunic

Sizes

Finished Bust Measurements: 42 (47½)"
Finished Length: 24"
Hat: 20¾" circumference

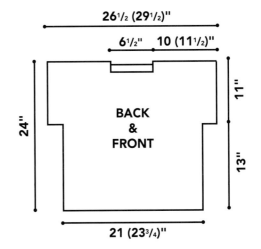

Materials

Trendsetter Yarns, *Sunshine* 85 g/75 yd (75% viscose, 25% nylon)
    5 (6) balls #49 Dark Green (A)
    5 (6) balls #28 Dark Blue (B)
    5 (6) balls #25 Light Blue (C)
    4 (5) balls #33 Violet (D)
Crochet hook US size F/5 (3.75 mm)

Gauge

In chevron pattern, measuring across a sc row, 1 3 sts = 3"; 12 rows = 3½"

Color Pattern Sequence

Alt 2 rows ea A, B, C, and D

Directions for
Cap-Sleeved Tee Top

Note: When working chevron pattern, you will have 91 (103) sc on pattern Rows 3 and 4.

BACK

With A, ch 121 (137) + 1 for turn. Work in wave and chevron pattern in color pattern sequence for 45 rows, ending after Row 2.

Underarm and Sleeve Shaping: Ch 13, sc in 2nd ch from hk and next 11 ch, sc across Back sts; turn—103 (115) sts. Rep this last row once more, then work in pattern across 12 Sleeve sts—115 (127) sts.

Work pattern Rows 5 and 6 on all sts—153 (169) sts, work Rows 1–6 for 5 reps, then work Row 1 once more.

Neck Shaping: Work pattern Row 2 on 57 (65) sts; turn, leaving rem sts unworked. Using same color as previous row, work pattern Rows 3 and 4. Fasten off.

To complete other side, leave center 39 sts unworked and work in rem 57 (65) to match 1st side. Fasten off.

FRONT

Work as for Back, working 1 less pattern 6-row rep before neck shaping. Shape neck as for Back, working even in pattern on ea side until same length as Back to shoulder, working last 3 rows in same color. Fasten off.

FINISHING

Sew shoulder seams.

Sleeve Trim: Row 1: Attach C at underarm, ch 1, work 97 sc evenly along edge of sleeve; turn.

Row 2: With C, work pattern Row 5; turn.

Rows 3 and 4: With D, work pattern Rows 6 and 1. Fasten off.

Sew underarm and side seams matching colors at sides.

Chevrons Cap

Directions for Juliet Hat

With B, ch 4, sl st in first ch to form ring.

Rnd 1: With B, ch 1, work 10 sc in ring; sl st in beg sc—10 sts.

Rnd 2: Ch 3 (counts as first dc), dc in same st; 2 dc in next and every st around; sl st in top of ch-3—20 sts.

Rnd 3: Ch 1, (sc in next st, 2 sc in next st) around; sl st in beg sc—30 sts

Rnd 4: Ch 3 (counts as first dc), dc in same st, dc in next 2 sts, * 2 dc in next st, dc in next 2 dc; rep from * around; sl st in top of ch-3—40 sts.

Rnd 5: Ch 1, (sc in next 3 sts, 2 sc in next st) around; sl st in beg sc—50 sts.

Rnd 6: Ch 3 (counts as first dc), dc in same st, dc in next 4 sts, * 2 dc in next st, dc in next 4 sts; rep from * around; sl st in top of ch-3—60 sts.

Cont as est, inc 10 sts every rnd and alt sc and dc rnds until 12 rds from beg, ending with a dc rnd—120 sts.

Color Brim: Rnd 1: With A, ch 1, sc in ea st around; sl st in beg sc.

Rnd 2: Ch 1, * sc in 2 sts, sc3tog, sc in 2 sts, 3 sc in next st; rep from * around; sl st with D in beg sc—14 chevrons around.

Rnd 3: With D, ch 3 (counts as first dc), * tr3tog in next 3 sts, dc in next st, hdc in next st, sc in next st, hdc in next st **, dc in next st; rep from * around, ending last rep at **; sl st in top of ch-3.

Rnd 4: Ch 1, sc in ea st around; sl st with C in beg sc—90 sc.

Rnd 5: With C, ch 1, sc in ea st around; sl st in beg sc.

Rnd 6: Ch 2 (counts as first hdc), * sc in next st, hdc in next st, dc in next st, 3 tr in next st, dc in next st **, hdc in next st; rep from * around, ending last rep at **; sl st with B in top of ch-2.

Rnd 7: With B, ch 1, * sc3tog in next 3 sts, sc in next 2 sts, 3 sc in next st, sc in next 2 sts; rep from * around; sl st in beg sc3tog.

Rnd 8: Rep Rnd 7; sl st with A in beg sc3tog.

Rnd 9: With A, ch 4, tr2tog in next 2 sts, * dc in next st, hdc in next st, sc in next st, hdc in next st, dc in next st **, tr3tog in next 3 sts; rep from * around, ending last rep at **; sl st in top of beg tr2tog (sk ch-4).

Rnd 10: Ch 1, sc in ea st around; sl st with D in beg sc.

Rnd 11: With D, ch 1, sc in ea st around; sl st with C in beg sc.

Rnd 12: With C, ch 1, * sc in next st, hdc in next st, dc in next st, 3 tr in next st, dc in next st, hdc in next st; rep from * around; sl st with B in beg sc.

Rnd 13: With B, ch 1, sc2tog in first 2 sts, * sc in next 2 sts, 3 sc in next st, sc in next 2 sts **, sc3tog in next 3 sts; rep from * around, ending last rep at **, sk last sc, sl st in beg sc2tog. Fasten off.

Designed by Gloria Tracy

Fans and Vees Tunic and Juliet Hat

The ability to be able to control the opacity of fabric by placing open areas at the shoulders and hemline and to close up the bust area inspired us to apply the stitches from Block 10 of the Learn-to-Crochet Afghan to a lovely tunic. Working both the body and the sleeves from the top down made the sleeve-cap shaping easier and showed off the scallop in the pattern to better advantage. A slight A-line shape was achieved by increasing hook size on the lower open fans pattern; and working the colors from light on the top to dark at the bottom was more flattering and practical.

Sizes

Finished Bust Measurements: 38 (41½, 45)"
Finished Length: 23 (25, 27)"
Hat: 18¼" circumference

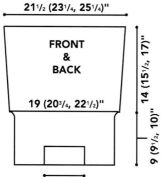

21½ (23¼, 25¼)"

FRONT
&
BACK

19 (20¾, 22½)"

14 (15½, 17)"

9 (9½, 10)"

5 (6½, 8¼)"

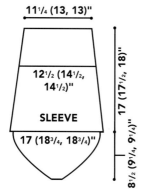

11¼ (13, 13)"

12½ (14½, 14½)"

SLEEVE

17 (18¾, 18¾)"

17 (17½, 18)"

8½ (9¼, 9¼)"

Materials

Muench Yarns *GGH Mystic*, 50 g/121 yd/114 m
(54% cotton, 46% viscose)
7 (8, 10) balls #36 Pale Ice Green (A)
8 (10, 12) balls #46 Medium Turquoise (B)
6 (7, 9) balls #31 Dark Turquoise (C)
Crochet hooks US sizes I/9 and J/10 (5.5 and 6 mm)

Gauge

Use 2 strands held tog for ea of the following:
In pattern 1 with I hk, 13 sts and 6 rows = 4"
In pattern 2 with I hk, 14 sts and 9 rows = 4"
In pattern 3 with I hk, 13.75 sts and 9 rows = 4"
In pattern 3 with J hk, 12.5 sts and 8 rows = 4"
In hdc with I hk, 12 sts and 11 rows = 4"

Stitches and Patterns Used

Chain, slip stitch, single crochet, half double crochet
FanCee vees, open shells, solid shells (Block #10)

FanCee Vees—Pattern 1
(multiple of 6 sts + 3)

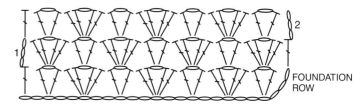

FOUNDATION
ROW

Foundation Row: Dc in 4th ch from hk, ch 1, dc in
same ch, * sk 2 ch, (2 dc, ch 1, 2 dc) in next ch,
sk 2 ch, (dc, ch 1, dc) in next ch; rep from *
across to last ch, dc in last ch; turn.

Row 1: Ch 3 (counts as dc), * (2 dc, ch 1, 2 dc) in
next ch-1 sp, (dc, ch 1, dc) in next ch-1 sp; rep
from * across to last ch-1 sp, (2 dc, ch 1, 2 dc)
in last ch-1 sp, dc in top of tch-3; turn.

Row 2: Ch 3 (counts as dc), * (dc, ch 1, dc) in next
ch-1 sp, (2 dc, ch 1, 2 dc) in next ch-1 sp; rep
from * across to last ch-1 sp, (dc, ch 1, dc) in
last ch-1 sp, dc in top of tch-3; turn.

Rep Rows 1 and 2 for pattern 1.

Solid Shells—Pattern 2
(multiple of 6 sts + 1)

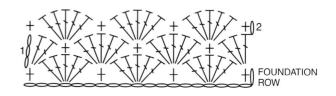

FOUNDATION
ROW

Foundation Row: Ch 1, sc in 1st ch, * sk 2 sc, 5 dc
in next ch, sk 2 ch, sc in next ch; rep from *
across; turn.

Row 1: Ch 3 (counts as dc), 2 dc in same st, * sk 2
dc, sc in next dc, sk 2 dc, work 5 dc in next sc;
rep from * across, ending last rep with 3 dc
instead of 5; turn.

Row 2: Ch 1, sc in 1st dc, * sk 2 dc, work 5 dc in next sc, sk 2 dc, sc in next dc; rep from * across; turn.

Rep Rows 1 and 2 for pattern 2.

Open Shells—Pattern 3

(multiple of 5 sts + 1)

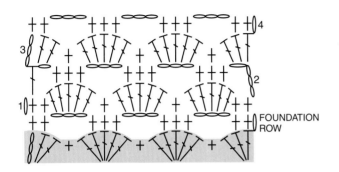

Row 1: Ch 1, sc in 1st 2 sc, * work 5 dc in next ch-3 sp **, sk next sc, sc in next sc, sk next sc; rep from * across, ending last rep at **, sc in next 2 sc; turn.

Row 2: Ch 4 (counts as dc and ch 1), sk 1st 2 sc and next dc, sc in next 3 dc, * ch 3, sk (dc, sc, dc), sc in next 3 dc; rep from * across, sk (dc, sc), ch 1, dc in last sc; turn.

Row 3: Ch 3 (counts as dc), work 2 dc in same st, sk ch-1 sp, * sk next sc, sc in next sc, sk next sc **, work 5 dc in ch-3 sp; rep from * across, ending last rep at **, work 3 dc in ch-4 sp; turn.

Row 4: Ch 1, sc in 1st 2 dc, ch 3, sk (dc, sc, dc), * sc in next 3 dc, ch 3, sk (dc, sc, dc); rep from * across, sc in last 2 sts; turn.

Rep Rows 1–4 for pattern 3.

Notes

1. For both the tunic and hat, hold two strands of yarn together throughout.

2. For the tunic, measure the length while the garment is hanging since the weight of fabric will affect the finished measurements.

3. The body and sleeves are worked from the top down. Use the smaller hook for all but bottom of body; change to the larger hook for that section to create a slight A-line shape.

4. The hat is worked from the top down in rounds with the smaller hook.

Directions for Tunic

BACK

With larger hk and 2 strands A held tog, ch 57 (63, 69) + 2 for turn. Work in pattern 1 for 7½ (8, 8½)" (see "Notes"), ending after Row 1—19 (21, 23) FanCee vee sts across. Cut one strand of A and attach B in its place.

With 1 strand of ea color held tog, work 1 more row pattern 1. Cut A and attach another B strand in its place.

With 2 strands B held tog, work across next row as follows: Ch 1, 2 sc in 1st dc, sk next dc, sc in (dc, ch-1 sp, dc), * sk next dc, sc in (dc, ch-1 sp, dc); rep from * across, 2 sc in last st; turn—61 (67, 73) sts.

Beg with Foundation Row of pattern 2, working into sts of previous row, to 9 (9½, 10)" from beg (see "Notes"), ending after Row 1.

Armhole Shaping: Ch 3 (counts as dc), (2 dc, sc) in same st, * sk 2 dc, 5 dc in next sc, sk 2 dc, sc in next dc; rep from * across, work 3 dc in same st as last previous st; turn—67 (73, 79) sts.

Cont working pattern 2 beg with Row 2. Work even in pattern 2 for 10 (11, 12)" more (see "Notes"), ending with Row 2. Cut both strands B.

With larger hk and 2 strands C held tog, work Row 1 of pattern 2 then work Row 4 of pattern 3. Cont in pattern 3 for 4 (4½, 5)" (see Notes) ending after Row 1 or 3. Fasten off.

FRONT

Working from the top down, work each shoulder section separately to neck, join then work down in one piece to complete.

Left Shoulder Section: With 2 strands A held tog, ch 21 + 2 for turn. Beg with Foundation Row, work pattern 1 for 4 rows—7 FanCee vee sts across. Fasten off.

Right Shoulder Section: Work as for Left Shoulder Section, but do not fasten off; turn.

Joining Row: Work across row in est pattern, sk last st, ch 15 (21, 27) for center section, work across Left Shoulder Section sk 1st st; turn.

Next Row: Work in est pattern making 7 FanCee vee sts to center ch, sk 1st ch, * (dc, ch 1, dc) in next ch **, sk next 2 ch, (2 dc, ch 1, 2 dc) in next ch, sk next 2 ch; rep from * across ch, making a total of 5 (7, 9) FanCee vee sts across, and ending last rep at **, sk last ch, complete row across 2nd shoulder in pat—19 (21, 23) FanCee vee sts across.

Complete Front to match Back.

SLEEVE (make two)

Work from the cap down to wrist.

With 2 strands A held tog, ch 13 + 2 for turn.

Cap: Row 1: Dc in 4th ch from hk and in next ch, (dc, ch 2, dc) in next ch, sk 2 ch, (2 dc, ch 1, 2 dc) in next ch, sk 2 ch, (dc, ch 1, dc) in next ch, dc in last 3 ch; turn—3 FanCee vee sts.

Row 2: Ch 3 (counts as dc), (dc, ch 1, dc) in same st, (2 dc, ch 1, 2 dc) in next ch-1 sp, (dc, ch 1, dc) in next ch-1 sp, (2 dc, ch 1, 2 dc) in next ch-1 sp, sk 3 dc, (dc, ch 1, 2 dc) in top of ch-3; turn—5 FanCee vee sts.

Row 3: Ch 3, (dc, ch 1, dc) in next dc, * (2 dc, ch 1, 2 dc) in next ch-1 sp, (dc, ch 1, dc) in next ch-1 sp; rep from * across to last ch-1 sp, (2 dc, ch 1, 2 dc) in next ch-1 sp, (dc, ch 1, dc) in next dc, dc in top of ch-3; turn—7 FanCee vee sts.

Row 4: Ch 3 (counts as dc), dc in same st, * (2 dc, ch 1, 2 dc) in next ch-1 sp, (dc, ch 1, dc) in next ch-1 sp; rep from * across to last ch-1 sp, (2 dc, ch 1, 2 dc) in last ch-1 sp, 2 dc in top of ch-3; turn.

Row 5: Ch 3 (counts as dc), (dc, ch 1, dc) in next dc, * (dc, ch 1, dc) in next ch-1 sp, (2 dc, ch 1, 2 dc) in next ch-1 sp; rep from * across to last 2 sts, (dc, ch 1, dc) in next dc, dc in top of ch-3; turn—9 FanCee vee sts.

Row 6: Ch 3 (counts as dc), dc in same dc, (dc, ch 1, dc) in next ch-1 sp, * (2 dc, ch 1, 2 dc) in next ch-1 sp, (dc, ch 1, dc) in next ch-1 sp; rep from * across, 2 dc in top of ch-3; turn.

Row 7 and 8: Rep Rows 3 and 4—11 FanCee vee sts.

Row 9: Cut one strand of A and attach B in its place. With 1 strand of each A and B held tog, rep Row 5—13 FanCee vee sts.

Row 10: Cut A and attach another B strand in its place. With 2 strands B held tog, rep Row 6.

Rows 11 and 12: Rep Row 3 and 4—15 FanCee vee sts.

Row 13: Ch 3 (counts as dc), dc in same dc, (2 dc, ch 1, 2 dc) in next dc, * (dc, ch 1, dc) in next ch-1 sp, (2 dc, ch 1, 2 dc) in next ch-1 sp; rep from * across to last 2 sts, (2 dc, ch 1, 2 dc) in next dc, 2 dc in top of ch-3; turn—17 FanCee vee sts.

For Sizes M and L only: Rep Row 13—19 FanCee vee sts.

Underarm to Wrist: Row 1: Ch 3 (counts as dc), * (dc, ch 1, dc) in next ch-1 sp, (2 dc, ch 1, 2 dc) in next ch-1 sp; rep from * across to last ch-1 sp, (dc, ch 1, dc) in last ch-1 sp, dc in top of ch-3; turn.

Row 2: Ch 3 (counts as dc), * (2 dc, ch 1, 2 dc) in next ch-1 sp, (dc, ch 1, dc) in next ch-1 sp; rep from * across to last ch-1 sp, (2 dc, ch 1, 2 dc) in last ch-1 sp, dc in top of ch-3; turn.

Row 3: Ch 3 (counts as dc), dc in next ch-1 sp, rep from * on Row 2 to last ch-1 sp, dc in last ch-1 sp, dc in top of ch-3; turn—15 (17, 17) FanCee vee sts.

Rows 4–6: Rep Rows 1 and 2, then Row 1 again.

Row 7: Ch 3 (counts as dc), dc in next ch-1 sp, rep from * on Row 1 to last ch-1 sp, dc in last ch-1 sp, dc in top of ch-3; turn—13 (15, 15) FanCee vee sts.

Row 8: Rep Row 2.

Cont working in pattern 1 until 11 (11½, 12)" (see "Notes") from underarm ending after a rep of Row 2. Cut B.

Next Row: With 2 strands C held tog, ch 1, sk 1st dc, sc in next dc and ch-1 sp, * ch 3, sk (2 dc, ch 1, 2 dc), sc in next (dc, ch 1, dc); rep from * across; turn leaving last st unworked.

Beg with Row 1, work in pattern 3 until 6" from color change, ending with Row 1 or 3. Fasten off.

FINISHING

Sew shoulder seams. Set in top of sleeve at opening. Sew underarm and side seams matching colors.

Directions for Juliet Hat

With 2 strands B held tog, ch 3, join with sl st in 1st ch to form ring.

Rnd 1: Ch 2 (counts as hdc), work 7 hdc in ring; sl st in top of ch-2—8 sts.

Rnd 2: Ch 2 (counts as hdc), hdc in same st, 2 hdc in rem sts; sl st in top of ch-2—16 sts.

Rnd 3: Ch 2 (counts as hdc), hdc in same st, hdc in next st, * 2 hdc in next st, hdc in next st; rep from * around; sl st in top of ch-2—24 sts.

Rnd 4: Ch 2 (counts as hdc), hdc in next and every st around; sl st in top of ch-2.

Rnds 5 and 6: Rep Rnds 3 and 4—36 sts.

Rnd 7: Ch 2 (counts as hdc), hdc in same st, hdc in next 2 sts, * 2 hdc in next st, hdc in next 2 sts; rep from * around; sl st in top of ch-2—48 sts.

Rnd 8: Rep Rnd 4.

Rnd 9: Ch 2 (counts as hdc), hdc in same st, hdc in next 5 sts, * 2 hdc in next st, hdc in next 5 sts; rep from * around; sl st in top of ch-2—56 sts.

Rnds 10–12: Rep Rnd 4. Cut B.

Rnds 13 and 14: With 2 strands A held tog, rep Rnd 4, dec 1 st in last rnd—55 sts. Cut A.

Rnd 15: With 2 strands C held tog, ch 1, sc in 1st 2 sts, * ch 3, sk 2 sts **, sc in next 3 sts; rep from * around, ending last rep at **, sc in last sc; sl st in 1st sc.

Rnd 16: Ch 1, sc in 1st sc, sk next sc, * work 5 dc in ch-3 sp **, sk next sc, sc in next sc, sk next sc; rep from * around, ending last rep at **, sl st in 1st sc.

Rnd 17: Sl st to 2nd dc of 5-dc group, ch 1, sc in 2nd, 3rd, and 4th dc, * ch 3, sk (dc, sc, dc) **, sc in next 3 dc; rep from * around, end last rep at **, sl st in 1st sc.

Rnd 18: Ch 1, sc in next sc, * 5 dc in next ch-3 sp **, sk next sc, sc in next sc, sk next sc; rep from * around, end last rep at **, sl st in 1st sc. Fasten off.

Designed by Gloria Tracy and Ruthie Marks

The Becoming Vest

This design is a flattering favorite. We call it The Becoming Vest because the double-breasted closure is "becoming" to any figure, but particularly to figures that are full through the middle. The circumference can also be easily changed up to 10 in. by simply moving the inside and outside buttons as you are "becoming" a different size.

We made two versions of this wonderful, adaptable pattern so you are sure to have one appropriate for any occasion. For the dressy, special-occasion version of the Becoming Vest, we held a strand each of Knit One, Crochet Too *Douceur et Soie* (baby mohair and silk yarn) with *Soufflé* (cotton and rayon) to produce an incredibly sensuous blend. For the practical, easy-care version, we chose Paton's *Canadiana*, a machine-washable easy-care fiber made of Acrilan acrylic. The looks are so different and the pattern is so easy, you may want to make both.

Sizes

Finished Bust Measurements: 45"/53" (48"/58")
Finished Back Width at Underarm: 22½" (24)"
Finished Length: 22½" (26½)"

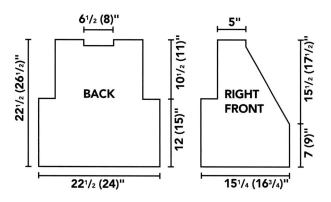

Materials

Version 1

Knit One, Crochet Too *Douceur et Soie* 25 g/
225 yd/ 206 m (70% baby mohair, 30% silk)
4(5) skeins #8146 Ivory (A)
Soufflé 50 g/104 yd/95 m (70% cotton, 30%
viscose)
8(9) skeins #7111 Bavarian Creme (B)

Version 2

Patons *Canadiana* 100 g/247 yd/225 m (96% Acrilan
acrylic and 4% viscose)
4(5) skeins Tweed
Two buttons
Crochet hook US size K/10.5 (7 mm)
Tapestry needle for finishing

Gauge

10 sts/9 rows = 4"

Stitches and Patterns Used

Chain, slip stitch, single crochet, double single crochet, double crochet, front post double crochet, back
post double crochet, single crochet decrease
Crunch Stitch (Block #4)
Post Stitch (Block #9)

Special Stitches

**Double crochet post stitches (front and back post
double crochet: = FPdc, Back = BPdc): FPdc:** Yo,
insert hk horizontally from front to back to front
around post of next st, yo and draw through 1 lp on
hk (3 lps rem on hk), (yo and draw through 2 lps)
twice (1 lp rem on hk)—FPdc completed.

BPdc: Yo insert hk horizontally from back to front
to back around post of next st, yo and draw through
1 lp (3 lps rem on hk), (yo and draw through 2 lps)
twice, (1 lp rem on hk)—BPdc completed.

sc2tog: Pull up lp in next 2 sts, yo, draw through all
3 lps on hk.

Body Pattern

(multiple of 2 sts; rep of 1 row)

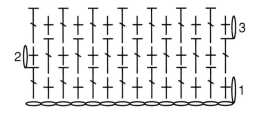

Row 1 (RS): Sc in 2nd ch from hk, * dc in next ch,
sc in next ch; rep from * across, dc in last ch;
turn.

Row 2: Ch 1, * sc in dc, dc in sc; rep from * across.

Rep Row 2 for body pattern.

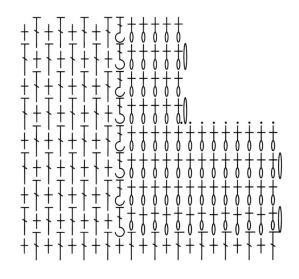

Directions for Vest

Note: Begin each row in the 1st st.

For Version 1, work with one strand of *Douceur et Soie* and one strand of *Bavairan Creme* held together.

BACK

Ch 57 (61) loosely. Mark RS of work with a pin. Work in pattern st for 10 (13)", ending with a WS row—56 (60) sts.

Armhole Edgings: With RS facing, ch 1, dsc on 11 sts, FPdc, work pattern st on 32 (36) sts, FPdc, dsc on 11 sts; turn.

Next Row (WS): Ch 1, dsc on 11 sts, BPdc, pattern st on 32 (36) sts, BPdc, dsc on 11 sts; turn.

Next 2 Rows: Rep last 2 rows.

Armhole Shaping: Row 1 (RS): Sl st across 7 sts, dsc on 4 sts, FPdc, work pattern st on 32 (36) sts, FPdc, dsc on 4 sts; turn—42 (46) sts.

Row 2: Ch 1, dsc on 4 sts, BPdc, work pattern st on 32 (36) sts, BPdc, dsc on 4 sts; turn.

Row 3: Ch 1, dsc on 4 sts, FPdc, work pattern st on 32 (36) sts, FPdc, dsc on 4 sts; turn.

Rep Rows 2 and 3 for 7 (8)" from Row 1 of armhole shaping, ending with a WS row.

Neck Edging: With RS facing, ch 1, dsc on 4 sts, FPdc, work pattern st on 3 sts, FPdc, dsc on 24 (28) sts, FPdc, work pattern st on 3 sts, FPdc, dsc on 4 sts; turn—42 (46) sts.

Next Row (WS): Ch 1, dsc on 4 sts, BPdc, work pattern st on 3 sts, BPdc, dsc on 24 (28) sts, BPdc, work pattern st on 3 sts, BPdc, dsc on 4 sts; turn.

Next 2 Rows: Rep last 2 rows.

Neck Shaping: With RS facing, ch 1, dsc on 4 sts, FPdc, work pattern st on 3 sts, FPdc, dsc on 4 (6) sts; turn—13 (15) sts.

Next Row: Ch 1, dsc on 4 sts, BPdc, work pattern st on 3 sts, BPdc, dsc on 4 (6) sts; turn.

Next 2 Rows: Rep last 2 rows. Fasten off 10 (11)" from beg of armhole shaping.

With RS facing, sk center 16 sts and join yarn in next st. Complete to match first shoulder, reversing shaping.

RIGHT FRONT

Ch 39 (43) loosely. Mark RS of work. Keeping first 4 sts at center edge in dsc and rem 34 (38) sts in pattern st, ch 1 at beg of each row and work even for 7 (9)", ending with a WS row—38 (42) sts.

Buttonhole and Front Shaping: Row 1 (RS): Ch 1, dsc in 2 sts, ch 1, sk 1 st, dsc on 1 st, sc2tog, work in est pattern st across; turn.

Row 2: Ch 1, work in pattern st across to last 7 sts, sc2tog, BPdc in next st 2 rows below, dsc in last 4 sts; turn.

Row 3: Ch 1, dsc on 4 sts, sc2tog, work in pattern st across; turn.

Row 4: Rep Row 2.

Keeping in pattern st and dsc on 4 sts at neck edge, rep. Rows 3 and 4 five times more (total 14 dec) until 13 (15 sts) rem, while at the same time, at 10 (13)" from beg, work armhole edging and then shape as for Back. Work even in est pat sts until same length as Back to shoulder. Fasten off.

LEFT FRONT

Work as for Right Front, reversing pat st placement and shapings.

FINISHING

Sl st shoulder seams and side seams tog.

Cross fronts, right over left for women and left over right for men, to a comfortable fit and mark placement for toggle button on outside of opposite front and sew in place. Sew flat button to inside opposite inside buttonhole.

Designed by Gloria Tracy

Windowpane Vest
and Matching Hat

This pattern is as versatile as any in this book. It can be used for a man or a woman, it can easily be adapted for a child, and it can be as casual or as dressy as the yarn you choose. You can even add sleeves and make the vest into a cardigan. We hope it will become a favorite of yours as it is of ours.

Sizes

Finished Bust Measurements: 37¾ (41¼, 45¾, 49¾, 56¾)"

Finished Length: 20 (21, 22, 23, 24)"

Hat: 18½" circumference

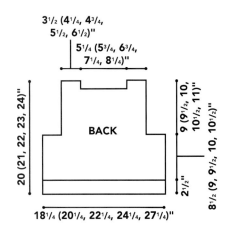

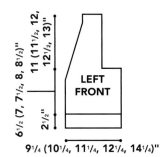

Materials

Knit One, Crochet Too *Parfait Solids* 100 g/
210 yd/192 m (100% wool worsted weight)
2 (3, 3, 4, 5) #1909 Jet (MC)

Mousse 50 g/105 yd/115 m (74% brushed
mohair, 22% wool, 5% nylon)
4 (5, 6, 7, 8) skeins #6333 Berry Sorbet (CC)

Crochet hook US size H/8 (5 mm)

Knit One, Crochet Too three 1" Squares Berry
Sorbet buttons

Gauge

In windowpane pattern, 16 sts and 16 rows = 4"
In dc in rnds, 13 sts = 4"

Stitches and Patterns Used

Chain, slip stitch, single crochet, double single crochet, half double crochet, front post double crochet, back post double crochet, front post treble crochet, linked double crochet

dc dec: Leaving last lp of each st on hk, work dc in each of next 2 sts, yo and draw through all 3 lps on hk.

Windowpane Pattern
(multiple of 4 sts + 1)

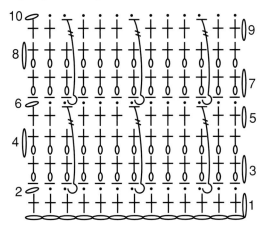

Row 1: With MC, sc in 2nd ch from hk and in ea ch across; turn.

Row 2: Ch 1, sl st in ea st across, changing to CC in last st; turn.

Row 3 (RS): With CC, ch 1, work dsc in back lp of ea sl st across; turn.

Row 4: Ch 1, work dsc through both lps on ea st across, changing to MC in last st; turn.

Row 5: With MC, ch 1, sc in 1st dsc, * sc in next dsc, FPtr around corresponding sc in Row 1, sk dsc behind post just made, sc in next 2 dsc; rep from * across; turn.

Row 6: Ch 1, sl st in ea st across; turn.

Rows 7 and 8: Rep Rows 3 and 4.

Row 9: With MC, ch 1, sc in 1st dsc, * sc in next dsc, FPtr around post of corresponding Fptr from Row 5, sk dsc behind post just made, sc in next 2 dsc; rep from * across; turn.

Row 10: Rep Row 6.

Rep Rows 7–10 for windowpane pattern.

Directions for Vest

BACK

With MC, ch 73 (81, 89, 97, 109) + 1 for turn. Work in windowpane pattern until approx 8½ (9, 9½, 10, 10½)" from beg, ending after Row 10. Fasten off and turn.

Armhole Shaping: Attach CC in 12th st from beg, beg with next st, resume pattern and work across to last 12 sts; turn, leaving rem sts unworked— 49 (57, 65, 73, 85) sts. Work even until approx 7 (7½, 8, 8½, 9)" above armhole, ending after Row 9.

Neck and Shoulder Shaping: Work across 16 (19, 21, 24, 28) sts; turn, leaving rem sts unworked. Cont in pattern dec 1 st at neck edge every row 2 times—14 (17, 19, 22, 26) sts. Work even until 9 (9½, 10, 10½, 11)" above armhole, ending after Row 9. Fasten off.

To complete other side, leave center 17 (19, 23, 25, 29) sts unworked, attaching yarn in last st, beg in next st complete row in pattern. Complete to match 1st shoulder.

LEFT FRONT

With MC, ch 37 (41, 45, 49, 57) + 1 for turn. Work in windowpane pattern until 6½ (7, 7½, 8, 8½)" from beg, or 2" less than Back underarm shaping.

Neck Shaping: On next dsc row, dec 1 (1, 2, 1, 1) st(s) at neck edge, then working 1 (1, 2, 2, 2) dec at neck edge in every 4-row pattern rep, while at the same time, work armhole shaping where needed to match Back. Cont neck shaping until 14 (17, 19, 22, 26) sts rem. Work even until same length as Back to shoulder. Fasten off.

RIGHT FRONT

Work as for Left Front, reversing armhole and neck shapings.

FINISHING

Sew shoulder and side seams.

Armhole Bands: Rnd 1: With RS facing, attach MC at side seam, and sl st a multiple of 3 sts evenly around armhole opening; sl st in 1st sl st to join; turn.

Rnd 2: Ch 1, sc in front lp of 1st 2 sl st, * sk next sl st, sc in front lp of next 2 sl st; rep from * to last sl st, sk last sl st; sl st in top of 1st sc; turn.

Rnd 3: Ch 1, sc in ea sc around adjusting to an even number of sts if needed; sl st in 1st sc; do not turn.

Rnd 4 (RS): Ch 2 (counts as 1st post dc), * FPdc around post of next sc, BPdc around post of next sc; rep from * around; sl st in top of 1st ch-2.

Rep Rnd 4 until ribbing is 1" wide; turn at end of last row.

Next Row (WS): Sl st in ea st around. Fasten off.

Bottom Ribbing: Row 1: With RS facing, attach MC at left front edge, and sl st an even number of sts evenly across lower edge to right front edge; turn.

Row 2: Ch 1, sc in front lp of ea sl st across; turn.

Row 3 (RS): Ch 2 (counts as 1st post dc), * FPdc around post of next sc, BPdc around post of next sc; rep from * across, end with hdc in last sc; turn.

Rep Row 3 until ribbing is 2½" wide.

Next Row: Sl st in ea st across. Fasten off.

Front and Neckband: Row 1: With RS facing, attach MC at right front edge, and sl st an even number of sts evenly around neck edge to lower left front edge; turn.

Work as for Bottom Ribbing until ½" from beg. Mark placement for 3 evenly spaced buttonholes on right front edge between lower edge and point where neck shaping begins.

Next Row: (Work in est pattern to marker, ch 2, sk next 2 sts) 3 times, complete row.

Next Row: Work in est pattern to ch-2 sp, work 2 hdc in sp, complete row.

Last Row: Work in rib pattern across row. Fasten off.

Sew buttons opposite buttonholes.

Directions for Hat

Note: Ch-3 at beg of each rnd counts as 1st dc.

With MC, ch 4, join with sl st in 1st ch to form ring.

Rnd 1: Ch 3, work 11 dc in ring; join with sl st in top of ch-3—12 sts.

Rnd 2: Ch 3, dc in same st, 2 dc in ea dc around; sl st in top of ch-3—24 sts.

Rnd 3: Ch 3, dc in same st, * dc in next st, 2 dc in next st; rep from * around, end dc in last st; sl st in top of ch-3—36 sts.

Rnd 4: Ch 3, dc in same st, * dc in next 2 sts, 2 dc in next st; rep from * around, end dc in last 2 sts; sl st in top of ch-3—48 sts.

Rnds 5–8: Cont as est inc 12 sts every rnd—96 sts after Rnd 8.

Rnds 9–11: Ch 3, dc in next and ea st around; sl st in top of ch-3.

Rnd 12 (dec rnd): Ch 3, dc in next 5 sts, dc dec over next 2 sts, * dc in next 6 sts, dc dec over next 2 sts; rep from * around; sl st in top of ch-3—84 sts.

Rnd 13 (dec rnd): Ch 3, dc in next 4 sts, dc dec over next 2 sts, * dc in next 5 sts, dc dec over next 2 sts; rep from * around; sl st in top of ch-3—72 sts.

Rnd 14 (dec rnd): Ch 3, dc in next 3 sts, dc dec over next 2 sts, * dc in next 4 sts, dc dec over next 2 sts; rep from * around; sl st in top of ch-3—60 sts.

Windowpane Band: Rnd 1: With MC, ch 3, Ldc in next and every st around; sl st with CC in top of ch-3—60 sts.

Rnd 2: With CC, ch 3, Ldc in next and every st around; sl st with MC in top of ch-3. Cut CC.

Rnd 3: With MC, ch 1, * sc in 2 sts, work FPtr around corresponding Ldc on Rnd 1, sk Ldc behind post just made; rep from * around; sl st in 1st sc.

Rnd 4: Rep Rnd 1; sl st with MC in top of ch 3. Fasten off.

Designed by Gloria Tracy

Tapestry Tabard and Matching Crusher Hat

Like the Amelia Jacket, this vest uses cuff-to-center horizontally worked shaping. We love this construction, and it's sure to become a favorite of yours too because it adapts to any size and produces flattering vertical lines. The side panels were worked in two solid wool colors, while the front and back sections were worked in a combination of solid wool for the crosses and a multicolor yarn for the bars. The matching hat makes efficient use of the leftovers.

Sizes

Finished Bust Measurements: 36 (38¾, 44¼, 46½, 51, 53½, 58½)" in parentheses
Finished Length: 21½"
Hat: 10½" diameter

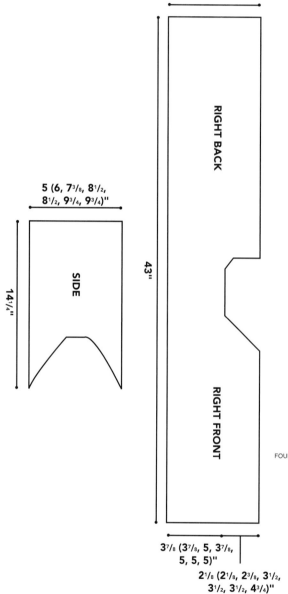

6 (6, 7⅜, 7⅜, 8½, 8½, 9¾)"

RIGHT BACK

5 (6, 7⅜, 8½, 8½, 9¾, 9¾)"

43"

SIDE

14¼"

RIGHT FRONT

3⅞ (3⅞, 5, 3⅞, 5, 5, 5)"

2⅛ (2⅛, 2⅜, 3½, 3½, 3½, 4¾)"

Materials

Knit One, Crochet Too *Parfait Solids* 100 g/
210 yd/192 m (100% worsted weight wool)
3 (3, 4, 4, 4, 4, 5) skeins #1292 Wine (MC; A)
1 (1, 1, 1, 2, 2, 2) skeins #1713 Plum (CC; C)

Mousse 50 g/105 yd/115 m (74% brushed mohair,
22% wool, 5% nylon)
4 (4, 4, 5, 5, 5, 6) skeins #6555 RazzleBerries
(CC; B)
Crochet hooks US size I/9 and J/10 (5.5 and
6 mm)
Yarn needle (optional)
Five 1" buttons

Gauge

In pat st, 14 sts = 4"; 17 rows = 5"

Stitches and Patterns Used

Chain, single crochet, double crochet, double treble
crochet
Crosses and bars pattern (Block #17)

Crosses and Bars Pattern Stitch

(multiple of 10 sts)
Note: Every 8-row rep of Pat st forms two 4-row
sections of pattern, one off-set over the other. When
following directions, a rep refers to one 4-row
rep only.

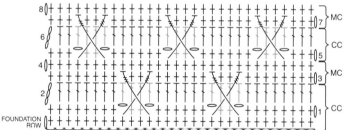

Foundation Row: With MC, sc in 2nd ch from hk
and in ea ch across, changing to CC in last st,
turn.

Row 1 (RS): With CC, ch 1, sc in 1st 8 sc, * ch 1,
sk next sc, sc in next 2 sc, ch 1, sk next sc, sc in
next 6 sc; rep from * across to last 2 sc, sc in last
2 sc, turn.

Row 2: With CC, ch 3 (counts as dc), dc in next
and every st and ch across, turn.

Row 3: With MC, ch 1, sc in 1st 8 sc, * dtr into
2nd sk sc 3 rows below, sk next st, sc in next 2

sts, dtr into 1st sk sc 3 rows below (thus crossing dtrs), sk next st, sc in next 6 sts; rep from * across to last 2 sts, sc in next st and in top of tch, turn.

Row 4: With MC, ch 1, sc in ea st across, turn.

Row 5: With CC, ch 1, sc in 1st 3 sc, * ch 1, sk next sc, sc in next 2 sc, ch 1, sk next sc, sc in next 6 sc; rep from * across working 3 sc instead of 6 for last rep, turn.

Row 6: Rep Row 2.

Row 7: With MC, ch 1, sc in 1st 3 sts, * dtr into 2nd sk sc 3 rows below, skip next st, sc in next 2 sts, dtr into 1st sk sc 3 rows below (thus crossing dtrs), sk next st, sc in next 6 sts; rep from * across working 3 sc instead of 6 for last rep, and working last st in top of tch, turn.

Row 8: Rep Row 4.

Rep Rows 1–8 for pattern st.

Notes

1. The vest is worked from side to side. The Left Body, Right Body, and Sides are worked separately then assembled later. Use the smaller hook throughout the garment. Use the larger hook for assembly only.

2. Carry unused colors loosely at the side of the work.

3. While working the neck shaping decreases, work single crochet decreases at the beginning of Rows 1, 3, 5, 7, and 8, and work double crochet decreases at the beginning of Rows 2 and 6.

Directions for Vest

LEFT BODY

Use B for CC when working Body.

With MC, ch 161. Work in pattern st on 160 sts until you have completed 3 (3, 4, 3, 4, 4, 4) 4-row pattern reps, ending after Row 4 (4, 8, 4, 8, 8, 8)—13 (13, 17, 13, 17, 17, 17) rows, approx 3⅛ (3⅛, 5, 3⅛, 5, 5, 5)" from beg.

Back Dividing Row (RS): Work in est pattern on 80 sts, turn leaving rem sts unworked.

Left Back: Working on this side only and cont in est pattern, dec 1 st at neck edge 3 times—77 sts. Work even until you have worked 5 (5, 6, 6, 7, 7, 8) 4-st pattern rep from beg of Left Body, ending after row 4 (4, 8, 8, 4, 4, 8)—21 (21, 25, 25, 29, 29, 33) rows, approx 6 (6, 7⅜, 7⅜, 8½, 8½, 9¾)" from beg. Fasten off.

Left Front (RS): Leave next 20 sts unworked for side of neck, attach yarn in next st, and beg with this st, work across rem 60 sts in est pattern. Cont in pattern and beg with next row, dec 1 st at neck edge every row until same number of rows have been worked as Back—53 (53, 53, 49, 49, 49, 45) sts rem. Fasten off.

RIGHT BODY

Work as for Left Body until same row as Left Back Dividing Row.

Right Front Dividing Row (RS): Work in est pattern on 60 sts, turn leaving rem sts unworked. Complete to match Left Front.

Right Back: Sk next 20 sts, attaching yarn in last sk st and work in pattern across next 80 sts. Complete to match Left Back.

SIDES (make two)

Use C for CC when working Sides.

With MC, ch 51. Work in pattern st on 50 sts, dec 1 st at right edge (armhole edge) every row 8 (9, 10, 13, 13, 13, 13) times—42 (41, 40, 37, 37, 37, 37) sts. Work even until 9 (12, 15, 16, 16, 20, 20) rows from beg. Inc 1 st at same edge every row 8 (9, 10, 13, 13, 13, 13) times—50 sts, 17 (21, 25, 29, 29, 33, 33) rows, approx 5 (6, 7⅜, 8½, 8½, 9¾, 9¾)" from beg. Fasten off.

FINISHING

Join Sides to Body with larger hk as follows:

Leave 1st 7 sts from lower edge of Body free. Holding Body and one Side with WS tog, and working on RS of work, work with MC in sc through both layers. Fasten off at end of seam. Rep on opposite side. Work in same manner to join center Back.

2-Color Trim (worked around body and armhole openings): With larger hk, use 2 strands held tog for each MC and CC, work as follows: Work sl st through both layers using MC for one st, then using CC for next st, alt colors in this manner.

Body Edging: With RS facing, work 2-color trim, evenly working 5 evenly spaced 2-color ch-10 button lp on edge of right front. Work around entire edge of garment, including lower edge of Sides. Fasten off.

Armhole Edging: Work as for Body Edging.

Sew buttons opposite button lps.

Directions for Crusher Hat

Materials

The model was made in the following color order, however, you can use your leftovers in any combination.
Parfait Solids Wine #1292 (A)
Mousse RazzleBerries #6555 (B)
Parfait Solids Eggplant #1730 (C)

With A ch 5, join with sl st into 1st ch to form ring. Do not turn.

Rnd 1: Ch 1, 10 sc into ring ending sl st into 1st st—10 sts.

Rnd 2: Ch 1, work 2 sc into 1st and every sc around—20 sts.

Rnd 3: Ch 3 (counts as dc), dc into same st, dc into next st, *2 dc into next st, dc into next st, rep from * around ending sl st into 1st st—30 sts.

Rep last rnd 5 times more working 1 more st between inc until 80 sts.

Work 3 rnds even in dc.

Work multicolor rnd as follows: ch 1, *sc with A, sc with B, rep from * around ending sl st into 1st st.

With B, work 1 rnd sc into back lp ending sl st into 1st st, changing to C.

Work 1 rep of the crosses and bars pattern in the rnd as follows:

Rnd 1: With C, ch 1, sc into same st and ea of next 2 sts, *ch 1, sk 1 sc, sc into ea of next 2 sc, ch 1, sk 1 sc, sc into ea of next 6 sc, rep from * around ending sc into last 3 sts ending sl st into 1st st.

Rnd 2: With C, ch 3 (counts as dc), dc into ea st to end of rnd ending sl st into 1st st, changing to B.

Rnd 3: With B, ch 1, sc into same and next 2 sts, *work dtr into 2nd sk sc 3 rnds below, sk 1 dc, sc into ea of next 2 dc, dtr into 1st sk sc 3 rows below (thus crossing 2 dtr), sk 1 dc, sc into ea of next 6 dc, rep from * ending last rep sc into last 3 dc, sl st into 1st st.

Rnd 4: With B, ch 1, sc into 1st and every st to end of rnd ending sl st into 1st st.

Work multicolor rnd as follows: ch 1, *sc with B, sc with A, rep from * around ending sl st into 1st st.

BRIM

Rnd 1: With A, ch 3, working into back lps, dc into same st, dc into ea of next 7 sts, *2 dc into next st, dc into ea of next 7 sts, rep from * to end of rnd ending sl st into 1st st.

Rnd 2: Ch 3, dc into same st, dc into ea of next 8 sts, *2 dc into next st, dc into ea of next 7 sts, rep from * to end of rnd ending sl st into 1st st.

Rnd 3: Work 1 rnd Rsc (crab stitch). Fasten off.

Designed by Gloria Tracy

Tasseled Shoulder Bag and Cloche Hat

By using the yarn double throughout, we cut the working time in half—you can easily make this clever set in a weekend. Made in a fabulous metallic yarn, this bag and hat will be perfect accents for any special-occasion outfit. If the set were made in a yarn with a casual look such as cotton or denim heathers, it would look entirely different. When buying yarn for your next project, add a couple of extra skeins and make this easy set to match.

Sizes

Bag: 8½" across x 13¾" long (open measurement)
Hat: 20½" circumference

Materials

> Skacel *Karat*, 50 g/143 yd/130 m (90% rayon,
>   10% polyester metallic)
>   Bag: 5 cones #19 Copper
>   Hat: 2 cones #19 Copper
> Crochet hook US size K/10.5 (6.5 mm)
> One large decorative button for bag
> Yarn needle
> Electric mixer (optional)

Gauge

In picot single crochet and 2 strands held tog,
14 sts and 12 rows = 4"

Stitches and Patterns Used

Chain, slip stitch, single crochet, double crochet,
picot single crochet

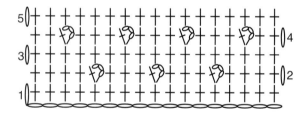

Special Abbreviations

sc dec: Pull up lp in 2 sts, yo, draw through 3 lps
on hk.

Notes

1. Use two strands held together throughout for both
   pieces.

2. The main section of the bag is worked from side to
   side. The bottom is worked from the outer edge to
   the center in rounds.

3. The cloche hat is worked from top to bottom in
   rounds.

Directions for Bag

Main Section: With 2 strands held tog, ch 47 + 1
   for turn.

Beg in 2nd ch from hk, work in Psc for 17". Fasten
   off. Sew beg and end edges tog.

Bottom: Rnd 1: With RS facing, attach 2 strands at
   seam, ch 1, work 56 sc evenly around edge of
   Main Section; sl st in 1st sc—do not turn.

Rnd 2: Ch 1, sc in blo around; sl st in 1st sc.

Rnd 3: Ch 1, * sc in 5 sts, sc dec; rep from *
   around—48 sts.

Rnd 4: Ch 1, * sc in 4 sts, sc dec; rep from *
   around—40 sts.

Rnd 5: Ch 1, * sc in 3 sts, sc dec; rep from *
   around—32 sts.

Cont in this manner dec 8 sts evenly in each rnd
   until 8 sts rem. Fasten off. Cut yarn and weave
   end in and out of rem sts. Pull tightly to close
   opening. Weave in end.

Top Trim: Rnd 1: With RS facing, attach 2 strands
   at seam, ch 1, work 60 sc evenly around top
   edge of Main Section; sl st in 1st sc—do not
   turn.

Place button across top of rnd and count how many
   sts equal width of button. Mark these sts on center front.

Rnd 2: Ch 1, sc in ea sc across to marked sts, ch as
   many sts as marked sts, sk marked sts, sc to end
   of rnd; sl st in 1st sc. Fasten off. Fold flap over to
   desired length. Sew button opposite button lp.

FINISHING

Shoulder Strap: Work twisted cord (see p. 57), using twenty-four 120" lengths of yarn. Knot each end of cording, leaving a 4" tail. Trim ends evenly. Sew back of knots to ea side edge of bag at fold.

Directions for Cloche Hat

With 2 strands held tog, ch 6, join with sl st in 1st ch to form ring.

Rnd 1: Ch 1, work 12 sc in ring; sl st in 1st sc—12 sts.

Rnd 2: Ch 3 (counts as dc), dc in same st, 2 dc in ea rem st around; sl st in top of ch-3—24 sts.

Rnd 3: Ch 3 (counts as dc), dc in same st, dc in next 3 sts, * 2 dc in next st, dc in next 3 sts; rep from * around, sl st in top of ch-3—30 sts.

Rnd 4: Ch 3 (counts as dc), dc in same st, dc in next 4 sts, * 2 dc in next st, dc in next 4 sts; rep from * around, sl st in top of ch-3—36 sts.

Rnd 5: Ch 3 (counts as dc), dc in same st, dc in next 5 sts, * 2 dc in next st, dc in next 5 sts; rep from * around, sl st in top of ch-3—42 sts.

Rnd 6: Ch 3 (counts as dc), dc in same st, dc in next 6 sts, * 2 dc in next st, dc in next 6 sts; rep from * around, sl st in top of ch-3—48 sts.

Rnd 7: Ch 3 (counts as dc), dc in same st, dc in next 7 sts, * 2 dc in next st, dc in next 7 sts; rep from * around, sl st in top of ch-3—54 sts.

Rnd 8: Ch 3 (counts as dc), dc in same st, dc in next 8 sts, * 2 dc in next st, dc in next 8 sts; rep from * around, sl st in top of ch-3—60 sts.

Rnd 9: Work 1 rnd Psc; sl st in 1st st.

Rnd 10: Ch 1, sc in ea st around; sl st in 1st st.

Rnd 11: Rep Rnd 9.

Rnd 12: Ch 3 (counts as dc), dc in same st, dc in next 9 sts, * 2 dc in next st, dc in next 9 sts; rep from * around, sl st in top of ch-3—66 sts.

Rnd 13: Ch 3 (counts as dc), dc in same st, dc in next 10 sts, * 2 dc in next st, dc in next 10 sts; rep from * around, sl st in top of ch-3—72 sts.

Rnds 14–16: Rep Rnds 9–11.

Rnd 17: Rep Rnd 10. Fasten off.

FINISHING

Work twisted cord (see p. 57) using twelve 60" lengths of yarn. Knot each end of cording, leaving a 3" tail. Trim ends evenly. Tack in place around hat between Rnds 12 and 13. Tie ends tog.

Designed by Gloria Tracy

Lacy Evening Wrap and Matching Juliet Cap

The inspiration for this lovely lacy wrap was from a baby afghan pattern from Spinrite Yarn Company. We liked the pretty pattern because it was reversible and because it had a delicate, lacy appearance that was easily adapted to a larger gauge. By holding a strand of soft merino wool together with a strand of metallic thread we created a festive, shimmering effect perfect for holiday dressing or any special occasion.

Size

Wrap: 22" x 60" (55 cm x 152 cm)
Cap: Approximately 25" (63 cm) circumference

Materials

Knit One, Crochet Too *Creme Brulee* DK (50 g/
    131 yd/120 m)
    9 skeins #565 Deep Evergreen (A)
Kreinik *Metallic Threads* 50 mm
    20 reels #850 FN Mallard (B)
Crochet hook US size J/10 (6 mm)

Gauge

In pat st, 1 pattern rep = 10½" across x 5" long

Stitches and Patterns Used

Chain, slip stitch, single crochet, half double crochet, double crochet
Lace (Block #20)
Twisted loops (Block #7)
Crumpled griddle stitch (Block #4)

Diamond Lace Pattern
(multiple of 20 sts + 17)

Foundation Row (RS): Sc in 2nd ch from hk, (ch 5, sk 3 ch, sc in next ch) twice, * sk 1 ch, 5 dc in next ch, sk 1 ch, sc in next ch, ** (ch 5, sk 3 ch, sc in next ch) 3 times; rep from * across to last 8 ch, ending last rep at **, (ch 5, sk 3 ch, sc in next ch) twice; turn.

Row 1: * (Ch 5, sc in next ch-5 arch) twice, 5 dc in next sc, sc in 3rd dc of next 5-dc group, 5 dc in next sc, sc in next arch; rep from * across to last arch, ch 5, sc in next arch, ch 2, dc in last sc; turn.

Row 2: Ch 1, sc in 1st dc, sk ch-2 sp, * ch 5, sc in next ch-5 arch, 5 dc in next sc, sc in 3rd dc of next 5-dc group, ch 5, sc in 3rd dc of next 5-dc group, 5 dc in next sc, sc in next arch; rep from * across, ending with ch 5, sc in tch-5 arch.

Row 3: Ch 3 (counts as dc), 2 dc in 1st sc, * sc in next ch-5 arch, 5 dc in next sc, sc in 3rd dc of next 5-dc group, ch 5, sc in next arch, ch 5, sc in 3rd dc of 5-dc group, 5 dc in next sc; rep from * across to last arch, sc in next arch, 3 dc in last sc; turn.

Row 4: Ch 1, sc in 1st dc, * 5 dc in next sc, sc in 3rd dc of next 5-dc group, (ch 5, sc in next arch) twice, ch 5, sc in 3rd dc of next 5-dc group; rep from * across, 5 dc in next sc, sc in top of tch-3; turn.

Row 5: Ch 3 (counts as dc), 2 dc in 1st st, * sc in 3rd dc of next 5-dc group, 5 dc in next sc, sc in next arch (ch 5, sc in next arch) twice, 5 dc in next sc; rep from * across to last 5-dc group, sc in 3rd dc of 5-dc group, 3 dc in last sc; turn.

Row 6: Ch 1, sc in 1st sc, * ch 5, sc in 3rd dc of next 5-dc group, 5 dc in next sc, sc in next arch, ch 5, sc in next arch, 5 dc in next sc, sc in 3rd dc of next 5-dc group; rep from * ending ch 5, sc in top of tch-3; turn.

Row 7: * Ch 5, sc in next ch-5 arch, ch 5, sc in 3rd dc of next 5-dc group, 5 dc in next sc, sc in next arch, 5 dc in next sc, sc in 3rd dc of next 5-dc group; rep from * across to last arch, ch 5, sc in next arch, ch 2, dc in last sc; turn.

Row 8: Ch 1, sc in 1st st, sk ch-2 sp, ch 5, sc in next ch-5 arch, ch 5, sc in 3rd dc of 5-dc group, * 5 dc in next sc, sc in 3rd dc of 5-dc group, (ch 5, sc in next arch) twice **, ch 5, sc in 3rd dc of 5-dc group; rep from * across, ending last rep at ** working last sc in tch-5 arch; turn.

Rep Rows 1–8 for pattern st.

Notes

Unless otherwise instructed, hold one strand each of *Creme Brulee* DK and metallic thread together throughout both projects.

Directions for Wrap

With 1 strand ea A and B held tog, ch 77 + 1 for turn.

Work pattern st Foundation Row, then rep Rows 1–8 until approx 60" from beg, ending after a rep of Row 8. Drop B.

Looped Top Border: Row 1: With A only, ch 1, sc in 1st sc, * (ch 5, sc in next arch) twice **, ch 5, sc in 3rd dc of next 5-dc group; rep from * across, ending at **, ch 5, sc in sc at beg of Row 8; turn.

Row 2: (Ch 7, sl st in next ch or sc) across. Fasten off.

Looped Bottom Border: With A only, attach yarn in 1st foundation ch, (7 ch, sl st in next st or ch) across. Fasten off.

Side Border: Row 1: Attach A in side of 1st row, ch 1, work an odd number of sc evenly along side taking care to keep work flat; turn.

TIP: *For a more tightly closed center when working a from-the-center-out motif, form a ring by wrapping the yarn twice around your finger, leaving an 8" tail. Work the first round into the ring, wrapping the yarn around the tail on each stitch. When the motif is completed, pull the tail to close the ring and fasten off.*

Row 2: Ch 1, sc in 1st sc, * dc in next sc, sc in next sc; rep from * across. Fasten off.

Rep for other side border.

Directions for Juliet Cap

Note: Two foundation rnds inc to 18 sts. Rnd 1 of the crown starts with 1 ch between each dc around, rnd 2 has 2 chs between dc, and so on until 5 chs make up sp between ea dc. At end of each rnd, sl st in 3rd ch of beg ch, then sl st to center of next sp. This will eliminate a visible joining seam.

With 1 strand ea A and B held tog, ch 4, join with sl st in 1st ch to form ring.

Foundation Rnd 1: Ch 1, work 9 sc in ring; sl st to first sc to join.

Foundation Rnd 2: Ch 1, work 2 sc in ea sc around; join—18 sc.

Rnd 1: Ch 4 (counts as dc and ch 1), * dc in next sc, ch 1; rep from * around, sl st in 3rd ch of beg ch-4, sl st in next ch (center of sp).

Rnd 2: Ch 5 (counts as dc and ch 2), * dc in next sp, ch 2; rep from * around, sl st in 3rd ch of beg ch-5, sl st in next ch (center of sp).

Rnd 3: Ch 6 (counts as dc and ch 3), * dc in next sp, ch 3; rep from * around, sl st in 3rd ch of beg ch-6, sl st in next 2 ch (center of sp).

Rnd 4: Ch 7 (counts as dc and ch 4), * dc in next sp, ch 4; rep from * around, sl st in 3rd ch of beg ch-7, sl st in next 2 ch (center of sp).

Rnd 5: Ch 8 (counts as dc and ch 4), * dc in next sp, ch 5; rep from * around, sl st in 3rd ch of beg ch-7, sl st in next 3 ch (center of sp)—18 sps around.

Rnds 6–9: Rep Rnd 5.

Rnd 10: Ch 1, 5 sc in ea ch-5 sp around—90 sc.

Rnd 11: * Working in flo of ea st, ch 7, sl st in next st; rep from * around.

Rnd 12: Working in rem back lp of ea st, ch 2, beg with next st, hdc in ea st around; sl st in top of ch 2.

Rnds 13–16: Rep Rnds 11 and 12 twice more.

Rnd 17: Rep Rnd 11.

Rnd 18: Working in rem back lp of ea st, ch 1, * sc in ea st around; sl st to 1st sc. Fasten off.

Designed by Bobbi Hayward

The Shawl-Collared Shawl

A shawl collar is one of the most flattering shapes you can choose to frame your face. When you make it out of a light-as-air yarn like this baby mohair and silk, you have a finished product suitable for a queen—or, better yet, for you. The top edge of the shawl lays out in a natural shawl-collar shape because it combines a variation of Faroese shaping and gradually decreasing hook sizes. The simple single crochet and chain stitches plus designerly decreases equal a fast and fun project you'll enjoy making and wearing.

Size

Approx 42" from point to center top; 76" across rounded beg edge

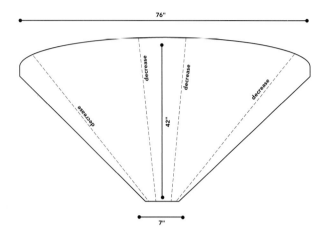

Materials

> Knit One, Crochet Too *Douceur et Soie* 25 g/ 225 yd/205 m (70% baby mohair, 30% silk) 6 skeins #8100 Snow
> Crochet hooks, US sizes G/6, H/8, I/9, J/10 and K/10.5 (4, 5, 5.5, 6, and 6.5 mm)
> Four split-ring stitch markers

Gauge

With largest hk and working in sc, 11 sts = 3"

Notes

1. Hooks: Begin the shawl with the largest hook, then change hook sizes as you progress, as indicated, to achieve the proper shaping.

2. Work all single crochet stitches in the back loop only, except the first and last stitches, which are to be worked through both loops. Chain 1 at the beginning of each row after the first row; turn at the end of each row. Move stitch markers up as you work each row.

Directions for Shawl

With K hook, ch 280.

Row 1 (RS): Sc in 2nd ch from hk and ea ch across—279 sc. Place markers on the following sts: 7, 130, 151, 274.

Row 2: Sc in ea st across, moving markers up as you go.

Change to J hook.

Rows 3 and 4: Rep Row 2.

Row 5: Sc in first 6 sts, sc2tog over next 2 sts, sc to 2 sts before next marker, sc2tog, sc in next 21 sts, sc2tog, sc to 2 sts before next marker, sc2tog, sc in last 6 sts—275 sts.

Row 6: Sc in ea st across.

Rows 7 and 8: Rep Rows 5 and 6—271 sts.

Change to I hook.

Rows 9–14: Rep Rows 5 and 6 for 3 times—259 sts.

Change to H hook.

Rows 15–20: Rep Rows 5 and 6 for 3 times—247 sts.

Row 21: Sc in 1st 6 sts, sc2tog, work (ch 2, sk 1 sc, sc in next sc) to 3 sts before last marker, ch 2, sk 1 sc, sc2tog, sc in last 6 sts—245 sts.

Row 22: Sc in ea sc and ch sp across—245 sts.

Rows 23–28: Rep Rows 21 and 22 for 3 times—239 sts.

Row 29: Sc in 1st 6 sts, sc2tog, sc to 2 sts before last marker, sc2tog, sc in last 6 sts—237 sts.

Row 30: Sc in ea st across.

Rows 31 and 32: Rep Rows 29 and 30—235 sts.

Rows 33–52: Rep Rows 21–32, then rows 21–28— 215 sts.

Rows 53–56: Rep Rows 5 and 6 twice—207 sts.

Row 57: Sc in 1st 6 sts, sc2tog, sc to 2 sts before next marker, sc2tog, sc in next 5 sts, (ch 2, sk 1 sc, sc in next sc) 6 times, sc in next 4 sts, sc2tog, sc to 2 sts before next marker, sc2tog, sc in last 6 sts—203 sts.

Rows 58, 60, 62, and 64: Sc in ea sc and ch sp across.

Row 59: Sc in 1st 6 sts, sc2tog, sc to 2 sts before next marker, sc2tog, sc in next 4 sts, (ch 2, sk 1 sc, sc in next sc) 7 times, sc in next 3 sts, sc2tog, sc to 2 sts before next marker, sc2tog, sc in last 6 sts—199 sts.

Row 61: Sc in 1st 2 sts, sc2tog, sc in next 2 sts, sc2tog, sc to 2 sts before next marker, sc2tog, sc in next 5 sts, (ch 2, sk 1 sc, sc in next sc) 6 times, sc in next 4 sts, sc2tog, sc to 2 sts before next marker, sc2tog, sc in next 2 sts, sc2tog, sc in last 2 sts—193 sts.

Row 63: Sc in 1st 5 sts, sc2tog, sc to 2 sts before next marker, sc2tog, sc in next 4 sts, (ch 2, sk 1 sc, sc in next sc) 7 times, sc in next 3 sts, sc2tog, sc to 2 sts before last marker, sc2tog, sc in last 5 sts—189 sts.

Row 65: Sc in 1st 5 sts, sc2tog, sc to 2 sts before next marker, sc2tog, sc in next 21 sts, sc2tog, sc to 2 sts before last marker, sc2tog, sc in last 5 sts—185 sts.

Row 66: Sc in ea sc across.

Rows 67 and 68: Rep rows 65 and 66—181 sts.

Row 69: Sc in 1st 5 sts, sc2tog, sc to 2 sts before next marker, sc2tog, sc in next 5 sts, (ch 2, sk 1 sc, sc in next sc) 6 times, sc in next 4 sts, sc2tog, sc to 2 sts before next marker, sc2tog, sc in last 5 sts—177 sts.

Rows 70, 72, 74, and 76: Sc in ea sc and ch sp across.

Row 71: Sc in first 5 sts, sc2tog, sc to 2 sts before next marker, (sc2tog) twice, sc in next 2 sts, (ch 2, sk 1 sc, sc in next sc) 7 times, sc in next st, (sc2tog) twice, sc to 2 sts before last marker, sc2tog, sc in last 5 sts—171 sts.

Row 73: Sc in 1st 5 sts, sc2tog, sc to 2 sts before next marker, sc2tog, sc in next 4 sts, (ch 2, sk 1 sc, sc in next sc) 6 times, sc in next 3 sts, sc2tog, sc to 2 sts before next marker, sc2tog, sc in last 5 sts—167 sts.

Row 75: Sc in 1st 5 sts, sc2tog, sc to 2 sts before next marker, sc2tog, sc in next 3 sts, (ch 2, sk 1 sc, sc in next sc) 7 times, sc in next 2 sts, sc2tog, sc to 2 sts before next marker, sc2tog, sc in last 5 sts—163 sts.

Row 77: Sc in 1st 5 sts, sc2tog, sc to 2 sts before next marker, sc2tog, sc in next 19 sts, sc2tog, sc to 2 sts before next marker, sc2tog, sc in last 5 sts—159 sts.

Row 78: Sc in ea st across.

Rows 79 and 80: Rep Rows 77 and 78—155 sts.

Row 81: Rep Row 73—151 sts.

Rows 82, 84, 86, and 88: Sc in ea sc and ch sp across.

Row 83: Sc in 1st 2 sts, sc2tog, sc in next st, sc2tog, sc to 2 sts before next marker, sc2tog, sc in next 3 sts, (ch 2, sk 1 sc, sc in next sc) 7 times, sc in next 2 sts, sc2tog, sc to 2 sts before next marker, sc2tog, sc in next st, sc2tog, sc in last 2 sts—145 sts.

Row 85: Sc in 1st 4 sts, sc2tog, sc to 2 sts before next marker, (sc2tog) twice, sc in next 2 sts, (ch 2, sk 1 sc, sc in next sc) 6 times, sc in next st, (sc2tog) twice, sc to 2 sts before last marker, sc2tog, sc in last 4 sts—139 sts.

Row 87: Sc in 1st 4 sts, sc2tog, sc to 2 sts before next marker, sc2tog, sc in next 2 sts, (ch 2, sk 1 sc, sc in next sc) 7 times, sc in next st, sc2tog, sc to 2 sts before last marker, sc2tog, sc in last 4 sts—135 sts.

Row 89: Sc in 1st 4 sts, sc2tog, sc to 2 sts before next marker, sc2tog, sc in next 17 sts, sc2tog, sc to 2 sts before next marker, sc2tog, sc in last 4 sts—131 sts.

Row 90: Sc in ea st across.

Rows 91 and 92: Rep Rows 89 and 90—127 sts.

Row 93: Sc in 1st 4 sts, sc2tog, sc to 2 sts before next marker, sc2tog, sc in next 3 sts, (ch 2, sk 1 sc, sc in next sc) 6 times, sc in next 2 sts, sc2tog, sc to 2 sts before last marker, sc2tog, sc in last 4 sts—123 sts.

Rows 94, 96, 98, and 100: Sc in ea sc and ch sp across moving markers as you go.

Row 95: Rep Row 87—119 sts.

Row 97: Sc in 1st 4 sts, sc2tog, sc to 2 sts before next marker, while at the same time, dec 5 additional sts evenly spaced; sc2tog, sc in next 3 sts, (ch 2, sk 1 sc, sc in next sc) 6 times, sc in next 2 sts, sc2tog, sc to 2 sts before next marker, while at the same time, dec 5 additional sts evenly spaced, sc2tog, sc in last 4 sts—105 sts.

Row 99: Rep Row 87—101 sts.

Change to G hook.

Row 101: Sc in 1st 4 sts, sc2tog, sc to 2 sts before next marker, (sc2tog) twice, sc to 2 sts before next marker, (sc2tog) twice, sc to 2 sts before last marker, sc2tog, sc in last 4 sts—95 sts.

Rows 102 and 104: Sc in ea st across.

Row 103: Sc in 1st 4 sts, sc2tog, sc to 2 sts before next marker, sc2tog, sc in next 15 sts, sc2tog, sc to 2 sts before last marker, sc2tog, sc in last 4 sts—91 sts.

Row 105: Sc in 1st 4 sts, sc2tog, sc to 2 sts before next marker, sc2tog, sc in next 2 sts, (ch 2, sk 1 sc, sc in next sc) 6 times, sc in next st, sc2tog, sc to 2 sts before last marker, sc2tog, sc in last 4 sts—87 sts.

Rows 106 and 108: Sc in ea sc and ch sp across.

Row 107: Sc in 1st 4 sts, sc2tog, sc to 2 sts before next marker, sc2tog, sc in next st, (ch 2, sk 1 sc, sc in next sc) 7 times, sc2tog, sc to 2 sts before last marker, sc2tog, sc in last 4 sts—83 sts.

Rows 109–112: Rep Rows 105–108—75 sts.

Row 113: Rep Row 103—71 sts.

Rows 114 and 116: Sc in ea st across.

Row 115: Sc in 1st 4 sts, sc2tog, sc to 2 sts before next marker, (sc2tog) twice, sc to 2 sts before next marker, (sc2tog) twice, sc to 2 sts before last marker, sc2tog, sc in last 4 sts—65 sts.

Row 117: Sc in 1st 4 sts, sc2tog, sc to 2 sts before next marker, sc2tog, sc in next st, (ch 2, sk 1 sc, sc in next sc) 6 times, sc2tog, sc to 2 sts before last marker, sc2tog, sc in last 4 sts—61 sts.

Rows 118 and 120: Sc in ea sc and ch sp across.

Row 119: Sc in 1st 4 sts, sc2tog, sc to 2 sts before next marker, sc2tog, (ch 2, sk 1 sc, sc in next sc) 6 times, ch 2, sk next st, sc2tog, sc to 2 sts before last marker, sc2tog, sc in last 4 sts—57 sts.

Rows 121–124: Rep Rows 117–120—49 sts.

Row 125: Sc in 1st 4 sts, sc2tog, sc to 2 sts before next marker, sc2tog, sc in next 13 sts, sc2tog, sc to 2 sts before next marker, sc2tog, sc in last 4 sts—45 sts.

Row 126: Sc in ea st across.

Rows 127–130: Rep Rows 125 and 126 twice—37 sts.

Row 131: Sc in 1st 4 sts, sc2tog, sc to 2 sts before next marker, (sc2tog) twice, sc to 2 sts before next marker, (sc2tog) twice, sc to 2 sts before last marker, sc2tog, sc in last 4 sts—31 sts.

Row 132: Rep Row 126.

Row 133: Sc in 1st 4 sts, sc2tog, sc to 2 sts before next marker, sc2tog, sc in next 11 sts, sc2tog, sc to 2 sts before last marker, sc2tog, sc in last 4 sts—27 sts.

Row 134: Rep Row 126.

Row 135: Sc in 1st 3 sts, sc2tog, sc in next 2 sts, sc2tog, sc in next 9 sts, sc2tog, sc in next 2 sts, sc2tog, sc in last 3 sts—23 sts.

Row 136: Sc in 1st 2 sts, sc2tog, sc in next 2 sts, sc2tog, sc in next 7 sts, sc2tog, sc in next 2 sts, sc2tog, sc in last 2 sts—19 sts.

Row 137 (Edging): Sc in 1st 3 sts, sc2tog, turn; ch 1, sc in each st, turn. Work back and forth over these 4 border sts working sc2tog using the last st of border and the next st on Row 136 on the shawl body eor until only 4 sts rem of Row 136.

FINISHING

Weave the 4 working sts tog with rem 4 sts of Row 136 to form an invisible seam.

Furry Hooded Scarf and Mittens

Flattering, face-framing furry loops make an easy band around the hood portion of our fun and practical Furry Hooded Scarf and Mittens. The same easy loop stitch edges the scarf and cuffs the mittens. A jaunty tassel tops the hood for a three-piece set to delight and warm women of all ages.

Sizes

Scarf and Mittens: One size fits all.

Materials

Patons *Canadiana Variegated*, 85g/205 yd/187 m
   (100% Acrilan acrylic with BounceBack fibers)
   3 skeins # 420 (A)
Patons *Canadiana Solid*, 100g/21 yd/195 m (100%
   Acrilan acrylic with BounceBack fibers)
   2 skeins #119 (B)
Crochet hooks US sizes G/6 and J/10 (4 and
   6 mm)
Yarn needle
5" cardboard square

Stitches and Patterns Used

Single crochet, chains
Twisted loops (Block #7)
Front porch and back porch patterns (Block #1)

Pattern Stitch

(any even number of sts; rep of 1 row)

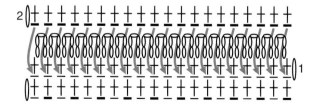

Ch 1, * sc in back lp of 1 st, sc in front lp of next st;
rep from * across; turn.
Rep this row for pattern st.

Fur Band Pattern

Row 1: Attach B in 1st st at beg of row and working
   in flo across, sc in 1st sc, * ch 5, sc in next sc;
   rep from * across, turn 20 sc and 19 ch-5 lps
   across.

Row 2: Ch 1, sc across in unused lp opposite previous row; turn.

Gauge

In pattern st and with G hk, 18 sts and 16 rows = 4"
In pattern st and with J hk, 16 sts and 11 rows = 4"

Directions for Hooded Scarf

SCARF, FIRST SIDE

With larger hk and A, ch 21.

Sc in 2nd ch from hk and in ea ch across 20 sc.
   Turn.

Work in pattern st with A until 6" from beg, changing to color B in the last st of last row.

Work 6 rows of Fur Band Pattern.

Attach A in 1st st at beg of row, and work in pattern
   st for 22" more. Fasten off.

SCARF, SECOND SIDE

Repeat as for First Side, reversing color placement.

HOOD

With larger hk and A, ch 29.

Sc in 2nd ch from hk and in ea ch across 28 sc.
   Turn.

Work in pattern st until 11" from beg. Fasten off A.

Attach B in 1st st at beg of next row, and work even
   in pattern st for 11" more. Fasten off.

ROLL-BACK EDGE

Row 1 (WS): With larger hk and A, work 64 sc evenly across long side of hood; turn.

Rows 2–5: Ch 1, sc in ea sc across; turn.

Rows 6–13: Work Rows 1 and 2 of Fur Band twice with A, once with B and once with A.

Rows 14–15: Rep Row 2. Fasten off.

Finishing: Fold cuff back to RS and tack ea end in place. Sew side end of scarf matching color to lower edge of hood. Fold hood in half and sew back seam of both hood and scarf.

TASSEL

Place 20" yarn length across 5" cardboard square. Wrap A around square 40 times. Tie yarn length tightly at top fold. Cut other end of tassel open. Use 2nd 20" yarn length to wrap around tassel about 1" from top. Hide ends at center of tassel and trim evenly. Attach tassel at tip of hood.

Directions for Mittens

Note: Work around without turning or joining at end of each rnd. Mark beg of each rnd. Begin at tip of mitten and work to wrist.

Rnd 1: With smaller hk and B, ch 2, work 8 sc in 2nd ch from hk.

Rnd 2: Work 2 sc in ea sc around—16 sc.

Rnd 3: (Sc in 1 sc, 2 sc in next sc) around—24 sc.

Rnd 4: (Sc in 3 sc, 2 sc in next sc) around—30 sc.

Work even in pattern st until piece measures 5½" from beg.

Next Rnd: Thumb Opening for Right Mitten: Sc in 4 sts, ch 6, sk 5 sts, sc in next 21 sts—30 sts.

Next Rnd: Thumb Opening for Left Mitten: Sc in 21 sts, ch 6, sk 5 sts, sc in next 4 sts—30 sts.

Next Rnd for both mittens: Work across in pattern st working 6 sc in ch-6 sp.

Work even in pattern st until mitten measures 7½" from beg.

CUFF

Rnd 1: With B and working through both lps around, sc in 1st 2 sts, * sc dec, sc in next 4 sts; rep from * around to last 4 sts, sc dec, 2 sc in last 2 sc—25 sts. Fasten off B.

Beg with RS facing and with A, work Rows 1 and 2 of Scarf Fur Band as follows:

Work Row 1 around; sl st in 1st st; turn.

Work Row 2 with WS facing, sl st in 1st st; turn. Rep these 2 rows 3 more times. Fasten off.

THUMB

Rnd 1 (RS): Working around thumb opening in pattern st, attach B in 1st ch of ch 6, 2 sc in 1st ch, sc in next 4 chs, 2 sc in last ch, sc in next 2 sc, sc inc, sc in last 2 sc—14 sc.

Work in pattern st until 2½" from beg or desired length.

Dec Rnd 1: Sc, sc dec, sc in 3 sc, sc dec, sc in 3 sc, sc dec—10 sc.

Dec Rnd 2: Sc, sc dec, sc in 2 sc, sc dec, sc—6 sc. Fasten off and cut yarn leaving an 8" sewing tail. With yarn needle, weave tail in and out of rem sts and pull tightly to close opening. Weave in end to WS.

Designed by Gloria Tracy

Loopy Bath Mat and Lid Cover

The inspiration for our bathroom set came from Gloria's husband when he remarked that her Twisted Loops Afghan Block would make a cozy rug. We designed a matching lid cover and came up with an attractive bathroom set. The rug alone would make a cozy addition to a baby's room, kitchen, or den.

Size

Finished Bath Mat: approximately 18" x 28"/ 45.5 cm x 71 cm

Finished Lid Cover: approximately 16" x 14"/ 40.5 cm x 35.5 cm

Materials

> Caron *Wintuk*, 100 g/213 yd/194 m (100% Acrilan acrylic, worsted weight)
> 4 skeins #3239 Teal (A)
> 2 skeins #3159 Colonial Blue (B)
> 1 skein #3001 White (C)
> 1 card 3-mm *Rainbow Elastic* #121 Dark Teal
> Crochet hooks US sizes F/5 and I/9 (3.75 and 5.5 mm)

Gauge

10 sts = 4"/10 cm
20 rows (10 rows of lps) = 6"/15 cm with larger hk

Notes

1. Each two rows of pattern form one row of loops.

2. The turning chain counts as a stitch. Be sure to work in the top of the turning chain at the end of the row. Confirm stitch count after each double crochet row.

3. Change colors as follows: In last stitch before changing to a new color, work until 2 lps remain on hk. With new color, yo and draw through last 2 lps on hk.

4. The lid instructions are for a lid that's 16" x 14" (40.5 cm x 35.5 cm) with a slight curve at the top and bottom (see diagram). There is a 1" (2.5 cm) border around all edges, except the back where the hinges are. The border around the edges will be gathered in with crocheted elastic for fit.

Stitches and Patterns Used

Twisted Loops Pattern

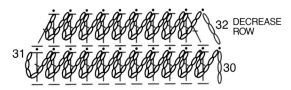

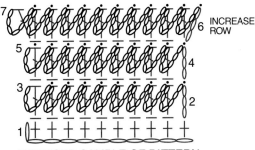

REDUCED SAMPLE OF PATTERN

Row 1 (WS): Starting in the 2nd st, *ch 7, sl st into blo of dc; rep from * across ending ch 7, sl st into top of tch, turn.

Row 2 (RS): Ch 3 (counts as 1 dc), sk 1st st, work 1 dc into blo of each st across ending with 1 dc into top of tch, turn.

Rep Rows 1 and 2 for pattern.

Directions for Bath Mat

With A and larger hk, ch 51. Dc into 4th ch from hk and in ea ch across—49 dc (counting beg ch-3). Work in twisted loops pattern for a total of 46 rows of lps in the following color sequence:

14 rows of lps in A

5 rows of lps in B

8 rows of lps in C

5 rows of lps in B

14 rows of lps in A.

Do not fasten off.

FINISHING

With A, work 2 sc into ea dc row along the sides (92 sc), and 49 sc along ea end working 3 sc into ea corner st; fasten off.

Directions for Lid Cover

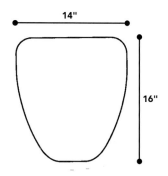

See "Note" below if your lid is a different size.

Work in twisted loops pattern for a total of 28 rows of lps in the following color sequence while following instructions for Rows 1–57:

9 rows of lps in A

3 rows of lps in B

4 rows of lps in C

3 rows of lps in B

9 rows of lps in A

With A and larger hk, ch 35.

Row 1: Sc into the 3rd ch from hk and in ea ch across, turn—34 sc (counting beg ch 2).

Work the following rows in twisted loops pattern in color sequence.

Rows 2–5: Work 2 rows of lps.

Rows 6–11: Inc at ea end of next 3 dc rows—40 sts.

Row 12–29: Work even in twisted loops pattern and color sequence until 9 more rows of lps have been completed—14 rows of lps total.

Rows 30–57: Dec 1 st at ea end of next dc row, then every other dc row 3 more time—32 dc, then every dc row 5 times—22 dc.

Cont working in twisted loops pattern and color sequence until 28 rows of lps total have been completed. Fasten off.

ELASTIC EDGING

Rnd 1: With smaller hk and elastic, sc around edges working 2 sc into ea dc row along the side edges and 1 sc into ea st at top and bottom.

Rnd 2: *Work 1 sc into ea of next 2 sc, sk 1 sc; rep from* around.

Rnd 3: Work 1 sc into ea st around; fasten off.

Note

If your lid is different from the model:

If it is shorter, just add or subtract rows in the color sections that are worked even.

If it is wider or shaped differently, make your own schematic by laying a piece of newspaper under the closed lid and drawing an outline around it. Add the 1" (2.5 cm) border around all edges except the back. Start the lid cover as directed for the beginning chain and the first two rows. Lay your work on your outline every few rows and shape your increases and decreases as needed to match your drawing. Finish as above.

Pretty Posies

We know you'll have fun with this unique project that uses Rainbow Elastic cotton-covered elastic thread. The three different bands are interchangeable with the three different flower patterns. Just make each band an inch or so smaller than the intended package and you have a package topper that is a gift on its own. Depending upon the size, the package topper can later be used as a scrunchy, a bracelet, a headband, a book marker, or a belt. We bet you'll think up even more uses for this fun project.

Finished Lengths

Woven Braid: 6"
Buttonhole Braid: 17"
Foxglove Braid: 17"

Materials

    K1C2 *Rainbow elastic thread*, 3 mm (bulky)/25 yd
        per card
    1 card each:
        Red (A)
        Orange (B)
        Yellow (C)
        Green (D)
        Blue (E)
        Violet (F)
    Crochet hook US size D/3 (3.25 mm)
    Tapestry needle

Stitches and Patterns Used

Chain, single crochet, half double crochet, double crochet, treble crochet, linked double crochet

Directions

Note: For all three braids, first measure circumference of box or item to be wrapped, then follow these guidelines for length of elastic braid:
Up to 12" — Make braid 1" shorter
Up to 24" — Make braid 2" shorter
Up to 36" — Make braid 3" shorter, etc.

Woven Braid

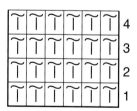

Note: Do not turn work. Work is done with RS facing at all times.
With F, ch 6.

Row 1: Placing hk under 2 lps of base ch, insert hk into 2nd ch, yo and pull through a lp. *Insert hk into next ch, yo and draw lp through. Rep from * to end—6 lps on hk.

Row 2: Working back along row from in opposite direction, yo and draw yarn through 1st lp. * Yo and draw through next 2 lps. Rep from * to end—1 lp on hk.

Row 3: Insert hk behind second vertical lp, yo and draw lp through. * Insert hk behind next vertical lp, yo and draw lp through. Rep from * to end—6 lps on hk.

Row 4: Rep Row 2.

Rep Rows 3 and 4 for desired length. Fasten off, leaving an 8" tail.

Overlap ends and sew tog with tapestry needle.

Chrysanthemum

With C, ch 6 and join with a sl st to 1st ch to form a ring.
Rnd 1: Ch 1, work 16 sc in ring.

Rnd 2: Working in flo, sl st in 1st sc. Ch 7, sl st in same sc, * ch 7, sl st in next sc, rep from * to last sc, ch 7 and sl st in blo of 1st sc in rnd.

Rnd 3: Sc in blo of ea st on Rnd 1—16 sc.

Rnd 4: Rep Rnd 2 in flo of ea st on Rnd 3, but ch 10 instead of 7.

Rnd 5: Rep Rnd 4, working in blo of ea st on Rnd 3. Fasten off.

Buttonhole Braid

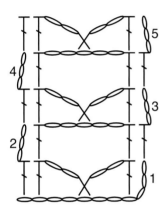

With A, ch 11.

Row 1: 1 dc in 4th ch from hk, ch 2, sk 2 ch, 1 sc in next ch, ch 2, sk 2 ch, 1 dc in ea of next 2 ch, turn.

Row 2: Ch 3 (counts as 1 dc), dc in 2nd dc, ch 5, dc in next dc, dc in top of tch, turn.

Row 3: Ch 3 (counts as 1 dc), dc in 2nd dc, ch 2, sc in 5-ch lp, ch 2, dc in next dc, dc in tch, turn.

Rep Rows 2 and 3 for desired length. Fasten off, leaving an 8" tail. Overlap ends and sew tog with tapestry needle.

Six-Petal Flower

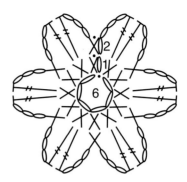

(Make 2 ea in B, E, and F, using C for ea center)

Rnd 1: With C, ch 6, join with a sl st to first ch to form a ring.

Rnd 2: Ch 1, work 12 sc in ring, sl st in 1st sc. Fasten off C.

Rnd 3: Join B, E, or F in any st. Ch 1, * 1 sc in next st, ch 3, 2 tr in next st, ch 3; rep from * around, sl st in 1st sc to join — 6 petals. Fasten off B, E, or F.

Foxglove Braid

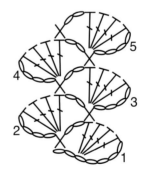

With D, ch 7.

Row 1: Work 4 dc in 5th ch from hk, ch 2, sk 1 ch, sc in next ch, turn.

Row 2: Ch 4, work 4 dc in sc, ch 2, sc in next dc, turn.

Rep Row 2 for desired length. Fasten off, leaving an 8" tail. Overlap ends and sew tog with tapestry needle.

Rainbow Flower

Note: Do not turn. Work is done with RS facing at all times.

Rnd 1: With C, ch 6, join with a sl st to 1st ch to form a ring.

Rnd 2: Ch 1, work 18 sc in ring, sl st in 1st sc. Fasten off C.

Rnd 3: Join F in any st. Ch 5, sk next 2 sc, * sc in next sc, ch 4, sk next 2 sc, rep from * to end. Join with a sl st into 2nd of 1st 5 ch—6 lps.

Rnd 4: Work (sc, hdc, 5 dc, hdc, sc) in ea ch-4 lp around, sl st in 1st sc. Fasten off F.

Rnd 5: Join A with sl st to 1st sc. * Ch 5, pass this ch behind 1st group of sts and work sc in 1st sc of next group of sts, inserting hk from behind. Rep from * around, sl st in 1st ch-5 lp.

Rnd 6: Work (sc, hdc, 10 dc, hdc, sc) in ea ch-5 lp around, sl st in 1st sc. Fasten off A.

Rnd 7: Join B with sl st to 1st sc. * Ch 7, pass this ch behind first group of sts and work 1 sc in 1st sc of next group of sts, inserting hk from behind. Rep from * around, sl st in 1st ch-7 lp.

Rnd 8: Work (sc, hdc, 15 dc, hdc, sc) in ea ch-7 lp around, sl st in 1st sc. Fasten off B.

Rnd 9: Join E with sl st to 1st sc. * Ch 8, pass this ch behind first group of sts and work sc in 1st sc of next group of sts, inserting hk from behind. Rep from * around, sl st in 1st ch-8 lp.

Rnd 10: Work (sc, hdc, 5 dc, 10 tr, 5 dc, hdc, sc) in ea ch-8 lp around, sl st in 1st sc. Join with a sl st into 1st ch. Fasten off E.

To finish each wrap, sew floral decoration on RS at seam.

Designed by Gloria Tracy

Gentle Waves Baby Afghan

This versatile pattern stitch is great for fringed projects because, when done in multicolors, the tails can be incorporated into a fringe, eliminating the need to weave in the ends. We chose a lightweight yarn and doubled it without making the afghan too heavy. Using this method we achieved a beautiful, shaded rainbow with only five colors (plus white) to create a project that is beautiful, practical, and fun. This technique could easily be adapted in different sizes and colors for any room in the house.

Size

Approx 40" x 52" without fringe

Materials

Herrschners 2-Ply Afghan Yarn 56 g/200 yd/182 m
(100% Acrilan acrylic)
8 skeins #0001 White (MC)
3 skeins #0014 Soft Pink(A)
3 skeins #0013 Soft Yellow (B)
3 skeins #0336 Baby Green(C)
3 skeins #0015 Soft Blue (D)
Crochet hook US size K/10.5 (6.5 mm)

Gauge

St: 1 motif = 3¾" wide, with two strands held tog
Rows: 1 motif = 1¼" high, with two strands held tog

Stitches and Patterns Used

Single crochet, half double crochet, double crochet,
treble, single crochet worked three rows below
Waves (Block #15)

Waves Pattern
(multiple of 12 + 10)

Row 1 (RS): With MC, work 1 sc into 2nd ch from hk, 1 sc into ea ch to end, turn.

Row 2: With MC, ch 1, work 1 sc into ea sc to end, turn.

Row 3: With CC, ch 3 (counts as 1 dc), sk 1st sc, 1 dc into next sc, 1 hdc into next sc, 1 sc into next sc, *ch 2, sk 2 sc, 1 sc into next sc, 1 hdc into next sc, 1 dc into ea of next 2 sc, 1 tr into ea of next 2 sc, 1 dc into ea of next 2 sc, 1 hdc into next sc, 1 sc into next sc; rep from * to last 6 sc, ch 2, sk 2 sc, 1 sc into next sc, 1 hdc into next sc, 1 dc into ea of last 2 sc, turn.

Row 4: With CC, ch 3, sk 1st dc, work 1 dc into next dc, 1 hdc into next hdc, 1 sc into next sc, *2 ch, 1 sc into next sc, 1 hdc into next hdc, 1 dc into ea of next 2 dc, 1 tr into ea of next 2 tr, 1 dc into ea of next 2 dc, 1 hdc into next hdc, 1 sc into next sc; rep from * to last 6 sts, ch 2, 1 sc into next sc, 1 hdc into next hdc, 1 dc into next dc, 1 dc into 3rd of ch 3 at beg of previous row, turn.

Row 5: With MC, ch 1, work 1 sc into ea of 1st 4 sts, [inserting hk from front of work, work 1 sc into ea of 2 free sc in MC 3 rows below], *1 sc into ea of next 10 sts, work 2 sc 3 rows below as before; rep from * to last 4 sts, 1 sc into ea of next 3 sts, 1 sc into top of tch, turn.

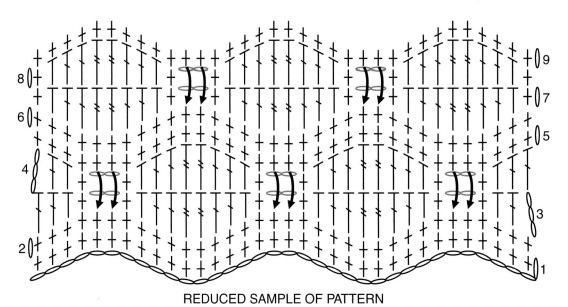

REDUCED SAMPLE OF PATTERN

Row 6: With MC, ch 1, work 1 sc into ea sc to end, turn.

Row 7: With CC, ch 1, *work 1 sc into 1st sc, 1 hdc into next sc, 1 dc into ea of next 2 sc, 1 tr into ea of next 2 sc, 1 dc into ea of next 2 sc, 1 hdc into next sc, 1 sc into next sc, ch 2, sk 2 sc; rep from * to end omitting ch 2 at end of last rep, turn.

Row 8: With CC, ch 1, *work 1 sc into next sc, 1 hdc into next hdc, 1 dc into ea of next 2 dc, 1 tr into ea of next 2 tr, 1 dc into ea of next 2 dc, 1 hdc into next hdc, 1 sc into next sc, ch 2; rep from * to end omitting ch 2 at end of last rep, turn.

Row 9: With MC, ch 1, *1 sc into ea of next 10 sts, inserting hk from front of work, work 1 sc into ea of 2 free sc in MC 3 rows below; rep from * to end omitting 2 sc at end of last rep, turn.

Rep Rows 2–9 for pattern. Rows 2–5 create 1 row of motifs, Rows 6–9, a second.

Notes

1. Hold two strands of yarn together throughout.

2. Add a new color yarn to your work as follows: When two stitches remain on the hook in the last stitch of the old color, draw through with the new color and proceed.

3. When adding a new color, leave 12" tails of both the old and new colors. They will be included in the fringe for finishing.

4. Every two rows of contrast color equals one row of motifs.

Directions for Baby Afghan

With 2 strands of MC, loosely ch 166 ch +s 1 ch for turn.

Row 1: Starting in the 2nd ch from hk, work 166 sc across.

Using 2 strands throughout, work the pat st in the following color sequence:

2 motif rows in AA

1 motif row in AB

2 motif rows in BB

1 motif row in BC

2 motif rows in CC

1 motif row in CD

2 motif rows in DD

1 motif row in DA

2 motif rows in DD

1 motif row in CD

2 motif rows in CC

1 motif row in BC

2 motif rows in BB

1 motif row in AB

2 motif rows in AA.

FRINGE

Loosely wrap leftover yarn around a 12" piece of cardboard, being careful to keep tension even. Cut along one end to make 24" lengths. Matching color of fringe to color of edge stitches on both ends, fold several lengths in half and add with a crochet hook as follows:

With WS facing, pull center of lps through edge st, pass cut ends through and pull tight. Trim to even edges.

Designed by Pat Kipperman

Traditional Plaid Afghan
and Pillow

We don't know of many other color techniques that are this easily learned and are so versatile. We've made this afghan and matching pillow in a simple five-color traditional plaid; however, you can easily change the colors to match any room in your home, or add colors or change the spacing of the stripes for a larger or smaller plaid. What could be easier?

We used 100 percent wool for our luxury afghan and pillow; however, a yarn of easy-care Acrilan acrylic would make a practical choice for a child's bedroom or family room.

Size

Afghan: approx 46" x 62" after lacing, excluding fringe.
Pillow: 18" square

Materials

Knit One, Crochet Too *Parfait Solids,* 100 g/ 210 yd/192 m (100% worsted weight wool)
11 skeins #1565 Deep Evergreen (A)
2 skeins #1108 Snow (B)
5 skeins #1656 Royal (C)
2 skeins #1460 Goldenrod (D)
5 skeins #1909 Jet (E)
Crochet hooks US sizes I/9 and G/6 (5.5 and 4.25 mm)
Yarn needle for lacing
18" pillow form

Gauge

Afghan: In dc: 16 sts = 4"; 2 rows = ½"
Pillow: In dc: 18 sts = 4"; 8 rows = 4"

Pattern Stitch for Afghan and Pillows

Row 1: Work dc in 5th ch from hk, *ch 1, sk next ch, dc in next ch; rep from * across row, turn.

Row 2: Ch 4 (counts as dc and ch 1), *dc in next dc, ch 1; rep from * across, ending dc in 3rd ch of tch, turn.

Rep Row 2 for pat st.

Note: Plaid pattern will be evident after lacing is worked.

Directions for Afghan

Note: Each row contains 76 ch-1 sps for laces to be threaded through later. Count these sps periodically to maintain correct amount throughout.

Using A, loosely ch 155.

Working in pat st, follow striping pattern as indicated in Color Sequence Charts (p. 204), rep entire color sequence twice more, ending with 4 rows of A and a total of 114 rows.

Weave in all ends along matching color stripes.

LACING

Spread afghan out on a smooth flat surface and measure total length. Use this measurement to determine length of crochet chains.

Following the Color Sequence Charts, make chains to your measurement plus 7" tail on *each* end to later include in the fringe.

Again following the color sequence, weave these strands vertically through ch-1 spaces. Begin at lower right-hand corner and lace chains vertically under and over striped rows, filling alternate spaces of each row. Chains should be pulled firmly so there are no loops, yet not too tightly or fabric may pucker. Continue as established, working two repeats across.

FRINGE

Cut 14" strands of yarn. Matching colors of vertical stripes, pull four strands through each hole across the first row. You may have to adjust the chains so that they come just to the end of the afghan. Knot strands with 7" tail at end of chains. Trim ends evenly.

Directions for Pillow

FRONT

Note: Ea row contains 35 ch-1 sps for laces to be threaded through later. Count these sps periodically to maintain correct amount throughout.

Using A, loosely ch 74. Working in pat st, follow striping pattern as indicated in the Color Sequence Charts (p. 204), ending with 35 rows. Fasten off after working last rows.

Weave in all ends along matching color stripes. Work lacing as for afghan.

BACK

With B, ch 62.

Row 1: Hdc in 3rd ch from hk and ea rem ch across; turn—60 hdc in row.

Row 2: Ch 2 (counts as 1st hdc), hdc in ea rem st across; turn.

Rows 3–8: Rep Row 2, changing to E in last hdc.

Row 9: With E, ch 1, sc in ea st across, changing to C in last st; turn.

Rows 10–12: With C, rep Row 2, changing to E in last st of Row 12; turn.

Row 13: Rep Row 9 with E, changing to A in last st; turn.

Rows 14–39: Rep Row 2 with A, changing to B in last st of Row 39; turn.

Row 40: Rep Row 9 with B, changing to D in last st; turn.

Rows 41–43: Rep Row 2 with D, changing to B in last st of Row 43; turn.

Row 44: Rep Row 9 with B, changing to E in last st; turn.

Rows 45–52: Rep Row 2 with E. Fasten off at end of Row 52.

FINISHING

With WS together, whip stitch the pillow front and back edges tog, leaving one side open. Insert pillow form and close rem side seam. If desired, make twisted cord (see p. 57) with 10 or more 260" strands of yarn in a mix of the rem yarn colors. This makes an approximately 94" finished and knotted cord, depending on how tightly you wind it.

Starting in middle of cord and at one corner of pillow, loosely stitch cording to pillow edge, slightly rounding corners as you go. Stitch other half of cording to last two sides of pillow. As you stitch last corner and the ends come together, tie the remaining cord in a large knot.

COLOR SEQUENCE CHARTS

AFGHAN	
# of Rows	**Color**
4	A
1	C
1	A
3	C
2	B
3	C
1	A
1	C
6	A
1	E
1	A
3	E
2	D
3	E
1	A
1	E
4	A

PILLOW	
# of Rows	**Color**
3	A
1	C
1	A
3	C
2	B
3	C
1	A
1	C
5	A
1	E
1	A
3	E
2	D
3	E
1	A
1	E
3	A

Carry-All Shoulder Bag

A ready-made fabric bag purchased many years ago was the inspiration for the unusual shaping in this handy Carry-All Shoulder Bag. Easily accessible outside pockets are custom sized for glasses, keys, and business cards. Creating even more pockets presents a great opportunity to try out other patterns. You can customize the pocket sizes to your own favorite uses.

Two- and three-color single crochet and crab stitch edgings present an easy way to use up scraps and to add a decorative touch—we don't know why these easy and clever edgings are so seldom used.

Size

Bag: 15¼" x 12" x 3"

Materials

Spinrite Sugar 'n Cream Solids 70.9 g/120 yd/
    109 m (100% 4-ply worsted weight cotton)
    1 ball #3 Pansy (B)
    1 ball #74 Blueberry (C)
Spinrite Sugar 'n Cream Ombres, 56.7 g/95 yd/
    86 m (100% 4-ply worsted weight cotton)
    2 balls #178 Potpourri (A)
Crochet hook US size H/8 (5 mm)
One 1" button for top closure
One ¾" button for Key Pocket closure

Gauge

In granite stitch, 18 sts and 18 rows = 4"

Stitches and Patterns Used

Chain, slip stitch, single crochet, double crochet,
reverse single crochet
Granite pattern (Block #14)
Trinity pattern (Block #14)
Floret stitch (Block #4)
Comma pattern (Block #2)

Pattern Stitch 1—Body Pattern

Granite pattern (see p. 45)

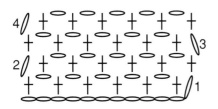

Pattern Stitch 2—Pocket C

Trinity pattern variation
(multiple of 2 sts + 1)

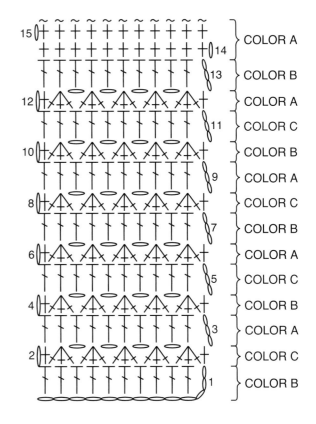

Foundation Row: Dc in 4th ch from hk and in ea
    ch across; turn.

Row 1: Ch 1, sc in 1st st, sc3tog inserting hk first
    into previous st, then into ea of next 2 sts, * ch
    1, sc3tog inserting hk into same st as 3rd leg of
    previous cluster, then into ea of next 2 sts; rep
    from * across, ending sc into same st as 3rd leg
    of previous cluster; turn.

Row 2: Ch 3 (counts as 1st dc), dc in next and
    every st across; turn.

Rep Rows 1 and 2 for trinity pattern variation.

Pattern Stitch 3—Pocket D

Floret stitch (see p. 45)

(multiple 2 + 1)

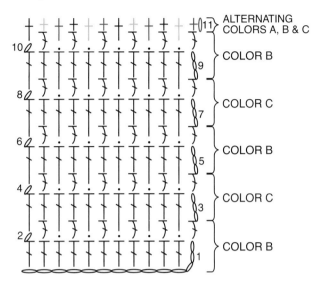

Pattern Stitch 4

Comma pattern (see p. 41)

(multiple of 4 + 3)

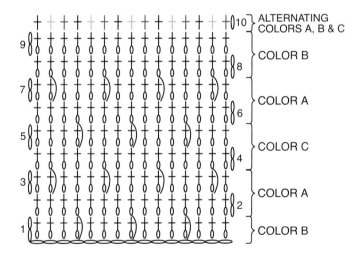

Directions for Shoulder Bag

BAG BODY

With A, ch 69 plus 1 for turn.

Starting in the 2nd ch from hk, work in pat st 1 for 12". Sl st across 1st 7 sts, work in pat st to last 7 sts, turn—55 sts. Work even for 3". Ch 7 on last row before turning. Work in pat st across the 62 sts, ch 7 before turning. Work for 12" on the 69 sts. Fasten off.

FINISHING

Sew sides of bag tog. With bag inside out, sew AA to B on both sides to close bottom of bag.

Sc around top edge alternating A, B, and C as follows: Starting at side seam, *draw up a lp of A, insert hk into next st and draw up a 2nd lp of A, draw B through both lps, insert hk into next st and draw up a 2nd lp of B, draw C through both lps, rep from * around top of bag. To keep yarns from tangling, draw colors in a consistent order, i.e., A on top, B in the center and C on bottom. Fasten off.

TIP: *Remember that an edging is just a decorative touch and doesn't need to be fortified. So when crocheting down the sides of your work, go around just one strand of yarn rather than the entire stitch. It will pull less and be less likely to leave an unsightly gap.*

STRAPS (make two)

With C, ch 5 plus 2 for turn.

Starting in 2nd ch from hook work in pat st 3 for 23". Mark centers of front and back of bag from seam lines. Mark 4 places 3" on each side of center marks. Sew center of end of straps at the 4 marked places, as shown in drawing.

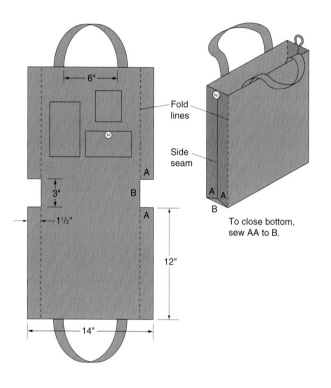

Fold lines

Side seam

6"

3"

1½"

12"

14"

A

B

A

A

A

B

To close bottom, sew AA to B.

POCKETS

Pocket C: For a 3½" wide pocket, with B ch 11 plus 3 for turn ch. Starting in 4th ch from hk, work in pat st 2 working 2 rows ea B, C and A for 26 rows or to desired length. With A work 1 row sc and 1 row Rsc (crab stitch) alt colors as in bag edging.

Pocket D: With B, ch 11 sts plus 2 for turn. Starting in 3rd ch from hk work in pat st 3 for 8 rows or to desired length alt 2 rows ea B and C ending with B and cont to sc around edge of piece to form a bottom finish. Pocket is sewn on sideways.

Pocket E: With B, ch 15 plus 2 for turn. Starting in 3rd ch from hk work in pat st 4 for 9 rows or to desired length alt B, A, C, A, B. Finish with three-color sc edging as for bag top.

At center top of pocket, make ch approx 2" long and attach to pocket to form lp. Sew button to bag.

Reversible Chenille Scarf and Hat

We fell in love with the fab-ulous feel and colors of this soft chenille. The three-color post stitch also became one of our favorite stitches for showing off multicolors. Since both sides of the pattern stitch have great merit, we felt it was a perfect choice for a scarf.

Size

Scarf: 8" x 60"
Hat: 20½" circumference

Materials for Scarf

Classic Elite *Persia* (100% rayon chenille)
  4 balls 50 g/104 yd #2478 Auburn (A)
  3 balls 50 g/121 yd #2425 Faded Rose (B)
  3 balls 50 g/121 yd #2463 Seashell (C)
I card 3 mm Rainbow Elastic thread #116
  Terra-Cotta
Crochet hook US size G/6 (4 mm)

Materials for Hat

Classic Elite *Persia* 50 g/104 yd/95 m (100% rayon)
  4 balls #2478 Auburn (A)
  3 balls *each* #2425 Faded Rose (B) and #2463
  Seashell (C)
K1C2 *Rainbow Elastic*, 3 mm (bulky)/25 yds/22 m
  #116 Terra-Cotta
Crochet hook US size G/6 (4 mm)

Gauge

In sc, 17 sts and 24 rows = 4"

Stitches and Patterns Used

Chain, slip stitch, single crochet, front post treble,
sc2tog
Three-color post stitch pattern (Block #19)

Three Color Post Stitch in the Round
(multiple of 3 sts; a rep of 6 rds)

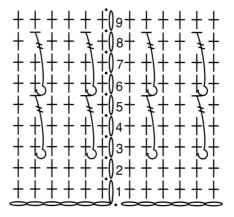

Rnds 1 and 2: With A, ch 1, sc in each st around; sl st in first sc.

Rnd 3: With A, rep Rnd 1.

Rnd 4: With B, rep Rnd 1.

Rnd 5: With C, sc in first st, * fp/tr in next st **, sc in next 2 sts; rep from * around, ending last rep at **, sc in last st; sl st in first sc.

Rnd 6: With C, rep Rnd 1.

Rnd 7: With B, rep Rnd 1.

Rnd 8: With A, rep Rnd 5 working fp/tr around post of fp/tr from 3 rows below.

Rnd 9: With A, rep Rnd 1.

Rep Rnds 4–9 for three-color post stitch in rnds.

Directions for Hat and Scarf

Make hat first and use remainder of yarn to make scarf.

HAT

With A, ch 3, join with a sl st in first ch to form ring.

Rnd 1: Ch 1, work 7 sc in ring; sl st in first sc.

Rnd 2: Ch 1, work 2 sc in each sc around; sl st in first sc—14 sc.

Rnd 3: Ch 1, sc in first sc, * 2 sc in next sc, sc in next sc; rep from * around to last sc, 2 sc in last sc; sl st in first sc—1 sts.

Rnd 4: Ch 1, sc in first 2 sc, * 2 sc in next sc, sc in next 2 sc; rep from * around to last sc, 2 sc in last sc; sl st in first sc—28 sts.

Cont in this manner inc 7 sts each rnd until 98 sts are obtained.

Dec Rnd: Ch 1, (sc in 7 sc, sc2tog) twice, * sc in 8 sc, sc2tog; rep from * around; sl st in first sc—88 sts.

Work 2 rnds even dec 1 st in 2nd rnd—87 sts.

Work three-color post stitch pat in rnds for Rnds 1–9 once, then rep Rnds 4–7 once.

Work 3 rnds sc with A, dec 1 st in last rnd—86 sts.

Last Rnd: Ch 1, * sc A in next st, sc B in next st; rep from * around; sl st in first sc. Fasten off.

FINISHING

Weave 2 or 3 rows Rainbow Elastic into brim.

SCARF

With A, ch 38 + 1 for turn. Work in three-color post ptitch (see p. 48–49) for 60" or desired length, ending with A row. Work 1 more sc row with A. Fasten off.

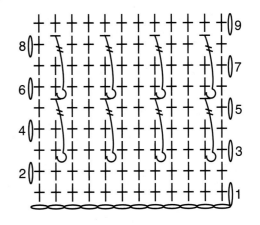

Resources

Bryson Distributing/ Notions & Accessories
4065 West Eleventh St. #39
Eugene, OR 97402
541-485-1884

Caron International
P.O. Box 222
Washington, NC 27889
800-868-9194

Classic Elite Yarns
12 Perkins St.
Lowell, MA 01854
978-453-2837

Coats Patons
1001 Roselawn Ave.
Toronto, Ontario
Canada M6B 1B8
416-782-4481

Herrschners
2800 Hoover Rd.
Stevens Point, WI 54492-0001
800-441-0838

JHB Buttons
1955 South Quince St.
Denver, CO 80231
303-751-8100

K1C2/Knit One, Crochet Too
2220 Eastman Ave. #105
Ventura, CA 93003
800-607-2462

Kreinik Manufacturing Company
3106 Timanus Lane #101
Baltimore, MD 21244
410-281-0040

Lion Brand Yarn Company
34 West Fifteenth St.
New York, NY 10011
212-243-8995

Muench Yarns
118 Ricardo Rd.
Mill Valley, CA 94941
415-883-6375

Plymouth Yarn Company
P.O. Box 28
Bristol, PA 19007
215-788-0459

Skacel Yarns
11612 SE 196th St.
Renton, WA 98058
253-854-2710

Spinrite Yarns
P.O. Box 40
Listowel, Ontario
Canada N4W 3H3
519-291-3951

Trendsetter Yarns
16742 Stagg St. #104
Van Nuys, CA 91406
818-780-5497

For more information about crochet or to
join the Crochet Guild of America contact:
The Crochet Guild of America
2502 Lowell Rd.
Gastonia, NC 28054
847-776-7941
CGOA@crochet.org

Appendix

EZ Reference Crochet Shorthand Chart

This chart lists fourteen crochet stitches in order of their height.
It also provides a fast and simple way of describing how each of the stitches is formed.

Definitions and explanations by column from left to right:

- **Stitch -** The UK refers to their crochet stitches by names a "step up" from US definitions. For example, the stitch called "single crochet" in the US is called "double crochet" in the UK. Where applicable, the UK term is given in italics.
- **Abbr.—**The abbreviation for the US term.
- **Symbol—**The international symbols for the stitch.
- **To form the stitch—**If "yo" is noted before the parentheses, yarn over or wrap the yarn around the hook *before* inserting it through the stitch and bringing it forward. ***If no "yo" is noted, none is required for that stitch.*** If there is a number given after the "yo," more than one yarn over is required. Each set of minuses and numbers inside the parentheses indicates a yarn over plus the number of loops to draw the yarn through on each step.

   For example: A double single crochet does not require a yarn over before inserting the hook into the stitch. Inside the parentheses it asks for two pull-through actions, dropping one loop the first time and two the second time. A double crochet calls for one yo before inserting the hook, then two pull-through actions dropping two loops each time.

- **# tch—**The number of chains needed to equal the height of the first stitch to be used in the next row.
- **# from hk—**The chain in which to insert the hook *when beginning.* Start counting in the chain next to the hook. Never count the chain on the hook.

Unfortunately, there is no single authority to determine hook size. When patterns indicate a hook by its letter size, use these guidelines. For best results, always work a gauge swatch before beginning.

Steel Crochet Hooks

U.S. (American)	Continental (metric)	U.K. (English)
00	3.5	-
0	3.25	0
1	2.75	1
2	2.25	1.5
3	2.1	2
4	2.0	2.5
5	1.9	3
6	1.8	3.5
7	1.65	4
8	1.5	4.5
9	1.4	5
10	1.3	5.5
11	1.1	6
12	1.0	6.5
13	0.85	7
14	0.75	-

Plastic and Aluminum Crochet Hooks

U.S. (American)	Continental (metric)	U.K. (English)
B/1	2.5	12
C/2	3	11
D/3	3.25	10
E/4	3.5	9
F/5	4	8
G/6	4.25	7
7	4.5	7
H/8	5	6
I/9	5.5	5
J/10	6	4
K/10.5	7	3
L/11	8	-
M/13	9	-
N/15	10	-
P/16	15	-
Q	16	-
S	19	-

EZ Reference Crochet Shorthand Chart (continued)

Stitch (UK term)	Abbr.	Symbol	To form the stitch	# tch	# from hk
chain	ch	⌒	yo(-1)		
slip stitch	sl st	− or •	(-1)	1	2nd
single crochet (*double crochet*)	sc	+ or X	(-2)	1	2nd
double single crochet	dsc	⊤ with ○	(-1-2)	2	3rd
half double crochet (*half treble*)	hdc	⊤	yo(-3)	2	3rd
half Elmore	hE	⊤ with ○	yo(-1-3)	3	4th
double crochet (*treble*)	dc	⊤ with ⧸	yo(-2-2)	3	4th
Elmore	E	⊤ with ⧸ ○	yo(-1-2-2)	3	4th
double Elmore	dE	⊤ with ⧸ ○ ○	yo(-1-1-2-2)	4	5th
treble (*double treble*)	tr	⊤ with ⧸⧸	yo2(-2-2-2)	4	5th
Elmore treble	E tr	⊤ with ⧸⧸ ○	yo2(-1-2-2-2)	4	5th
double treble (*triple treble*)	dtr	⊤ with ⧸⧸⧸	yo3(-2-2-2-2)	4	5th
Elmore double treble	E d tr	⊤ with ⧸⧸⧸ ○	yo2(-1-1-2-2-2)	5	6th
Tall Texan	TT	⊤ with ○⧸○⧸○⧸	yo2(-1-2-1-2-1-2)	6	7th

Index

Note: References in italic indicate a photo or illustration.